VORTEX CITIES TO
SUSTAINABLE CITIES

PHIL MCMANUS is a Senior Lecturer in the School of Geosciences at the University of Sydney and is a National Councillor of the Australian Conservation Foundation.

He has qualifications in Urban and Regional Planning, Environmental Studies and Geography, and has studied in Australia, Canada and England. Within Australia, McManus has lived in rural Western Australia, Perth, Newcastle and Sydney.

VORTEX CITIES TO SUSTAINABLE CITIES

Australia's Urban Challenge

Phil McManus

UNSW PRESS

To Caitlin, her generation and future generations

A UNSW Press book

Published by
University of New South Wales Press Ltd
University of New South Wales
Sydney NSW 2052
AUSTRALIA
www.unswpress.com.au

National Library of Australia
Cataloguing-in-Publication entry:

McManus, Phil, 1966- .
    Vortex cities to sustainable cities : Australia's urban
    challenge.

    Includes index.
    ISBN 0 86840 701 1.

    1. City planning – Australia. 2. Regional planning -
    Australia. 3. Sustainable development – Australia. I. Title.

    711.40994

Printer Ligare
Cover design Di Quick
Cover image PhotoLibrary.com
Layout Lamond Art & Design

CONTENTS

ACKNOWLEDGEMENTS

As usual with a project of this magnitude, there are many people without whom it would not have been possible to complete the work. Thanks are extended to John Elliot and Stephanie Harding from UNSW Press for commissioning and supporting the work which has taken longer to complete than was envisaged. Thanks also to David Hedgcock and Jenny Barrett for their constructive and insightful feedback on earlier versions of the manuscript. Their comments and suggestions for changes were very welcomed, and the book is very much improved thanks to their support. Thanks also to Eleanor Bruce and David Hobson for their generous assistance with organising and preparing a number of the images used in this publication, and to Angela Damis for editing the manuscript.

A number of people have helped on particular chapters, or at specific time periods in the research and preparation of the manuscript. I would like to acknowledge the assistance given by Nahrel Dallywater, Mark Diesendorf, David Gibbs, Sonia Graham, Michael Krockenberger, Daniel Montoya and Gary Peel. I am very grateful for the contributions these people have made and I have enjoyed working with each and every one of them. Many other friends, activist colleagues, teachers and students in various places around the world have helped in the development of my thinking about sustainable cities. These contributors are too numerous to mention individually, but it is important to acknowledge them. While there is no doubt that the project has benefited enormously from the help of all of these people, any errors in this book are my responsibility.

INTRODUCTION

During the 12th century Angkor in present-day Cambodia was the largest city in the world. Today it is ruins. In the Great Plague of 1665 at least one-quarter, or over 100 000, of London's inhabitants died. By way of comparison, the official death toll from the September 11 bombings in New York City in 2001 was 3021. On 7 April 2003 an asteroid measuring 150 metres in diameter passed within 1 153 401 kilometres of the Earth. If it had struck the Earth, the impact area is estimated to have been the size of Los Angeles. The potential cumulative impacts of gigantic waves, rivers changing course, dams collapsing, and so on, would extend far beyond the area of direct impact.

These three last-mentioned scenarios all challenge our thinking about cities and sustainability. In countries such as Australia, our imagined and desired cities have changed from colonial capitals or the 'dirty old town' of the Industrial Revolution to scenarios ranging from ecological cities (somewhat akin to Ernest Callenbach's 1975 novel *Ecotopia*) through to high-technology cities modelled on Silicon Valley, as in elements of the aborted multi-function polis that was proposed for South Australia (Downton and Ede, 1995).

There is widespread agreement that we need a process such as sustainable development for the future of Australian cities. After all, who would advocate unsustainability? The revived interest in urban sustainability and issues pertaining to the built environment is exemplified in the Australian House of Representatives Standing Committee on Environment and Heritage's Inquiry into Sustainable Cities 2025. The discussion paper for this inquiry was released in September 2003, allowing time for submissions in the lead-up to 2004, the Year of the Built Environment.

The notion of sustainable development raises a number of questions. For instance, what do we mean when we say that we want sustainable development? What do we mean when we advocate a 'clean and green' city, an eco-city or a sustainable city? At what scale, and over what period, are we talking about? How do we know if a city is sustainable, or even if it is possible for a city to be sustainable? Is the concept of a sustainable city an oxymoron?

If sustainable cities are not possible, or if the anticipated effort to move towards sustainability more generally is too great relative to the perceived benefits, why should we bother? Many of Australia's largest cities have grown from isolated colonial settlements to being crucial parts of a 'lucky country'. These cities sit like pegs on the outside of a massive Hills hoist, attaching the patchwork quilts of agriculture and mining to the coast and the world beyond this country. Why bother with ideas such as sustainability? In this country we have land, the air is clean, we're not squashed together as in older European or rapidly growing mega-cities (those cities with populations in excess of ten million people) in Asia and Africa. Most of our major cities are growing rapidly, but we do not experience the population explosion of the world's mega-cities. In short, our urban future is looking promising, isn't it?

If the 2001 Census figures are any indication, it appears that more and more Australians are choosing, for a variety of reasons, to live in our largest cities. We may dream of the Man from Snowy River, but the reality is that most Australians have more in common with the man from the Yarra River or the woman from the River Torrens. More and more Australians are living in the largest cities, watching stereotypical images of drought-stricken rural and regional Australia. In a little over 100 years since Federation, the urban population of Australia has grown significantly in relation to inland agricultural and mining towns. Many Australians who have sought to escape the largest cities have moved to or along the coast. How do these trends in Australia articulate with current thinking about sustainable cities and our perceptions of Australian cities?

This book sets out to challenge many perceptions about cities, rural and regional Australia, sustainability, and our future. This is necessary because if we want to improve things, whatever they may be and however we may define 'improve', then it is necessary to have a more sophisticated understanding of what it is that we may want to change or sustain, why change is necessary, and how may this change be undertaken. Although change is inevitable, as this book demonstrates, the rate and types of changes are contested. Ideas and material for the book are drawn from a range of intellectual traditions and disciplines, including geography, environmental studies, sociology and urban and regional planning. It is the interdisciplinary nature of this material that makes it both challenging to write a book such as this one, but also makes the process intellectually richer, and ultimately, I believe, more useful for dealing with the issues addressed here.

The diversity of issues highlights the need to consider each city in its historical, geographical, social, political, economic and cultural contexts. Indeed, there is no reason to think that what is appropriate for a large, rapidly growing city such as Sydney will work in Hobart, or in the more tropical city of Darwin. Each city is unique. Honadle (1999) explains the difference between 'homogenous thinking', which lacks a specific context and produces a mentality of 'one best way' to be implemented everywhere, and 'situational thinking', which takes account of local conditions, cultures and other specific factors. This book builds on the idea that the best way of doing something means the best way for a specific area at a particular time. Having said that, it is important to see beyond the confines of a local area. As will be demonstrated in the early chapters of this book, drawing on the insights of actant network theory, ideas travel and can be translated into a form that is suitable in a particular area. It is possible also to learn from the experiences of other cities and to avoid some of the mistakes that have been made elsewhere.

As the last part of this book emphasises, it is important that we learn, and that we act on this learning. This action must have a sense of urgency and a sense of humility, a recognition that we could be wrong, and it must be meaningful and not simply expedient. As was noted in the 2003 NSW State of the Environment Report, 'very few authorities believe that the current pace of change to sustainable actions and behaviours across the community has reached the speed and breadth needed to overtake and correct an underlying path of degradation' (EPA NSW, 2003, 7). This particularly applies to Australian cities, and their impacts on regional hinterlands, distant locations and the choices of future generations of Australians.

This book is written with these thoughts in mind. Hopefully it will contribute to more critical thinking about cities and sustainability and inspire actions to create cities that are suitable for the 21st century and beyond.

STRUCTURE OF THE BOOK

The book is divided into three sections: section 1, covering patterns and processes in historical perspective (chapters 1–4), section 2, on sustainability issues (chapters 5–10), and section 3, addressing future directions (chapter 11). Chapter 1 traces the actual growth, and the impacts of this growth, of Australia's largest cities since about the mid-19th century. It relates the changing urban pattern of Australia to wider trends in industrialisation, focusing on Sydney, Newcastle, Wollongong, Melbourne and Adelaide, and to the rise of so-called lifestyle-oriented cities such as the Gold Coast, Sunshine Coast and Cairns. More importantly, the chapter engages in, for the purpose of critiquing, the stereotyping of Australian cities. It is necessary to move beyond stereotypes of cities in order to develop and implement plans, policies and grassroots action that move towards sustainability. Chapter 1 provides the historic basis for accepting diversity in Australia's cities and their environments, and thus establishes the framework for potential sustainability initiatives to have common elements in various cities, and at the same time to be tailored to the specific context of each city.

Ideas in urban planning have had a significant impact on Australian cities. Chapter 2 explores the history of ideas that have impacted, or were in their time thought likely to impact, on Australian cities. The chapter examines historical changes so that readers can understand how what was considered ideal in one era, for example, large private gardens for health, becomes the antithesis of planning wisdom in another era, where such private gardens are seen as contributing to urban 'sprawl' and reducing the viability of public transport systems. It is impossible, and unnecessary, to present the myriad of plans and policies for every major Australian city here. The overall picture that emerges from this chapter is of various Australian cities sharing similar ideas, but different translation of these ideas into plans and actions, by virtue of the presence or other influence of powerful individuals and organisations. Another picture that emerges, discussed later in the book, is that of the resistance and dissent generated by some plans and the process of resistance leading to changes in planning and in the physical form of cities. Chapter 2 also explores the implementation of some of these ideas in Australia through Commonwealth government initiatives such as the Better Cities and Building Better Cities Programs of the 1990s, and through state and local planning processes. The chronology of government involvement in Australia's cities described in this chapter provides a necessary context to understand current approaches to urban issues in Australia.

Chapter 3 explores the governance and planning of Australia's largest cities in the contemporary era. It begins with a discussion of the Howard Government's lack of commitment to urban issues, a problem highlighted in the example of Local Agenda 21 in Australia. The chapter also explores the governance and metropolitan planning of Australia's five largest cities, before introducing three ideas that may have potential to make Australian cities more sustainable in the 21st century. These ideas are 'new urbanism', 'smart growth' and bioregionalism.

Chapter 4 discusses what is largely a contemporary idea: the move from a focus on environmental protection to thinking about creating sustainable cities. The idea of protecting the environment is introduced and critiqued because of its construction of cities and of 'the environment'. The evolution of environmentalism and sustainability is traced so that we can see how these ideas came to be seen as relevant to cities. The notion of sustainability is questioned. In particular, this chapter looks at the possibility that 'sustainable cities' is an oxymoron. The chapter raises the possibility that we should be focusing on David Satterthwaite's (1997) question of 'sustainable cities, or cities that contribute to sustainable development?' This book is premised on the idea that sustainable cities *must* contribute to sustainability. We cannot have 'islands of sustainability' if they are exporting unsustainable practices beyond their borders. Sustainability in this book refers to the integration of ecological, economic, social and cultural factors. The emphasis is on ecological factors because without ecology, there is no society and no economy. Social, economic and cultural aspects of sustainability are recognised as important and are emphasised at appropriate points in this book, but ecological sustainability is prioritised. The ecological sustainability focus of this chapter leads to the perception of Australian cities in their current form, and no doubt other cities throughout the world, as being 'vortex cities'.

In most cases, the vortex effect is increasing. This leads to section 2 of the book where we explore the vortex effect in practice by examining a range of contemporary issues that must be addressed in order for Australian cities to become more sustainable. The first chapter in the section, chapter 5, looks at the concept of population and in particular how it relates to national planning. Commonwealth involvement in urban planning was attempted by the Whitlam Government in the early 1970s, and in a different form during the Hawke–Keating era of 1983–1996. In this book I am arguing that currently 'the market' is the de facto national population planner after immigration levels have been set. This is because Australia's major source of population growth is the net increase in migration, and most migrants move to the large cities, with approximately 40 per cent of new migrants settling in Sydney. This is occurring at a time when many small country towns are declining, some regional cities are expanding at the expense of their hinterlands (the so-called sponge cities) and most large cities and coastal locations are experiencing urban expansion pressures. This chapter looks at changes in population pressures, housing occupation rates and demand for new housing, and establishes the context and reasons for the expansion of urban areas and the creation of land use conflicts.

This expansion of direct and indirect impacts of cities is affecting a number of fragile environments and critical resources. One such impact is the impact of Australian cities on water. This issue is acute in a dry country such as Australia. Chapter 6 considers the limited, and limiting, factor of water, and how Australian cities may manage water supply and water quality issues. The key argument in this chapter is that a focus on water demand management and on implementing 'water sensitive urban design' can limit the need for new water supplies. Still, the chapter recognises that, while these approaches are not a panacea to fix water issues, they provide positive actions that can make a significant difference in the way Australian cities are developed and the impacts these cities have on nature both in and beyond their built-up area.

Another important issue in Australian cities is transport. This issue has been discussed by many authors in relation to sustainability. The existence of automobile dependence and the appropriateness of various modes of public transport and privately operated collective transport have been the subject of heated debates. In chapter 7 all major forms of urban transport, including walking, cycling, buses and rail-based transport, are considered. Transport is an issue that impacts on the sustainability of cities in a significant way. It also has impacts far beyond the city, and is one activity that can be, and needs to be, significantly modified if Australian cities are going to become more sustainable and in a position to contribute to sustainability at a global level. Given that transport is a major, but of course not the only, user of energy in Australian cities, chapter 7 includes material on energy use (including changes in the type of energy). One logical consequence of fossil fuel energy power, considered in a later chapter, is the impact of transportation on air quality.

Chapter 8 on waste addresses the concept of what we used to call 'waste', but is now often described as a 'resource'. It considers the unsustainability of waste generation, the limited effectiveness of recycling initiatives and the need to 'close the loop' on industrial processes so that 'waste' becomes the inputs for downstream industrial production. The chapter draws on and critically assesses current ecological modernisation and industrial ecology literature, as well as examples from Australia and overseas to demonstrate what is possible, and what is necessary, to do in order to reduce our generation of waste and to genuinely turn waste into a resource.

Chapter 9 examines the issue of climate change and air quality. Climate change is understood as being a natural phenomenon, but it is the change caused by human impacts that is of interest here. Climate change has become the major environmental issue for the early 21st century. This chapter distinguishes between climate change, ozone depletion and other localised forms of deterioration in air quality. It focuses on emissions and considers their impacts at a number of levels. The chapter covers some of the energy and air quality issues that are not addressed in the earlier chapter on transport.

The final issue to be considered in section 2 is biodiversity. The conservation of urban nature will contribute to biodiversity maintenance. The limited expansion of urban areas, especially into remnant vegetation and habitats, can maintain biodiversity in areas near Australian cities. Chapter 10 on biodiversity uses examples from Australian cities to demonstrate how biodiversity is an urban environmental issue. It considers how Australian cities have fared in biodiversity conservation, including marine biodiversity and the maintenance of fragile coastal ecosystems, and the specific threats and challenges facing each of the five largest Australian cities.

The overview of specific issues in section 2 leads into a discussion about the future. Chapter 11, the single chapter in section 3, focuses on process and navigates the gap between the ecologically necessary and the politically possible. The chapter includes discussions on scale, the importance of education and what is required for ongoing, meaningful action towards sustainability. It raises the process-oriented question of whether we need leadership or grassroots decision-making. Any debate about how to achieve sustainability requires a consideration of structures and leadership roles. While the image of activists defending remnant vegetation and species is important and conducive to media coverage, many achievements occur, or are consolidated, through mundane decision-making processes and legal actions. This chapter looks at the impact of individual leadership, the establishment of appropriate structures and the role of professional people in working with communities and environmental organisations to move towards sustainable cities. It is not advocating an abdication of leadership, nor even of what may be seen as top-down planning by some people, but it does call for improved planning processes in order to achieve better outcomes in terms of sustainability. The other side of this issue addressed by this chapter is the perceptions, functions and actions of local urban activists. It is very easy for these activists to position themselves as romantically defending a neighbourhood in a David versus Goliath struggle, while similarly it is easy for qualified planners, elected officials and other representative decision-makers to see grassroots activists as 'nimbys' (from 'Not In My Back Yard') who are only concerned to protect their own narrow interests. Chapter 11 discusses these community groups and looks at their role in moving cities towards sustainability. It includes material about recent initiatives such as the Protectors of Public Lands, a coalition of community groups in Sydney, and analyses what impacts similar groups have had, or may have, on moving Australian cities towards sustainability. The chapter considers the complexities of local activism, including its motivations, structures and links with urban professionals, and the impacts of local activism in terms of sustainability.

It is challenging to write a conclusion to a book that is about analysis, action and change. These are ongoing processes. There is, however, a need to emphasise the main points of the book and to leave readers with a message of optimism about the future. Without hope, we abandon the future. At the risk of sounding naive to some urban planners, environmental scientists, consultants and government officials who have been trained in technical and scientific logic and methods, it must be acknowledged that their way is only part of the answer. Despite our fantastic technological developments and incredible increase in particular forms of knowledge relative to previous generations, it appears that hope, humility, love, ethics, wisdom and courage will be our greatest assets in creating a more sustainable future.

SECTION 1

PATTERNS AND PROCESSES IN HISTORICAL PERSPECTIVE

This section comprises four chapters. Chapter 1 traces the growth, and the impacts of this growth, of Australia's largest cities from about the mid-19th century to the present day. The changing urban pattern of Australia is related to wider economic, social and demographic trends. As is demonstrated in this chapter, Australia's cities and their environments are diverse, and have been for a long time. It is important to recognise this point. It means that the sustainability initiatives discussed in later chapters may have common elements in various cities, but be tailored to the specific context of each city.

Chapter 2 explores the history of ideas that have impacted, or were thought likely to impact, on Australian cities. This chapter examines changes in ideas and their implementation through time. The chapter assists to explain some of the logic that was used to construct cities that are now considered unsustainable. The picture that emerges from this chapter is one of similar ideas influencing various cities, but different translations of these ideas into plans and actions in each Australian city.

Chapter 3 explores the governance and planning of Australia's major cities in the contemporary era. The chapter also explores the governance and metropolitan planning of Australia's five largest cities, before introducing three ideas that may have potential to make Australian cities more sustainable in the 21st century. These ideas are 'new urbanism', 'smart growth' and bioregionalism.

Chapter 4 discusses what is essentially a contemporary idea: the move from a focus on environmental protection to the creation of sustainable cities. This chapter traces the evolution of environmentalism and sustainability, and their articulation, to understand how these ideas came to be seen as relevant to cities. The notion of sustainability is questioned. In particular, this chapter looks at the possibility that 'sustainable cities' is an oxymoron. The ecological sustainability focus of this chapter highlights that Australian cities, in their current form, are 'vortex cities' rather than sustainable cities. In the following section of the book we examine a range of contemporary issues to be addressed for Australian cities to become more sustainable.

CHAPTER 1

AUSTRALIA'S LARGEST CITIES

INTRODUCTION

Australia's largest cities have a unique individual and collective history. The English colonial experience, including the specific time of settlement of each colony, meant that particular ideas about health, planning and defence have influenced the initial location and form of the city. While there have been some changes, as in Governor Phillip's decision in 1788 to relocate the planned settlement from Botany Bay to the south side of Port Jackson, often the site of initial settlement in each colony in Australia has become the contemporary city centre.

Australian cities have not been founded on earlier cities, although they have all been built on the sites and using the materials of Aboriginal communities. Australian cities do not have ancient or medieval city centres. Unlike English industrial cities of the 19th century, Australia was not the centre of a vast colonial empire. The initial penal or free settlements of Australian cities grew slowly until the big gold rushes of the 1860s in Victoria and the 1890s in Western Australia.

In the 20th century, Australia's people and cities were fortunate to largely escape the destruction of war that befell cities such as London, Berlin, Dresden, Warsaw, Leningrad (now St Petersburg) and Hiroshima. More recent events in Baghdad, Sarajevo and Kabul highlight the potential for massive destruction. While Darwin was bombed by Japanese planes in 1942 and more than 243 people were killed, the only other significant recorded damage in an Australian city was the sinking of HMAS Kuttabul in Sydney Harbour by one of three Japanese midget submarines in 1942, with the resulting loss of 21 lives.

What has emerged in Australia is a system of coastal cities with a high degree of primacy within each state (see table 1.1). In contrast to many large American cities (for example, New York, Los Angeles, Chicago), these Australian cities are the centre for both economic and political power within a state. Similar to countries such as Canada, Brazil and the United States, but unlike most major European cities, Australia has established a national capital in Canberra, thereby avoiding the concentration of political and economic power at the national level.

Table 1.1 Population and primacy of the six state capital cities in Australia, 2001

Statistical divisions	2001 population (000's)	State	2001 population (000's)	Degree of primacy (%)
Sydney	4154.7	NSW	6609.3	63
Melbourne	3488.8	Victoria	4822.7	72
Brisbane	1653.4	Queensland	3635.1	45
Perth	1397.0	WA	1906.1	72
Adelaide	1110.5	SA	1514.9	73

Source: Derived from Australian Bureau of Statistics, 2003a, 2003b

Understanding the urban environmental history of cities is important for sustainability concerns because some contemporary environmentalists and urban commentators equate the evils of the modern city with one of two factors – industrialisation or the dominance of the automobile (Newman and Kenworthy, 1999). The first factor begets the second. The critique of industrialisation assumes that prior to the Industrial Revolution in Wales, Belgium and England there was a golden age of cities that was somehow ruined by pollution, rapid urban expansion and poor housing. It is undeniable that these were some of the outcomes of industrialisation, as noted by Friedrich Engels about the northern English city of Manchester. Engels (1845, 73) wrote, 'The dwellings of the workers are everywhere badly planned, badly built, and kept in the worst condition'. However, ancient cities had (and caused) environmental problems, including pollution from bakeries, coin-making, and wood burning for the Roman baths. Julius Caesar banned wheeled traffic in Rome from sunrise to two hours before sundown in order to alleviate congestion in what was then the world's largest city.

This last example highlights the importance of transport in cities and the emergence of urban problems and attempted solutions prior to the Industrial Revolution. Congestion occurred in Ancient Rome, was present in London for hundreds of years and was a problem in 19th-century Manhattan, New York City, which in 1900 was home to 130 000 horses, used mostly for pulling wagons. The problems of horsedrawn vehicles included the deaths of pedestrians, the accumulation of manure (estimated to be 136 000 tonnes in Manhattan in 1900) and diseases such as tuberculosis (McShane, 1994).

This historical context is important when considering Australian cities, which, although founded in the late 18th and during the 19th century, have grown and been shaped most noticeably in the post–World War II era of automobile dominance. Without at least a rudimentary understanding of urbanisation in other countries through history, we are not in a position to identify the similarities and differences in the Australian experience. For example, relative to English cities, some Australian cities were spread over large areas from an early stage in their development prior to the invention of the automobile. Rather than being seen by governments, planners and many ordinary people as a problem, the spread of the city was seen as being good for health and sunlight and reducing the risk of disease. It was also considered part of the moral health of citizens to garden and demonstrate pride in maintaining their dwelling and yard.

This chapter presents an overview of Australia's largest cities. This is initially achieved through a chronological approach, one which relates the changes in these cities to particular international and internal dynamics. The focus of the chapter then moves to understanding the similarities and differences between Australia's largest cities by investigating perceived defining characteristics, such as the industrial city or the gateway city. In doing so, this chapter highlights that sustainability was not a major concern in the historical development of Australian cities. The chapter does, however, demonstrate the diversity in Australia's cities and their environments, thus establishing the framework for potential sustainability initiatives that are discussed in later chapters. These initiatives can have common elements in various cities, yet be tailored to the specific conditions of each city.

CHRONOLOGY

THE ORIGINS OF AUSTRALIAN CITIES

Sydney was founded in 1788 as a penal colony on the shores of Port Jackson, or what the local Eora people called 'Werrong'. Melbourne was established as a settlement by private settlers. Newcastle was settled after soldiers in chase of escaped convicts observed exposed coal seams at the mouth of what the local Wonnarua people called the 'Coquun', now known as the Hunter River. Perth was originally settled as a free colony in 1829, but imported convict labour from 1842 onwards. The origins of these cities were very different. McCarty (1970) identifies Sydney, Hobart, Launceston and Brisbane as being convict rather than commercial settlements. Newcastle can be added to McCarty's list (Dunn, et al, 1995). By way of contrast, McCarty (1970) argues that Perth, Melbourne and Adelaide were established as commercial centres. It is notable that in these cities, the port (Fremantle, Port Melbourne and Port Adelaide respectively) was some distance from the administrative centre of the colony.

The visions of the European settlers and planners in each colony led to further differences in the development of each city. Early settlement generally spread either in accordance with the traditional colonial grid plan, as Robert Hoddle established for Melbourne in 1837 and Colonel Light for Adelaide in the same year, or it followed land contours and Aboriginal travelling routes, as occurred in Sydney along the modern Parramatta Road. It was apparent that from an early stage in the settlement process, environmental issues were going to be controversial, with Governor Phillip failing in his attempt in 1795 to prevent the pollution of the Tank Stream, Sydney's initial water supply (Warner, 2000).

In short, there were errors in the choice of location for cities, an inaccurate understanding and/or representation of the site and the hinterland of these settlements (often to ensure that settlers would come to the colony), and an unplanned expansion of settlements contrasting with designated planning of what McCarty (1970) calls the 'planted city'. By the late 19th century, some of the key components of Australia's urban pattern, and the structure of individual cities within this urban pattern, were in place.

THE LATE 19TH CENTURY

If Sydney grew as a result of being the foremost administrative centre with the largest agricultural hinterland, then the rapid growth of Melbourne in the late 19th century can be attributed to the discovery of gold in inland Victorian centres such as Ballarat and Bendigo. Melbourne's population rose from 29 000 in 1851 to 473 000 in 1891, compared to Sydney's growth in the same period from 54 000 to 400 000 (McCarty, 1970). The definition of boundaries is crucial in calculating the population, and hence the density and primacy, of Australian cities. McCarty (1970) included the port as part of the city (for example, combining Fremantle and Perth), which results in his population figures and the degree of primacy generally being slightly higher than those of other authors.

The comparative populations of the capital city in each colony in the late 19th century can be seen in table 1.2. This table also highlights the degree of primacy (that is, the dominance of the largest city) of these cities in relation to the rest of each colony/state. It can be seen that in Sydney, Adelaide and Brisbane there is a trend towards increasing primacy between 1851 and 1901, although the degree of primacy was (and still is) less in Queensland due to the presence of other large urban centres. In the late 19th century the second largest city in Queensland was Rockhampton, which in 1900 was one-seventh the size of Brisbane (McCarty, 1970). Today it is seven-hundredths the size of Brisbane and has been surpassed in South-East Queensland by the Gold Coast, Sunshine Coast and the northern cities of Cairns and Townsville.

The remaining capitals demonstrate varying degrees of primacy. Melbourne's primacy declined from 38 per cent of Victoria's population in 1853 to 23 per cent in 1861, due to the rapid growth of regional centres such as Ballarat and Bendigo. Thereafter the trend was generally a rise in the primacy of Melbourne, although it stabilised in the 1890s as Melbourne's population growth rate slowed dramatically. The degree of primacy of Perth in Western Australia was virtually unchanged between 1861 and 1901, despite a rapid increase in population (an annual average increase in population of 14.3 per cent from a low base) between 1891 and 1901 due to the gold rush. The explanation for this primacy being unchanged is that while Perth's population grew rapidly between 1891 and 1901, by 1901 the population of the Eastern and Northern Goldfields had also increased dramatically and was 32.3 per cent of the state's total (Government Statistician's Office, 1957). In Tasmania, the level of primacy declined in each decade from 28 per cent in 1861 to 21 per cent in 1901. Northern Tasmania, especially Launceston, grew as an alternative settlement to Hobart. The lack of a major hinterland, and its location within Tasmania, meant that while it was the fourth largest town in 1861 (four times the size of Brisbane), by 1901 Hobart was already the smallest of the six state capitals of Australia (McCarty, 1970).

The degree of primacy was a concern for some commentators in the late 19th century (as it was later in the Whitlam era of the early 1970s and in more recent debates about the population of Australia's cities and coastal centres). Parkin (1891, 690 in McCarty, 1970, 111–12), was concerned about urban population growth at the expense of country towns and smaller districts:

Table 1.2 Population and primacy of the six colonial capital cities in Australia, 1851–1901

City	1851 pop. (000's)	% of colony	1861	% of colony	1871	% of colony
Sydney	54	28	96	27	138	27
Melbourne	29	38	125	23	191	26
Brisbane			6	20	15	13
Perth			5	33		
Adelaide	18	28	35	28	51	27
Hobart			25	28	26	25

City	1881	% of colony	1891	% of colony	1901	% of colony
Sydney	225	30	400	35	496	37
Melbourne	268	31	473	41	478	40
Brisbane	31	14	94	24	119	24
Perth	9	30	16	32	61	33
Adelaide	92	33	117	37	141	39
Hobart	27	23	33	22	35	20

Source: McCarty, 1970

> Population flocks into the towns of Australia in a proportion not known anywhere else. Melbourne contains nearly one-half of the people of Victoria, Sydney more than a third of the population of New South Wales. The abnormal aggregation of the (Australian) population into their capital cities is a most unfortunate element in the progress of the colonies.

These statistics have a spatial element. People had to live somewhere in the city. Infrastructure was needed to service the population. Frost (1991) argues that the Australian cities can be divided into two distinct groups – those that followed the 'new frontier' pattern of development found in cities in America's West, and those cities that tended to be high-density cities akin to European and US East Coast cities. Frost (1991) placed Melbourne, Perth and Adelaide in the former category, while he situated Sydney, Brisbane and Hobart in the high-density category. The major difference between these two categories of cities in Frost's typology was that in the 'new frontier' cities the pattern of growth was low-density suburban housing for both the working class and the middle class, whereas in Sydney, Brisbane and Hobart the working class generally lived in high-density housing and the attainment of additional space was generally the privilege of the elite.

This typology is perhaps best represented spatially. Figure 1.1 shows that in 1891 the built-up area of Melbourne was seven times that of Sydney, which has a layout similar in size to the English city of Birmingham. Sydney was restricted in its growth by the harbour and rugged terrain, while Melbourne had expanded on flatter and accessible land, combined with railway and tram infrastructure development and fare structures that enabled working class people to live in suburbs distant from their workplace (Davison, 1970; Frost, 1991). Mark Twain (1897 in Frost 1991, 18), the famous American author, noted that 'Melbourne spreads over an immense area of ground'.

Figure 1.1 Population and built-up area of Melbourne, Birmingham and Sydney, 1890–91

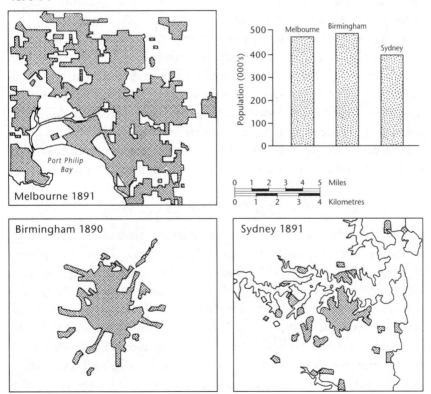

Source: Frost, 1991, 27

FEDERATION AND BEYOND

By 1901 Australia had a population of 3 773 801, excluding Aboriginal people who were not counted in the census. The largest city was Sydney, with a population of 496 000. Other significant cities included Melbourne (478 000), Adelaide (141 000) and Brisbane (119 000). Perth had a population of 61 000, while 32.3 per cent of the state's people lived in the Goldfields region of Western Australia, in thriving centres such as Kalgoorlie–Boulder, Coolgardie and Kanowna, the latter of which is now a ghost town.

The early part of the 20th century was most notable for the absolute and relative decline of mining centres, the increased primacy of the very largest Australian cities within their states, and the growth of the industrial cities of Newcastle and Wollongong. Despite this growth, as Forster (1999) observed, the largest cities retained their primacy by attracting many of the manufacturing and manufacturing-related jobs.

The chronology of Australian urban history in the 20th century has been addressed by many authors, including Burnley (1980), Maher (1982) and Forster (1999). These chronologies tend to focus on the largest cities, because of the population growth, increase in primacy and urban conflicts that growth and change generated in these cities. The remainder of this chapter moves from the chronological structure used to examine the early development of settlements, to looking at Australia's largest cities based on their popularly perceived dominant characteristics. We pick up the chronology of urbanisation in the following chapters when we look more closely at urban planning ideas and their implementation in Australia's largest cities during the 20th century.

CITY TYPES

A note of caution is needed when considering Australia's largest cities in terms of their perceived dominant characteristics. These perceptions of cities, while usually containing some degree of accuracy, are not always supported by empirical evidence. Further, the largest Australian cities embody many of the characteristics that are used to define smaller cities. For example, Sydney is more industrial than Newcastle. This was the case even when the BHP steelmill was operational in Newcastle.

The purpose of this structure is therefore not to classify Australia's largest cities by simple stereotypes, but to show the futility of this approach and to highlight the complexity of Australian cities. A limited range of stereotypes, reflecting both popular imaginings of some Australian cities (for example, industrial cities) and the recent use of terminology to define a particular type of city (for example, lifestyle cities and gateway cities), have been selected. The examples of sustainable cities and agricultural cities are also discussed, again to highlight the limitations of this approach.

Despite frequent media attempts to stereotype cities, and efforts by city leaders to repackage and present cities to be more favourably positioned within contemporary international service-oriented economies, the analysis that follows demonstrates that Australia's major cities are a kaleidoscope of characteristics. Some of these characteristics may be more prevalent in particular cities, and in certain areas of cities at historic moments. What is important for this book is that in the move towards sustainability, cities cannot be easily stereotyped. Attempts to do so will lead to the omission of significant activities and important ecological impacts of cities.

INDUSTRIAL CITIES

Australia generally does not have an image of being heavily industrialised like the north of England, the so-called rust belt of the United States or the Ruhr Valley of Germany. There are, however, concentrations of industrial activity. Arguably the most significant of these concentrations are in the largest cities, but areas such as Auburn and Clyde in Sydney or Laverton and Altona in Melbourne do not form the dominant image of these cities. These industrial areas are important, not so much in terms of the proportion of employment in a city, but for reasons such as the value they contribute to the city's production either directly or through the provision of industrial goods for use in other sectors of the economy.

There are, however, other smaller cities in Australia that have gained an image of being an industrial city, even though this may not be the city's most important economic activity. One such city is Newcastle, north of Sydney. Newcastle originated as a penal colony, became a free settlement, then an area of significant coal mining activity, and in 1913 commenced construction on the BHP steelworks (Dunn, et al, 1995). The city gained the image as Australia's premier industrial city. The agglomeration of mining villages were physically and administratively united in what Maitland (1997) called the 'Lost Cities of the Borehole Seam'. Even within so-called industrial cities such as Wollongong, to the south of Sydney, and Newcastle, there are significant differences. Wollongong became seen as Australia's second major industrial city with the development of the Port Kembla steelworks. Most of the migrants to Newcastle were English, whereas Wollongong, due largely to its time of expansion, attracted more southern European migrants.

The notion of cities having an industrial base is crucial in Australian urban history. Major cities such as Perth (through the development of the coastal new town of Kwinana to the south) and Adelaide (through the development of the General Motors Holden plant at the new town of Elizabeth to the north of the city) were keen to develop their industrial base and to prosper during the 'long boom' of the 1950s (Forster, 1999).

Other smaller cities also developed important industrial bases, and sometimes grew rapidly during periods of industrial expansion. For example, the cities of Geelong, south-west of Melbourne, and Gladstone, on the central Queensland coast, have important industrial functions which largely service Australia's five major cities. In summary, the notion of an industrial city is very likely to be based on an important characteristic of particular cities, but it has limited value in helping us understand the complexity and diversity of Australian cities.

GATEWAY CITIES

Australian cities had become 'gateways to Asia' before the former prime minister, Paul Keating, embarked on reorienting Australia's diplomacy efforts towards having us accepted as a 'southern tiger' economy. A number of Australian cities have been labelled 'gateways'. Brisbane was projected as a gateway city for trade purposes; part of this was developing a 'gateway ports area' for inter-modal transportation links and a 'gateway strategy' for the regional development of Brisbane and South-East Queensland (Stimson and Taylor, 1999). The gateway metaphor has been used to link cities for the purposes of comparison. For example, Sydney and Vancouver were identified as gateways to Asia (Ley and Murphy, 2001). The metaphor is continued in the Canadian urban context by Ley and Tutchener (2001) and Ley, Tutchener and Cunningham (2002).

Another Australian city that has been seen as a gateway is Perth. This city grew rapidly in the 1960s, largely as a result of iron ore discoveries in the Pilbara region in north-west Western Australia. Iron ore was exported to Japan, and Perth's city centre was transformed as a result of key financial and administrative service functions for resource development being located in the south of the state. These service functions have expanded given Perth's location relative to growing markets in South-East Asia.

The notion of a gateway is problematic, whether it relates to material flows or to investment capital and lifestyle (as in South-East Queensland and as was attempted near Adelaide with the multi-function polis). It is a discourse that is favoured by politicians and business people because it positions cities favourably relative to growth opportunities. In doing so, it marginalises other cities to a 'backyard' status. There is some accuracy in the discourse in that cities such as Perth, Brisbane, Cairns and Darwin have grown because of their proximity to emerging markets, while cities such as Adelaide and Hobart have not grown, largely because of their geographic position. The metaphor of a gateway does not, however, address the variety of functions and orientations existing within a city.

LIFESTYLE CITIES

Bernard Salt (2001) attributes the growth of the Gold Coast, Sunshine Coast and other rapidly growing coastal cities to 'lifestyle'. This is a challenging variable to isolate, because like industrial cities and gateway cities, so-called lifestyle cities also contain other functions. The leaders of Australia's major cities are also very concerned about the capability of their city image to attract tourism and highly paid international executives and retain residents. The promotion of Melbourne as the world's 'most livable city' highlights the values embodied in notions of lifestyle. What does 'livability' mean? Is it cleanliness, open space, a sunny climate, affordability, good food, a dynamic city, the provision of nature within urban areas, and so on?

Cities are also very concerned about negative images and poor urban environmental quality. For example, Newcastle's image as an industrial city has been seen as a barrier to development (Dunn, et al, 1995). Perth's air quality, Adelaide's water quality and Sydney's cost of living and congestion are seen as negative images that reduce the quality of lifestyle available in these cities (as will be further explored in section 2 of this book).

One issue that is emerging, particularly in Sydney, is the notion of overpopulation as a negative impact on a city's lifestyle (and ecological attributes). It seems strange to people outside of Australia that we are having debates about the concept of 'overpopulation'. Australia, the world's sixth largest country, having a population of 20 million living in a land area of over 7.6 million square kilometres! By way of comparison, China has just over 9.5 million square kilometres of land and a population of over 1.25 billion, or over 60 times the number of people in Australia (National Bureau Statistics of the PRC, 2000).

We will examine the notion of overpopulation in more detail in section 2. At this stage it is sufficient to say that some people, including Bob Carr, the Premier of New South Wales, perceive overpopulation to be a threat to lifestyle.

SUSTAINABLE CITIES

We explore the notion of sustainable cities in more detail in chapter 4. The concept warrants mention at this point because some cities around the world have promoted themselves as green or sustainable cities, in much the same way as some cities are perceived to be industrial cities. No major Australian city has promoted itself as a 'green' or 'sustainable' city similar to Leicester in England. The closest is Newcastle in New South Wales, which promotes an image of 'clean and green' and was responsible for hosting the Pathways to Sustainability Conference in 1997. In Newcastle, sustainability has come to mean a neo-traditional, high-density form of urban development (known as 'Newcastle urbanism'), exemplified by projects such as the Honeysuckle development and the nearby suburbs of Wickham and Carrington.

Other cities have adopted various aspects of sustainability, include the City of Melbourne's 'triple bottom line' (economic, social and ecological) framework for decision-making (McManus and Pritchard, 2001). Examples of particular actions to promote sustainability (such as purchasing decisions, organising conferences to promote the concept, initiating major projects to show what is possible and development control that constrains unsustainable practices) can be found in every major Australian city. Again, the stereotyping of cities fails to highlight the complexities of modern Australian cities.

One additional complexity worth discussing is the significance of agriculture in Australian cities and its contribution to both sustainability and environmental problems. Urban agriculture (on the urban-rural fringe), near-urban agriculture, semi-rural land, peri-urban land, or whatever other 'in-between' terminology we may coin, has long been seen by developers and others as an area waiting to be developed for housing, industry and other uses associated with cities. Consideration of cities often excludes the importance of agriculture, but earlier studies such as Wills (1945, 29) noted 'that no less than 40 per cent of the vegetables (excluding potatoes) consumed by Sydney's one and a third million inhabitants come [sic] from farms within twenty-five miles of the heart of the city', while Golledge (1960) emphasised the importance of land values and proximity to markets to enable capital investment in irrigation and fertilisers to create land suitable for intensive agricultural production. Golledge also noted the tendency among some farmers who 'allowed their land to deteriorate in anticipation of subdivision', and he identified the seeds of contemporary conflicts such as the one of continuing agricultural production versus capitalising on land value that may only be valorised through subdivision (Golledge, 1960, 253). Rutherford et al (1966) noted the changing patterns of what they term 'near-urban agriculture' in the Sydney Region. They also noted the importance of agriculture in the Sydney Region in terms of production, land area occupied, and supplying the nearby market of Sydney with its needs – especially fruit, vegetables and poultry products. Sinclair (1996) has observed that agricultural production in the Sydney Region was valued by NSW Agriculture at approximately $1 billion per annum, not including the value of the horse bloodstock industry which could add another $1 billion to this figure. In 1994–95 Sydney produced 44 per cent of New South Wales' poultry meat and 48 per cent of the state's eggs. Sydney was also very significant in terms of nurseries (44 per cent), flowers (55 per cent) and turf (58 per cent) in New South Wales (Sinclair, 1996). A recent study by Gillespie and Mason (2003) found that the Sydney Region accounts for 12 per cent of total agricultural production, by value, in New South Wales, using only 1 per cent of the state's land. Agriculture in the Sydney Basin is an economically significant activity with production valued at over $1 billion per annum (Gillespie and Mason, 2003).

Recent studies by McManus (2002a) indicate that while each Australian city is unique in its agricultural production, Sydney is important for lemon/lime and strawberry production, Melbourne for cherry production, Adelaide for cherry and strawberry production, and Perth is vital for producing lemons/limes, strawberries, peaches and plums/prunes. Similar studies of vegetable production reveal that with the exception of bulky vegetables requiring more space for growth, for example, potatoes and pumpkins, Australian cities produce significant quantities of vegetables and have high yields (McManus, 2002a). We do not, however, label our cities 'agricultural cities', again highlighting the deficiencies that are inherent in the process of stereotyping.

Despite its economic importance, much of the remaining agriculture in Australian cities will be lost unless we change our geographical imaginations about cities. This loss is likely to result in food travelling over even greater distances from its production to its consumption.

Agriculture in metropolitan Australia should not be romanticised as being sustainable. Senn et al (2000), for example, note the impact of agricultural practices, especially market gardening, on the Hawkesbury–Nepean River. The provision of healthy, sustainably produced food close to where it is being consumed is an important part of sustainable cities. Sustainable food production is, however, only one part of a sustainable city. Still, in the moves towards sustainability, agriculture is often overlooked and many of the issues discussed in the section 2 of this book, particularly population growth, impact negatively on agriculture.

SUMMARY

Australian cities all developed on Aboriginal land from the late 18th century onwards, the era of what Frost (1991) calls the 'new frontier'. Even so, the density of Australian cities varied significantly, with Sydney, Brisbane and Hobart being more compact cities in the late 19th century. The 20th century saw the rise of the automobile (a rise that was facilitated by urban planning decisions), major industrial development and changes in political and economic conditions that gave rise to the idea of gateway cities and lifestyle cities. It was understood that high environmental quality was important for competitiveness. The categories used in this chapter are not mutually exclusive, and all Australian cities have made efforts towards introducing sustainable development. Whether this warrants the label of a 'sustainable city' or a 'green city' will be discussed later in this book. Before doing so, it is important to explore aspects of the planning and environmental history of Australia's largest cities in order to learn from previous attempts to imagine and build our cities, and to understand how the contemporary Australian cities that we want to make more sustainable are a palimpsest of ideas and their translation into the urban fabric.

CHAPTER 2

AUSTRALIAN CITIES AND PLANNING

INTRODUCTION

Urban planning is an important activity in contemporary Australia, and in many other countries throughout the world. While some people may perceive planners to be faceless bureaucrats impeding the efficient operation of market forces through development control, in fact the opposite is often the case. The so-called free market could not survive without the planning and regulation of activities and of the land that they use.

Urban planning originated in the late 19th century in response to concerns about health (both physical and moral). It often included a reformist agenda. There is nothing, however, that is necessarily progressive about urban planning (see Yiftachel, et al, 2002). The formal activity of urban planning can reinforce and perpetuate injustice, environmental degradation and vested interests as easily as it can reform, mitigate or even improve environmental quality.

One of the major tools used by urban planners has been the map. This includes subdivision, land use and zoning maps. Legal zoning plans identified which land uses were permitted, and under what circumstances, in particular zones. The corollary was that certain activities and land uses were not permitted in particular zones. Ideally these zones related to the capability and suitability of specific land to accommodate the permitted land uses, but unfortunately this was not always the case. This process is not values-neutral because, as was understood in earlier planning traditions like the City Beautiful Movement (see below), the ability to use land in particular ways influences the financial value of the land.

Contemporary versions of urban planning tend to be less restrictive and more 'flexible' in their goals and in the tools that they use. The language of planning has changed and ideas that were fashionable in one era are often contrary to planning wisdom at a later date. For example, the separate house on a large lot of land that allowed for well-kept gardens, sunlight and safe areas for children to play has been identified as contributing to urban 'sprawl' and is often seen as wasteful given the contemporary trends towards smaller household size, more women in the workforce and the lifestyle benefits of inner-city living (see chapter 5).

Planning ideas may change faster than plans. The plans are often conduits that transfer ideas from one era to another. For example, the impact of 1960s transport planning that was primarily focused on mobility and developing facilities for the automobile (see chapter 7) is continued today as road constructors complete the 'missing link'. Transport planners facing opposition from community groups some-times justify their actions by saying that they are implementing plans that have been in the public domain for many years. The plans may now be cloaked in the language of sustainability (indeed, they have to be due to legislative requirements regarding ecologically sustainable develop-ment), even if through the perpetuation of a car-oriented city these plans are actually reinforcing unsustainability.

This chapter explores some of the key urban planning ideas that have influenced the development of Australian cities. These ideas are varied in their focus, scale, objectives and implementation. The diverse ideas considered in this chapter are development control, the Garden Cities and Green Belts Movement, the City Beautiful Movement, the high-rise aspirations of Le Corbusier, the 'neighbourhood unit', metro-politan planning and decentralisation. While it may be argued that other economic and social trends have been more influential in shaping Australian cities and that planners have largely responded to these trends (McLoughlin, 1992), and also that other urban planning ideas are interesting or have been influential, this chapter is based on the belief that the above ideas were either influential in Australian cities or, if they were less influential than anticipated, it is important to under-stand why. Understanding the impact of these ideas is assisted if we adopt a perspective of translation, following the work of actant network theorist Michel Callon (1986). 'Translation' emphasises the modifica-tion of ideas and their implementation as they move from one location to another. This is in contrast to a notion of diffusion that traces the spread of (but not necessarily the changes in) an idea or practice from its point of origin.

The ideas discussed in this chapter have, to varying degrees, helped produce the contemporary Australian cities which are often highly regarded in terms of human well-being and environmental quality, but which now stand accused of being entirely unsustainable, at least in sectors such as transport (Newman and Kenworthy, 1999). Ideas are, however, not sufficient to explain the history of Australia's largest cities. Their history is understood by the relationships between planning ideas, the implementation of plans and the multiple forces that influence the growth and development of Australian cities. These relationships are explored in more detail at the national, state and local levels in the latter part of the chapter. If, as suggested in the following chapters, we are to move Australian cities towards sustainability, it is important to understand the planning ideas that have produced the contemporary cities and to avoid repeating any fundamental mistakes in the plans or their implementation as we plan for sustainability.

SEVEN IMPORTANT IDEAS IN THE DEVELOPMENT OF AUSTRALIAN CITIES

DEVELOPMENT CONTROL

Development control is generally viewed as the most mundane aspect of urban planning. Arguably, however, it has been the most effective tool in shaping Australian cities because of its widespread implementation, although this should be seen as a secondary factor in relation to economic forces (see McLoughlin, 1992).

Development control is often projected as the progressive actions of urban planning that fetter market forces. In its absence, unfettered capitalism would produce disorderly and unhealthy cities, as was in evidence in Australia in the 1890s (Huxley, 1994). The emergence of development control includes zoning plans that permit certain uses on particular pieces of land and therefore prevent other uses of that land, and the regulations about how the permitted uses will be allowed to be developed. Yiftachel (2001, 11) has stated that 'most social systems devise mechanisms of legitimation, which tend to obscure, appease or even partially negate the oppressive and regressive effects of control policies'. Development *control* (my emphasis) is the intervention by educated professionals in processes of land development. It has often been underpinned by a discourse of greater community benefit (McManus, 2001), but has also been criticised for being restrictive, responsible for worsening problems of urban poverty (Simmie, 1993) and regulating out sustainability innovations (Duany and Talen, 2002). Despite these criticisms, drawn from various parts of the world where development control is practiced, and despite the influence of neo-liberal agendas in some places, there is little likelihood of development control disappearing altogether (see Gleeson and Low, 2000). Indeed, as Nankervis (2003, 316) has identified in the Australian context, 'much of a planner's day-to-day work involves statutory or regulatory work'. In this sense, the concept of planning as regulation has been a powerful influence in the development of Australian cities, but this influence is often secondary to economic forces.

'GARDEN CITIES'

The 'garden cities' vision of Ebenezer Howard (1850–1928) is part of a longer tradition of concern about livability and environmental quality in English and Scottish cities. As part of this concern, in 1845 Friedrich Engels published *The Condition of the Working Class in England*, based on 20 months of living in Manchester. In this condemnation of deplorable urban conditions, and the capitalist class that was primarily responsible for their creation, Engels claimed:

> The dwellings of the workers are everywhere badly planned, badly built, and kept in the worst condition, badly ventilated, damp and unwholesome. The inhabitants are confined to the smallest possible space, and at least one family usually sleeps in each room. (Engels, 1845, 173)

The housing scenario described by Engels was common to many rapidly growing industrial cities (the largest of which was the established metropolis of London). It was a scenario that fitted with Charles Dickens' 'Coketown' in the novel *Hard Times*, which describes the monotony of the city and of working-class life in the industrial cities (Dickens, 1856). There were attempts prior to and following the release of Engels' publication to change the physical conditions of the working class. Early urban reformers in England and Scotland were capitalist factory owners who may have been altruistic, or to varying degrees were seeking controlled and productive workers. Examples of these individuals, and the towns that they developed, include:

- Robert Owen (New Lanark, 1800 – south-east of Glasgow, UNESCO World Heritage-listed in 2001)
- Titus Salt (Saltaire, 1853 – near Bradford, UNESCO World Heritage-listed in 2001)
- George Cadbury (Bourneville, 1879 – near Birmingham)

• William Lever (Port Sunlight, 1888 – near Birkenhead, across the Mersey
  River from Liverpool).

Ebenezer Howard was influenced by spiritualism, anarchism and socialism (including the role of the Land Nationalisation Society). Having
lived in America, he had witnessed the changes occurring in the boom-
ing city of Chicago (see Cronon, 1991) and seen the possibilities of
landscape in the plan for Riverside, Chicago, which was prepared by
Frederick Olmstead in 1868 (Miller, 1989; Fulton, 2002). Howard's
plans for a new type of city were inspired by an American utopian novel
(*Looking Backward* by Edward Bellamy, published in 1888) and they
built on the earlier plans for Victoria (1849) by James Silk Buckingham
and for Hygeia (1876) by Dr Benjamin Ward Richardson (Miller,
1989). Howard's ideas and plans were introduced in his book
Tomorrow: A Peaceful Path to Real Reform (1898). In 1902 this book
was republished with the title *Garden Cities of Tomorrow*. The change
of title reflects the change in emphasis from the social to the physical
elements of Howard's ideas, a move that was reinforced through the
membership of the Garden Cities Movement (see Sandercock, 1975;
Ward, 2002).

Howard's concept of a central city surrounded by garden cities and
a green belt, with citizens working the land for agriculture, was developed as a social goal. Howard, like Buckingham and Richardson, was
attempting to show that it was possible to take the best from rural and
urban life and to create a new kind of city that was emotionally and
physically healthy for its inhabitants.

> I will undertake, then, to show how in 'Town–Country' equal, nay
> better, opportunities of social intercourse may be enjoyed than are
> enjoyed in any crowded city, while yet the beauties of nature may
> encompass and enfold each dweller therein. (Howard, 1898 in
> LeGates and Stout, 1996, 349)

Despite the significant attention given in England to Howard's proposals, including the formation of the Garden City Association, only two
examples of Howard's original garden city idea, as opposed to translations of this idea into garden suburbs, garden villages or later satellite
housing estates such as Wythenshawe near Manchester, were built in
England (see Deakin, 1989; Rudlin and Falk, 1999). These two examples (with Wythenshawe sometimes seen as England's third garden city)

were both north of London. Letchworth was built in 1903 and Welwyn Garden City in 1919 (see Busby, 1976; Miller, 1989; Parsons and Schuyler, 2002). In these two privately developed examples, Howard's ideas of cooperatively owned land and social reform were overlooked in favour of physical design, although Hardy (2000, 69, following Miller, 1989) has noted that Letchworth 'attracted a utopian following, so much so that the settlement as a whole acquired a reputation for "crankiness"'. The garden city concept was also influential in England in the aftermath of World War II when, through the Abercrombie Plan of 1944, the English New Towns Movement emerged and led to the development of new towns and the expansion of some existing settlements outside a number of larger English and Scottish cities. Birch (2002, 172) identifies 'five generations of garden city planners who have experimented with Howard's design concepts – just as he envisioned they would'. While Birch's chronology is American-centric, there is growing awareness that his fifth stage, comprising 'new urbanism', 'smart growth' and sustainable development, with examples such as the towns of Seaside and Celebration in Florida, draws on many of the same ideas as Howard's garden city concept (Birch, 2002). (See chapter 4.)

The concept of the garden city is important in Australian urban history because Australia was considered by Ebenezer Howard to be ideal for the development of garden cities. However, to date this scenario has not eventuated and it appears unlikely that it will in the future. Howard wrote:

> As population increases and flows to Australia, it is not difficult to picture that every important new town will be based upon garden city practice and ideas. I can see no way of correcting the current overpopulation of big cities and interesting people in productive enterprises of the soil, except by taking to the country all the advantages of the modern town or city. (Howard, 1920 in Freestone, 1981, 35)

'GREEN BELTS'

Notwithstanding the creation of environments planned on the garden cities concept (see Garnaut, 2000), as well as the decentralisation policies pursued by the Whitlam Government between 1972 and 1975, perhaps the closest that Australia has come to the idea of 'garden cities and green belts' was the establishment of a green belt for Sydney in the

1948 County of Cumberland Plan. This plan included green belts and limited satellite towns in the garden city tradition, but despite the green belt existing on paper, it was rapidly eroded by developers, including the Housing Commission, in the post–World War II boom that saw Sydney's population exceed the growth rates predicted in the 1948 plan (Wright, 2001; Bunker, 2002). As Freestone noted, '[t]he Australian path to reform was to improve the physical environment of the existing city – the low density city' (Freestone, 1981, 46). In a limited number of cases, this included 'garden suburbs' that were inspired by the garden city idea (these were Daceyville and Haberfield in Sydney, Coolbinia and Wembley Downs in Perth, Hamilton South and parts of Stockton in Newcastle; see also Garnaut, 2000).

Experience suggests that the concept of a greens belt has a number of significant problems. Freestone (2002, 82–3) highlights ten major concerns about green belts (see box 2.1).

Box 2.1 Ten major concerns about green belts identified by Robert Freestone

1. Greenbelts increase land and house prices.
2. Greenbelts can protect land of average environmental quality.
3. Greenbelts increase car travel.
4. Greenbelts divert development deeper into the countryside.
5. Greenbelts increase development pressures within existing centres.
6. Greenbelts can have a range of unpredictable effects.
7. Greenbelts do not necessarily increase public access to non-urban land.
8. Greenbelts are not always environmentally just.
9. Greenbelts are a negative and inflexible means of development control.
10. Greenbelts do not constitute a regional settlement strategy.

Source: Freestone, 2002, 82–3

The idea of a green belt occasionally emerges in Australia, in part because the original reasons for its creation, such as urban expansion and the desire to protect agriculture, still exist. Green belts exist in larger cities such as London and Seoul, and these examples provide models for other cities. As one small part of a visionary strategy for the development of Western Sydney, a new green belt of protected public space was proposed by the State Government-funded Greater Western Sydney Economic Development Board in 2003. This green belt was 'planned' (it was embryonic and deliberately lacked detail) to protect agricultural land. In this sense the green belt had much in common with Ebenezer Howard's original green belt, which was a 'working green belt' rather than a zone of environmental preservation of natural ecosystems. According to O'Rourke (2003, 7), this green belt 'would act as the lungs of the city, by preserving thousands of hectares of land along the Hawkesbury, Nepean and Cataract river system [sic)]'.

The visions of Ebenezer Howard are important for Australian cities and sustainability because they exemplify what can happen in the translation of utopian plans into practice, and because the accusations against Howard range from being 'the father of the modern suburb' (Rudlin and Falk, 1999, 33) to a promoter of 'private cities', a forerunner of the modern gated community (Webster, 2001). Sustainable cities should be moving away from these outcomes. A potential lesson here is the importance of the role of the state: Howard's initial plans faltered for lack of investment, but were implemented in a later generation (following Birch, 2002) because of the resources and legislative support of the British state. In the absence of state support for heroic projects, it appears that if garden cities of any description are going to be produced, it will be by private land developers.

THE CITY BEAUTIFUL MOVEMENT

At approximately the same time as the Garden City Movement was developing in England, the City Beautiful Movement rose to prominence in America and was very influential in some other locations between 1890 and 1910. The movement was based on the idea that cities should be works of art. It has been aptly described by Freestone (1997, 223) as 'a middle-class reform impulse directed to the renewal of urban fabric in the interests of social stability and economic growth'.

The reference point for this movement was the modernisation of Paris between 1853 and 1870 by Baron Haussmann during the reign of Napoleon III, although Wilson (1989, 9) from an American perspective claimed that 'the taproot of the City Beautiful Movement lies in 19th-century landscape architecture, personified by Frederick Law Olmsted'. In Paris, the creation of boulevards and vistas was primarily for military reasons, but other aspects of the redevelopment of Paris that appealed in an age of modernity were the boldness of the plan, the concentration on geometry and form, the provision of air and light in a medieval city, and the modernisation of sewerage and other infrastructure as part of the works. Importantly, Haussmann argued that the 'cost of urban renewal was justified by the enhanced property values along the new streets' (Stelter, 2000, 100).

The City Beautiful Movement became very influential in Rio de Janeiro and Buenos Aires, where the leaders of these cities were francophiles (Stelter, 2000). It also spread to North America (more so in the United States than Canada, and less in the southern states – see Wilson, 1989), where the leaders of cities such as Washington DC, Kansas City, Seattle, Cleveland, Denver, Chicago and San Francisco adopted this approach to the development of their cities.

'Australia was well placed to draw upon city beautiful thought at the turn of the century', argued Freestone (1998, 92). The movement has indeed had an impact in Australia, although this impact is not consistent between cities (see Freestone, 1998). Freestone (1997, 230) writes that the implementation was strongest in Canberra but that in many cases the discourse is about cities 'that might have been'. The concept was imported into Australia via the United States, rather than emerging directly from Paris or through a French connection. Walter Burley Griffin's award-winning design for Canberra (and some of the designs that did not win the award) were based on city beautiful thinking and practice. Burley Griffin had seen the Chicago World Fair of 1893, and had admired Daniel Burnham's ambitious city beautiful-inspired 1909 Plan for Chicago (Stelter, 2000). The geometry of Canberra incorporates the geometry of Washington DC, itself inspired by the geometry of Haussmann's Paris.

The City Beautiful Movement was also influential in Perth, which grew rapidly after the gold rush of the late 1880s and early 1890s. The population of Perth and Fremantle grew from 16 000 in 1891 to 107 000 in 1911 (McCarty, 1970). The major influential figure in shaping Perth was William Ernest Bold, who was the city's town clerk from 1901 to 1944. The report on his 1914 world tour emphasises the aesthetic, efficiency and cost–recovery aspects of boulevards in cities such as Kansas City and Denver. These examples were the inspiration for creation of The Boulevard in the Perth suburb of Floreat Park and Riverside Drive along the Swan River, and later Forrest Place in the city centre (Bold, 1914; Freestone, 2000; McManus, 2002b).

Sydney was unique among Australia cities in that it had undertaken a major demolition project as a result of the Bubonic Plague of 1900 (see Spearritt, 2000). Parts of older inner-city fringe suburbs such as The Rocks and Ultimo were demolished. The subsequent 1909 Royal Commission on the Improvement of Sydney and Suburbs was heavily influenced by the redevelopment of Paris, which one critic and champion of Sydney, Jack Fitzgerald, regarded as a 'wonder city', '[the] most beautifully ornate and spacious city in the whole world' (in Spearritt, 2000, 16). The designs of Sir John Sulman were based on Haussman's Paris (which he had first visited in 1873), his extensive travelling in the United States and the City Beautiful and Garden Cities Movements, but it should be noted that the 1909 Plan for Sydney was very much focused on the area between Central Station and Circular Quay (Freestone, 1996; Spearritt, 2000). It was not a metropolitan plan, even allowing for Sydney's smaller built-up area compared to Melbourne.

The legacy of the City Beautiful Movement in Australia varies between cities. In Melbourne, a number of parks, monuments and the boulevard of St Kilda Road are the legacies of the movement (Freestone, 1997). Freestone (2000, 44) has noted that 'the city beautiful ethos was more muted in Adelaide, still basking in its status as the original parkland city and with the local planning agenda set by Charles Reade more oriented to administrative concerns'.

The City Beautiful Movement, unlike the Garden Cities Movement, was not attempting to address social inequities. The City Beautiful Movement was inspired by the idea of beauty and value-capturing. Both movements wanted to improve environmental quality, and one way in which this was achieved was through the spacious layout of the city. Both fostered the spread of urban areas, but while this was once seen as a positive phenomenon for emotional, moral and physical health reasons, it is now the subject of intense criticism and debate.

LE CORBUSIER AND THE HIGH-RISE CITY

Le Corbusier was born Charles-Edouard Jeanneret in 1887 (he died in 1969). He grew up in Switzerland and changed his name when he moved to Paris. He was a major proponent of purism, which he founded in 1918 (Harrison and Wood, 1992; Kleiner, Mamiya and Tansey, 2001). This movement maintained that 'machinery's clean functional lines and the pure form of its parts should direct the artist's experiments in design, whether in painting, architecture or industrially produced objects' (Kleiner, Mamiya and Tansey, 2001, 1019). Le Corbusier designed houses as 'machines for living'. Le Corbusier abhorred the inefficiency and lack of space in old cities. He embraced modern technology and incorporated it into his designs. There was no place to fit this technology into Europe's old cities, so the cities would be razed and rebuilt. He proposed vertical cities for residential, business and service functions, the development of linear industrial cities linking the vertical cities, and separate centres for people involved in intensive agricultural production (Kleiner, Mamiya and Tansey, 2001). Le Corbusier is generally known for his vertical city proposals.

In 1922 Le Corbusier presented a plan for 'a contemporary city of three million people'. Unlike many other utopian plans, Le Corbusier's city was not to be a city of the future, but the city of today. He proposed to build it by knocking down several hundred acres of the existing city on the Right Bank of Paris. Le Corbusier wanted to increase densities to 1200 people per acre, almost ten times the existing Paris density. While there is little tradition of this approach in Australia (the clearance of The Rocks following the rat plague of 1901 being an exception), in Paris during the 1860s Haussmann had pushed boulevards through the old quarters to divide and isolate rebellious citizens and to enable troops access to the city (Harvey, 1989).

Le Corbusier's planned city consisted of symmetrical rows of evenly spaced geometrical skyscrapers. His theme was the 'skyscraper in the park', developed conceptually as 'the 'Ville Radieuse' in 1933. In this sense Le Corbusier's aims 'are similar to those of Howard ... to decongest the centre of cities, increase mobility and increase the amount of parks and open space' (Rudlin and Falk, 1999, 34). The Contemporary City attempted to achieve sunlight, open space (comprising about 95 per cent of the land), mobility, technological innovation, a transport hierarchy and control. 'We must build *in the open*: both within the city and around it', wrote Le Corbusier (1929 in LeGates and Stout, 1996, 375).

Another important aspect of Le Corbusier's work was the destruction of World War I. The metaphor of war infuses his notion of planning a city: '[W]e can take control and decide in what direction the forthcoming battle is to be waged ... [f]or the desire to rebuild any great city in a modern way is to engage in a formidable battle' (Le Corbusier, 1929 in LeGates and Stout, 1996, 369).

The legacy of Le Corbusier's ideas includes schemes in Marseilles, the city of Chandigarh in India and, indirectly, many high-rise public housing estates. In Australia this is most obvious in the inner suburbs of Melbourne, where 'during the 1960s the Housing Commission of Victoria established an international reputation as the foremost construction authority in the field of slum reclamation and high-rise public housing' (Tibbitts, 1988, 123). The commission razed blocks of housing in older suburbs to construct 47 high-rise towers in locations such as South Melbourne, Fitzroy, Collingwood, North Melbourne, Carlton, Kensington, Flemington and Footscray (Tibbitts 1988; Ecumenical Housing, 2001).

It is prudent to be cautious about the legacy of Le Corbusier because the inheritors of Le Corbusier's ideas often tried to save money and in doing so were not faithful to his vision of a skyscraper in the park. Green spaces became car parks, buildings were cheaply constructed, and so on. In a number of English and Scottish cities, including Manchester, Liverpool and Glasgow, a number of these high-rise public housing estates have been or are being demolished (see Coleman, 1985). In Australia, many of these estates are being refurbished, but one tower at 72 Derby Street in Kensington (in Melbourne) was demolished in 1999 (Ecumenical Housing, 2001). The legacy of the high-rise public housing estates is similar to the low-density fringe public housing estates found in cities such as Sydney, Adelaide and Perth. They both have their genesis in the desire to house greater numbers of people as cheaply as possible, rather than housing fewer people in better conditions.

THE NEIGHBOURHOOD UNIT

There is general acceptance in planning history that the concept of the neighbourhood unit was developed by an American urban planner called Clarence Perry in 1929 while working on the Regional Plan of New York (Schubert, 2000), although Miller (2002) traces the evolution of this idea to English planning in the 19th and early 20th centuries. Birch (2002) claims that Perry was influenced by the Chicago School's sociological work on the development of community, and by the efficiency movement known as Taylorism. The neighbourhood unit has been used for the extension of existing cities through the process of suburban development, but it is probably more famous for the iconic (sub)urban planning of the new settlements of Reston (in Virginia, in 1961) and Columbia (in Maryland, in 1963) at a time when the suburban population was rapidly approaching the population of the cities in the United States (Birch, 2002).

Of the ideas discussed so far, apart from development control, the neighbourhood unit has been the most widely applied in Australia's largest cities. It has been concerned with improving livability and environmental and social quality. It was conceived as a response to the rise of the private car, and Australia's largest cities have grown significantly during the age of the automobile. It was based on a maximum of 5000 people surrounding an elementary (primary) school, with local shops, internal open space and a road network that discourages through-traffic. The layout was in contrast to the grid street pattern found in earlier American planning. This facilitated the passage of the automobile through cultural neighbourhoods, which were perceived to have reduced environmental quality as a result.

The neighbourhood unit was suited to the development of low-density Australian suburbs emanating from a central city. Forster (1999, 17) claims that between World Wars I and II, 'life in the new suburbs – poorly designed or not – was much better than in the traditional working-class inner areas which had suffered severely from the unemployment and hardship of the Great Depression in the early 1930s' (see Park, 1948 and 1949). The building of new dwellings, and the attraction of life in the suburbs, was promoted in building and women's magazines in the 1920s and 1930s (Spearritt, 1978 and 2000). It was made possible by rapid increases in car ownership (Forster, 1999; McManus, 2002b), especially in the period following the conclusion of World War II.

The neighbourhood unit has provided the foundation for modern Australian suburbia. While there have been radical departures from the traditional neighbourhood unit, such as the Radburn-inspired design for Crestwood in the Perth suburb of Thornlie, these are few and far between. The segregation of passing traffic from the internal traffic of a neighbourhood unit has generally been achieved by a hierarchy of roads and the use of crescents and cul-de-sacs. In comparison to the older grid-based suburbs, this form of development is difficult to redevelop to higher densities in a comprehensive and coordinated manner because of the road pattern, lot layout and infrastructure provision. Redevelopment is possible, but it sometimes requires modifications to the design of the suburb in order to facilitate high-density development. As Wheeler (2003, 318) has observed, 'street patterns are probably the most important single element of urban form, since these networks determine so much else about neighbourhood design and are difficult to change once they become established'.

METROPOLITAN PLANNING

The earliest 'metropolitan' plans in Australia were developed prior to World War I. The 1909 Plan for Sydney 'fell short of a truly comprehensive metropolitan strategy' (Freestone, 2000, 37). Hutchings (2000) discusses early attempts at metropolitan planning, but the initial enthusiasm was rarely translated into practice.

The emphasis during the interwar period moved to attempts to create metropolitan governments, rather than numerous small local governments working together to develop metropolitan plans. Only Brisbane, merging 19 local governments into one in 1925, and Newcastle amalgamating 12 municipalities into a single unit in 1933, were successful in adopting a metropolitan-wide unitary system of government, although there was partial success in inner Perth (Alexander, 1986; Yiftachel, 1991; McInerney, 1993; Maitland and Stafford, 1997).

It may be argued that an increased role for urban planning was more socially acceptable as the population had become accustomed to government involvement in many aspects of the economy and society during World War II. In addition, the dreams of a new post-war society (in Britain this meant a modern society in new towns not so vulnerable to aircraft attack on the established, industrialised, large cities) could be fulfilled by the same planning that had helped win the war. Australia followed the lead of Britain, where in 1944 the Abercrombie Plan laid out the post-war urban vision for London and satellite cities.

In Australia the first post-war urban plan was the 1948 County of Cumberland Plan for Sydney. This plan was based on 1947 population forecasts for Sydney (Bunker, 2002). The plan created a green belt stretching from Ku-ring-gai Chase National Park in the north, the agricultural settlements of Blacktown and St Marys in the west and beyond Liverpool in the south to link up with Royal National Park.

The problems with the County of Cumberland Plan included an underestimatation of Sydney's future population (admittedly fuelled by an unprecedented post-war immigration boom) and, unlike London, inadequate planning for satellite towns beyond the green belt (see Wilmoth, 1987). The resulting erosion of the green belt in the early 1960s enabled the development of Sydney's vast western suburbs, including many large public housing estates (see Wright, 2001).

The 1968 Sydney Region Outline Plan was based on the notion of corridor growth, as had been practiced in Scandinavian cities such as Stockholm, Copenhagen and Helsinki (Meyer, 2000). The idea was to have open space in between the 'fingers' of growth, and that these corridors would be serviced by existing rail networks and proposed motorways. The corridors would use existing towns as nodes of growth –

these being Campbelltown in the south-west, Mt Druitt and Penrith in the west and Gosford and Wyong north of Sydney (Morison, 2000). The plan assumed a population of five million by 2000, and with this assumption (based on the rapid post-war growth that exceeded 1948 predictions), the area set aside for residential development has been used with a population of about four million people because the density of residential development has been much lower than the 1968 Plan envisaged (Meyer, 2000).

The Melbourne and Metropolitan Board of Works, which was the organisation responsible for providing Melbourne's major infrastructure (including water, sewerage, stormwater drains and main roads), produced a plan for Melbourne in 1954 (see Bunker, 2002). The planned area was less than half the size of the County of Cumberland Plan, there was no attempt to restrict suburban growth and the plan reinforced Melbourne's south-easterly growth orientation (Wright, 2001; Bunker, 2002). Importantly, the plan ensured that areas for water catchment were not encroached on by urban growth (see chapter 6).

The revised Melbourne Statutory Scheme of 1971 was the result of a major conflict between the planning agencies and the powerful Melbourne and Metropolitan Board of Works (see Logan, 1986; Huxley, 2000; Morison, 2000). This organisation had Alastair Hepburn as its chief planner since the late 1950s. Its plan was for seven corridors and a satellite town to be developed at Sunbury, with green wedges between the corridors. The intention was to orient growth towards the less attractive northern and western areas of Melbourne, in order to reduce pressure on the south-east and the Dandenong Ranges (although growth to Berwick and to a lesser extent Lilydale was encouraged). This plan was adopted as government policy.

The 1955 Metropolitan Plan for Perth and Fremantle prepared by Gordon Stephenson and Alistair Hepburn (it is known as the Stephenson–Hepburn Plan) was a response to planned industrial development on the coast south of Fremantle at Kwinana (see McManus, 2002b). This plan was notable because it established a metropolitan system of parks 'which incorporated the river corridors and coastline as well as wetlands and the escarpment' (Wright, 2001, 42). This built on the earlier regulation by the previous town planning commissioner which reserved land adjacent to the coast and waterways as public land (Wright, 2001). The impact on the contemporary city is enormous – Perthites have access to the rivers and coasts, conservation is facilitated and the later provision of cycleways (particularly for recreation) has been possible because of the land tenure. The 1955 plan was also important in that it recommended a density of 20 dwellings per hectare in new suburbs, whereas by the early 1990s the average was about 8 dwellings per hectare (Yiftachel and Kenworthy, 1992). The plan also envisaged a maximum population of 1.4 million by 2000, after which any overspill growth would occur in smaller towns away from the urban fringe (Yiftachel, 1991).

In Perth the 1963 Metropolitan Region Scheme, and later the 1970 Corridor Plan, confirmed that the city was to be spread out and reliant on automobile transport. The railways in the Stephenson–Hepburn Plan were omitted and the length of actual and planned freeways in kilometres exceeded the combined total of existing freeways (those under construction and those being designed) by a factor of ten (McManus, 2002b).

In Adelaide the 1962 Metropolitan Development Plan envisaged a linear city, one comprised of a number of districts with populations ranging from 80 000 to 150 000, each with its district centre (Wright, 2001; Bunker, 2002). The subsequent planning for Adelaide was based on this plan well into the 1970s because population growth was slower than expected and there was less pressure to review the plan (see Huxley, 2000).

Brisbane is unique in not having metropolitan planning as such, largely because the Brisbane City Council has been, until recent times, the de facto metropolitan planner.

The metropolitan plans described above variously aimed to coordinate development, manage infrastructure provision, encourage and manage growth, protect agriculture and the environment and make housing affordable by releasing land for development. Where the plans were successful, these aims were often achieved at the expense of sustainability – of stocks in the city, in the hinterland and particularly in other places of the planet that Rees (1997) has called the 'distant elsewhere'.

DECENTRALISATION

When one thinks of the concept of decentralisation in Australian urban planning, the usual association is with the Whitlam Labor Government and the Department of Urban and Regional Development in the early 1970s. This period is much later than the decentralisation move in England, encapsulated in the 1944 Abercrombie Plan for London. At the 1951 conference during which the Australian Planning Institute was formed (later becoming the Royal Australian Planning Institute and then the Planning Institute of Australia), decentralisation was viewed very positively (Wright, 2001). The long era of the Liberal Party's domination at the national level, and the unwillingness of prime ministers such as Robert Menzies to become involved in planning, meant that it was only in the 1970s that decentralisation became a focus for urban policy and planning.

The focus on decentralisation was very political. The Federal Whitlam Government's priorities were Albury–Wodonga (on the NSW–Victoria border), Townsville (in northern Queensland) and Campbelltown (in the south-west of Sydney). South Australia was promoting the proposed new town of Monarto, near Murray Bridge about 80 kilometres east of Adelaide. New South Wales wanted Bathurst–Orange as a focus for development. Victoria wanted Geelong as a focus, while the vast differences in political values between the Whitlam Government and the National Party led by Joh Bjelke-Petersen in Queensland meant that support for Townsville was not forthcoming (see Wright, 2001).

The legacy of the decentralisation push is mixed, especially given the financial resources devoted to this idea. In 1972 it was proposed that Albury–Wodonga was to have a population of 300 000 by 2000. In 1978 the target was revised to 150 000. When the Albury–Wodonga Development Repeal Bill was debated in the NSW Legislative Council in mid-2000, the population of the combined cities was about 72 500 (NSW Hansard, 2000). The financial resources devoted to Albury–Wodonga up until 30 June 1998 were said to be in the order of $139 million (with $83.7 million spent between 1974 and 1976, mostly on land purchase), but the income generated to 30 June 1999 was claimed to be approximately $327 million (NSW Hansard, 2000). While Albury–Wodonga is a thriving inland centre (one of the three largest inland centres in Australia), it does little to siphon population growth away from Australia's largest cities. By way of contrast, Monarto is vacant, due largely to the slower than anticipated growth in Adelaide. The focus on inland Australia has been less than successful. Decentralisation due to market forces is occurring, particularly in Sydney where house prices are forcing people out of Sydney – mostly to Queensland or the NSW Central Coast. This is placing additional pressures on coastal areas (Burnley and Murphy, 2004).

Unless there is a major focus for employment, as in Canberra with the machinery of government and diplomatic relations, there is little likelihood of major growth (relative to the annual increase in population in Sydney of about 50 000 people) in inland Australia. Decentralisation to coastal areas is environmentally damaging, which means that population growth is likely to be distributed between the consolidation of existing large cities, the outward expansion of these cities and the seemingly unstoppable growth of coastal areas (Gosford, Gold Coast, Mandurah, and so on) near major Australian cities.

Decentralisation may imply an anti-urbanism agenda, but this is not necessarily so. It may represent a 'frontier mentality' that sees 'green-field' sites beyond the existing cities, and the opportunity to start anew without the baggage of history. As this chapter has demonstrated, these concepts are not new.

RECENT HISTORIES OF AUSTRALIA'S LARGEST CITIES

The approach taken to Australian cities during the period 1975–1996 may be analysed by identifying two major sub-periods, 1975–1983 and 1983–1996. These sub-periods are defined by changes in government at the Commonwealth level that have had a major impact on national urban policy. It is possible to structure this chapter based on other changes at the international level or at the state and metropolitan levels (the rise and fall of the Kennett Government in Victoria, for example), but the approach taken here is to review the national and various state and local governments within the distinct periods of national leadership. This does not mean that national leadership was always more important than other levels of government or than the rise of public participation in planning. The challenges to government and planning bureaucracies from local communities was often important in altering official plans. This is particularly the case for issues such as heritage and transport planning. Recognising this caveat, the structure sets the scene for our understanding of contemporary cities and the challenges posed by the concept of sustainability.

WITHDRAWAL FROM A NATIONAL APPROACH TO URBANISATION: 1975–1983

When elected in 1975 the Fraser Coalition Government systematically slashed programs of the Whitlam Government as it pursued a policy of monetarism that aimed to reduce government expenditure. The Fraser Government implemented what it called 'new federalism', whereby the government withdrew from a range of activities which it saw as being in the realm of the states. Further, the Fraser Government moved away from the tied and special grant programs of the Whitlam era by providing a generic pool of funds for states to administer.

The removal of funding for the Whitlam Government's decentralisation program was crucial in shaping Australia's settlement patterns. There is no guarantee that decentralisation would have worked, and if it did from a perspective of population distribution, there was an upfront financial cost to be paid that may or may not have been effective use of money. By removing funding and by scrapping plans to relocate government staff in Albury–Wodonga as a stimulus to growth, the Fraser Government ensured that decentralisation did not work. Since the mid-1970s, there has been a reinforcing of capital city growth, particularly if the capital cities are considered the focus of a mega-region such as Sydney–Newcastle–Wollongong or South-East Queensland. Forster (1999) identifies that between 1971 and 1996, Sydney's population grew by 33 per cent, Melbourne's by 25 per cent, Brisbane's by 72 per cent, Perth's by 77 per cent and Adelaide's by 24 per cent. Between 1996 and 2001, the four largest cities grew by at least 7 per cent, with Adelaide's growth over the period being slower at 2.4 per cent (derived from census data in Australian Bureau of Statistics, 1996 and 2001).

The withdrawal of the Fraser Government from urban and regional planning meant that the emphasis returned to the individual states, particularly the capital cities and their hinterlands. Unfortunately, little innovation occurred during this period – most cities continued to implement, or to struggle to implement, the plans of the late 1960s and early 1970s. The major change was in the growth of environmental awareness, the creation of environmental legislation and the formation of environmental departments. These departments were often seen as competition by the older planning departments.

In New South Wales, the *Environmental Planning and Assessment Act 1979* was introduced. This Act represented a shift towards policy-based urban governance, but while it has been important in shaping local planning in Sydney, the Act it did not substantially address metropolitan-level issues. The sum of the parts do not necessarily make a coherent whole, and despite policies, Sydney continued to expand through land releases, largely as it had done prior to the new legislation. Significantly, much of the land that was released was not serviced by rail or public transport, thereby leading to greater automobile use (see chapter 7). Meanwhile, Sydney surged ahead of Melbourne to become Australia's major financial and international city. By 1983, 73 per cent of the head offices of merchant banks in Australia were in Sydney, although the largest 14 merchant banks were at that time divided equally in location between Sydney and Melbourne (cited in Rich, et al, 1987).

In Melbourne, the battle in the early 1970s over which metropolitan plan to adopt gave way to land scandals and debates about urban form in the late 1970s (Logan, 1986; Huxley, 2000). The 1980 Metropolitan Strategy Plan was about consolidating growth in inner Melbourne, which the chairman of the powerful Melbourne and Metropolitan Board of Works claimed was becoming 'the hole in the middle of a swelling doughnut' (cited in Logan, 1986, 149). The battle about consolidation versus dispersal, which became a focal point for academics, policy-makers and planners in the era of the Hawke and Keating Federal Labor Governments (1983–1996), was initiated in the 1980 Metropolitan Strategy Plan which attempted to reduce expenditure on providing new infrastructure at the fringe of Melbourne's built-up area.

Brisbane and surrounding areas, now known as the South-East Queensland Region, grew very rapidly during 1975–1983, despite losses of population in the inner suburbs (Stimson and Taylor, 1999). Attempts to produce a metropolitan region strategy in the 1970s amounted to 'little of substance' and the '1976 plan for Brisbane City was little more than a traditional regulatory zoning scheme (Stimson and Taylor, 1999, 292).

The planning focus in the rapidly growing city of Perth during 1975–1983 was accommodating urban development in four corridors (north-west, south-west, south-east and east) as recommended in the 1970 Corridor Plan, which had been adopted in 1973 (Stokes and Hill, 1992). This was important because the growth of the north-west corridor, in particular, towards the new subregional centre of Joondalup, was almost entirely based on automobile transport.

Meanwhile, the Department of Conservation and Environment, which was formed in 1972, was busily dividing Western Australia into 'systems' for conservation purposes. System 6, officially known as the 'Darling System' after the Darling Ranges east of Perth, covered the south-west of the state, including the entire Perth Metropolitan Region. In 1981 the System 6 Report was released. It 'advocated an essentially "preservationist" approach to conservation' and, despite its flaws, 'it has had a major impact on the protection of many nominated habitats and environments that would otherwise have been destroyed' (Singleton, 1992, 241) (see chapter 10).

In Adelaide, the focus shifted from making plans to urban governance. The Dunstan Labor Government, which lasted until 1979, reorganised departments and created a structure that subsumed urban planning within housing. The earlier approach of 'blueprint' planning was superceded by 'systems planning' that monitored infrastructure development and land release to ensure efficiency, coordination and equity (Huxley, 2000).

Despite some important initiatives at the level of individual cities, it was not until the late 1980s that urban planning regained some of the momentum it had in the early 1970s. This was largely brought about by changes at the national level and the passing of time which had exposed some of the weaknesses in earlier plans. The new generation of plans were based on the idea of 'strategic planning'.

DOMINANCE OF THE AUSTRALIAN LABOR PARTY: 1983–1996

The era of the Hawke and Keating Labor Governments in retrospect can appear like a return to Whitlam-style policies (Alexander, 1994), yet it is important to note distinctions over this period. Housing and planning for new housing on smaller lots was important in the 1980s. The Joint Venture for More Affordable Housing's (1989) proposals for 'cost-effective residential land development' were popularly known as 'Green Street'. In the latter years of Labor's reign, particularly from 1991 onwards, numerous reports relevant to urban and regional development were produced (see Alexander, 1994). The flagship of this armada was the Better Cities Program, later to become the Building Better Cities Program, which was launched in the 1991–92 budget with $800 million in funding over five years. Hamnett (2000, 170) claims that 'the Better Cities Program of the early 1990s marked a significant renewal of interest in the cities on the part of the Federal Labor Government'.

The Building Better Cities Program has become associated with sustainability because of the United Nations Conference on Environment and Development (the 'Earth Summit') in Rio de Janeiro in 1992. There certainly was an urban sustainability emphasis within the program, particularly in the funding of model urban consolidation projects such as Pyrmont in Sydney and the former industrial area of East Perth. There were also occasional papers on topics ranging from water management in subdivision design to the issue of contaminated sites. The program was, however, largely about infrastructure development and, commentators such as Alexander (1994) have suggested, about securing urban votes for the Australian Labor Party. In 1994–95 the program was reviewed as being a success, and the federal budget for 1995–96 allocated a further $236 million for a new program, Better Cities Two. This was, however, immediately ended with the election of the Howard Coalition Government in 1996 (Hamnett, 2000).

While the Building Better Cities Program dominated the national urban policy agenda in the early 1990s, there were important develop-ments in state- and metropolitan-level governance and planning that were having significant impacts in Australia's largest cities. Individual cities were faced with particular challenges and opportunities over this period. Cities such as Sydney, Melbourne and particularly Brisbane and Perth experienced rapid increases in population between the 1981 and 1996 Census dates.

The population of Sydney rose from 3.2 million in 1981 to 3.7 million in 1996. This represents a 16 per cent increase in 15 years, or an average annual population increase of 1.1 per cent. The rapid growth in Sydney's population was largely accommodated in western and south-western local government areas such as Liverpool (22.3 per cent increase in population between 1996 and 2001), Blacktown (which increased in population from 211 710 in 1991 to 232 219 in 1996, a rise of 9.7 per cent in five years) and Penrith (which rose by 9 per cent between 1991 and 1996) (Australian Bureau of Statistics, 2001).

The major metropolitan planning document released in this era was the 1988 Metropolitan Strategy. This, as with the 1968 Sydney Region Outline Plan, was not a gazetted document. The strategy aimed to increase residential densities, particularly in the form of more multi-unit dwellings, and increase the number of lots in the new subdivisions from an average of 8 per hectare to 10 per hectare (see Meyer, 2000). Basically, the idea of a concentrated, rather than a dispersed city, was the planning option to be pursued.

The urban consolidation approach was reinforced in the 1995 docu-ment *Cities for the 21st Century*, which called for what Hamnett (2000, 174) termed 'fairly heroic' increases in residential density. The medium-level population projection for 2021 was 4.48 million (Meyer, 2000). The move towards a more consolidated city also included the develop-ment of subregional centres such as Parramatta and Chatswood, the redevelopment of inner harbour sites such as Darling Harbour for tourism and entertainment, and the redevelopment of industrial land (contested in, for example, the 'Battle for Balmain', as noted by

Bonyhady, 1995) and government-owned land, as in Pyrmont. These major developments have been the forerunner of significant residential development in the city, inner suburbs and along Sydney Harbour and the Parramatta River.

The major change to affect Melbourne during this period was the replacement of the Kirner Labor Government by the Kennett Liberal Government. The democratically elected Melbourne City Council was replaced in 1993 by commissioners appointed by the state, who promptly approved Southbank along the Yarra River (see Hamnett, 2000). During the Kennett era, 1992–99, there was an emphasis on business growth and making the city competitive. The city was restructured by business, with government approval and assistance, to meet the needs of business. Planning for the central city was outlined in the 1994 document *Creating Prosperity: Victoria's Capital City Policy* (Hamnett, 2000). The Kennett Government outlined its vision in a document that Gleeson and Low (2000, 110) called the 'cynically labelled "Agenda 21" in provocative contrast to the world program for sustainable development agreed at the Rio Earth Summit in 1992'. Fast-tracking of major projects became standard practice under the Kennett Government. In late 1995 the Kennett Government released *Living Suburbs: A Policy for Metropolitan Melbourne into the Twenty-First Century.* Hamnett (2000) has noted that this document claimed that Melbourne had 20 years of urban land supply at the fringe, and that the usual environmental issues such as energy efficiency and water management were part of this document (see chapter 6).

Brisbane experienced rapid growth between 1981 and 1996 (Stimson and Taylor, 1999; Haveri and Siirila, 1999). According to Haveri and Siirila (1999, 108) the Brisbane region (now incorporated by the South-East Queensland (SEQ) region) was 'one of the fastest growing western urban areas in the whole world'. The major change that occurred in the planning of Brisbane in this period was the realisation that a regional strategy was necessary to address the pressures of growth not just in Brisbane, but in the SEQ region. The region stretches from north of Noosa on the Sunshine Coast, west to Toowoomba and south to the Gold Coast on the border of New South Wales. Between 1991 and 1996, the SEQ region accounted for 77 per cent of the rapid population growth in Queensland (Minnery, 2001). In late 1990 the South-East Queensland 2001 Regional Growth Management Project was initiated by the recently elected state Labor government (Minnery, 2001). The project evolved from the 1990 document *The Brisbane Plan: A City Strategy*, which 'fell foul of politi-cal changes in the City Council in 1990 and was eventually published in 1991 simply as a discussion document' (Lennon, 2000, 161). The evolution of the SEQ region was important for sustainability in that it was addressing a scenario of rapidly growing population, the necessity for regional coordination of planning and the need to provide appro-priate infrastructure and services if this population was going to reside in South-East Queensland.

In Western Australia the election of the Burke Labor Government led to significant changes in urban planning (see Stokes and Hill, 1992). These changes included the restructuring of the planning institutions in 1985, and the release of the 1987 document *Planning for the Future of the Perth Metropolitan Region*. This was a critique of the 1970 Corridor Plan that had channelled Perth's growth into ever lengthening corri-dors. The late 1980s were characterised by a growing popularity of urban consolidation, as a reaction to 'sprawl', car-use, inefficient use of land, and so on. Three years later *Metroplan* (1990) reverted to the corridor planning philosophy, but was less about modernist blueprint planning and more about urban management processes (see Stokes and Hill, 1992).

The rapid growth of Perth was facilitated by major infrastructure development, particularly in the field of transportation. The Burke Government reopened the Perth–Fremantle railway line that had been closed in the late 1970s, electrified the three existing suburban railway lines and developed the new Northern Suburbs Transit System (see McManus, 2002b). At the same time freeways adjacent to the new rail-way were widened, thus increasing the total capacity to extend the suburban growth boundary. The public transport is significant because it enables comparisons to be made between Perth and Adelaide (see chapter 7) and for this reason alone puts Perth forward as an example of best practice for sustainable cities (see Taplin, 1999).

Adelaide's own history combined with its slow population growth relative to other major Australian cities influenced urban planning during the period 1983–1996. The city's population grew from 883 000 in 1981 to 1.05 million in 1996 (Australian Bureau of Statistics, 1996). When the 1962 Metropolitan Development Plan was released Adelaide was growing rapidly. In percentage terms it was the fastest growing of the five major Australian cities between 1961 and 1966 (Huxley, 2000). This context, and the subsequent slowing of growth rates, was partly responsible for the 1962 plan surviving until the 1980s. The most significant planning action in Adelaide during 1983–1996 was, arguably, the review of planning in South Australia (carried out between 1990 and 1992), which in turn led to the release of *2020 Vision*, a planning strategy for Metropolitan Adelaide. This strategy emphasised urban consolidation, partly due to concerns that the city of a million people extended approximately 100 kilometres from north to south (Self, 1988). Consolidation had been happening in Adelaide prior to this time, including work done by the South Australian Housing Trust, which produced most developments and housing units in inner Adelaide between 1970 and 1988 (Badcock and Browett, 1992), but this was possible because the land could be acquired relatively cheaply when the dominant pattern was peripheral urban growth. This north–south growth threatened the vineyards at McLaren Vale to the south of Adelaide, which were given greater protection in *2020 Vision* by directing the peripheral growth to the north of the city (Bunker, 1990; Lennon, 2000).

The other significant planning issue was the highly controversial multi-function polis (MFP), a Japanese-backed futuristic city planned for Australia. The proposal emerged in 1987, and after competition from a number of Australian cities, the eventual site chosen in 1990 was '3460 hectares of environmentally degraded land at Gillman' in the northern suburbs of Adelaide (Haughton, 1994, 47). From a sustainability perspective, the MFP presented challenges because the site was degraded and was surrounded by heavy industry (thereby creating land, water and air pollution and limiting the design possibilities of the site), but also a potential opportunity to revitalise the site, on par with the development of Homebush Bay in the lead up to the 2000 Sydney Olympic Games. The MFP concept eventually collapsed.

SUMMARY

Australian cities have been influenced by a range of planning ideas. It has been important to present and analyse these ideas and their impacts because these ideas have aimed to improve the livability of cities in an efficient manner. They have also aimed to maintain environmental quality in the city, and to some extent, they have included equity considerations. There are elements of these ideas that would likely be included in contemporary planning for sustainable cities.

While some of the ideas were translated from theory and applied in practice, others were ignored. In some cases, the original application of the ideas has been superceded by later developments, whereas in other cases planning has been very important in shaping the contemporary city, or at least parts of it. Planning since 1975, as demonstrated in this chapter, is marked by a move away from ideas based on land socialisation. However, it is possible to observe the return of earlier ideas in new guises. Ideas, their incorporation into plans, their application and their legacy, are important in understanding the development of Australian cities. In the next chapter, we look at Australia's largest cities today and some 'new' ideas that may influence Australian cities and urban sustainability in the future.

CHAPTER 3

AUSTRALIAN CITIES TODAY: ISSUES, GOVERNANCE AND PLANNING

INTRODUCTION

Each of Australia's major cities is unique, yet each city experiences many of the same forces that operate in other cities around the world. These forces include globalisation processes, changes in transport technology, problems of ageing infrastructure, additional population with minimal room for expansion given environmental constraints, and the emergence of new planning ideas.

The issues and relationships are complex. Australian cities are situated on Aboriginal land and are linked to 'sister cities' in various parts of the world. Some of these issues, ideas and relationships have been raised in earlier chapters, while the environmental issues will be addressed in depth in section 2 of this book.

This chapter builds on the overview, planning history and growing awareness of the need for sustainable cities that have been discussed in earlier chapters. The chapter discusses the Commonwealth approach to urban issues before looking at current governance and planning arrangements at the state and local government levels in each of Australia's five largest cities. State governments are invariably the most powerful and active government players in shaping Australian cities, because they are responsible for metropolitan planning, environmental protection, public housing and delivery of public transport services. Local governments are important because they are often responsible for development control and for the provision of necessary infrastructure such as local roads and waste management services, and because of their diversity they represent important opportunities for innovation. The chapter concludes with a discussion of three ideas that may be important for making Australia's major cities more sustainable in the 21st century. These ideas are 'new urbanism', 'smart growth' and biore-gionalism. The links between these, and other possible, ideas and the governance and planning of Australia's largest cities have yet to be developed in the Australian context. The argument emerging from this chapter is that changing the structure and names of state departments and restructuring local governments and planning to manage urban growth are insufficient actions in the search for ways to achieve more sustainable cities. Bold thinking is required, but, drawing on the lessons of history, these ideas must be articulated with governance structures, plans and cultural values in order to facilitate their implementation (see Cocks, 2003).

THE HOWARD GOVERNMENT: 1996 TO THE PRESENT

The election in 1996 of the Liberal–National Coalition Government led by John Howard saw the ascendancy of neo-liberalism at the national level. In Victoria this meant that there was a neo-liberal agenda being vigorously pushed at all levels, because by this stage the local governments had been sacked and restructured and were being run by administrators appointed by the state government for three years.

The election of the Liberal–National Coalition in 1996 meant the decline of sustainability as an issue, the emergence of an isolationist and obstructionist approach on a number of environmental issues at the international level (notably climate change), and the withdrawal from urban programs. It meant the immediate demise of the second stage of the Better Cities Program. It also meant that the Local Agenda 21 Program, which emerged from the United Nations Conference on Environment and Development (the 'Earth Summit') in Rio de Janeiro in 1992, was quietly downgraded in importance. The Better Cities Program has been discussed in chapter 2. Local Agenda 21 is worthy of closer inspection because it highlights the potential of sustainability initiatives, but also some vulnerabilities.

Agenda 21 was the major document to emerge from the Earth Summit in Rio de Janeiro in 1992. It put forward 2509 actions; as Chapter 28 of Agenda 21 identified, approximately two-thirds of these actions required the involvement of local government (Mercer and Jotkowitz, 2000). In recognition of this fact and the slow rate of implementation at the local level, the Pathways to Sustainability Conference, held in Newcastle, New South Wales in 1997, called on all local authorities throughout the world to 'develop action plans by the year 2000 to implement Agenda 21' (Mercer and Jotkowitz, 2000, 165). This is Local Agenda 21, which may involve new programs and actions by council, or may simply involve bringing together a 'council's existing commitments to local environment, justice and local democracy' (Whittaker, 1997, 320; see also Mercer and Jotkowitz, 2000).

A 1996 survey reported in Whittaker (1997) indicated that of the then 770 local governments in Australia, only 34 responded to say that they were undertaking or were planning a Local Agenda 21. Allowing for the self-selection biases and the possibility that other councils may have been doing something, but failed to respond to the survey (a point noted by Whittaker, 1997 and Mercer and Jotkowitz, 2000), it was apparent that most local governments were not rushing to implement Local Agenda 21. Whittaker (1997) identified the lack of national and state government support, and the lack of support by local government associations, as being major barriers to implementation.

A survey of the ten leading Victorian local authorities in relation to Local Agenda 21 again highlighted a lack of progress in developing and implementing Local Agenda 21 (Mercer and Jotkowitz, 2000). Barriers to progress that were identified included the restructuring of local government in Victoria between 1994 and 1996, the lack of Commonwealth government support, the tight financial situation of local authorities, the compulsory process of competitive tendering and the lack of standardisation in reporting requirements in Victoria (Mercer and Jotkowitz, 2000). A web-based survey of Local Agenda 21 implementation in Western Australia by the 142 local governments (which received a 42 per cent response rate) highlighted the main barriers to implementation as being inadequate resources (97 per cent of respondents), a lack of awareness of the aims of Agenda 21 (53 per cent) and inadequate expertise in environmental management (52 per cent). Only 16 per cent of respondents attributed the problem to inadequate legislative authority (Price, 2003). Hine (2003), like Whittaker (1997), highlights the importance of support from higher levels, in this case the South Australian government through the Partnerships for Local Agenda 21 Program, in encouraging and assisting local authorities to implement Local Agenda 21 plans and programs.

Local Agenda 21, and its lack of widespread and effective implementation, is an excellent example of the need for an environmental ethic and good governance at all levels of government and within society. National leadership, in conjunction with the Australian states and the national- and state-level local government associations, could have made an enormous difference in the adoption and commitment to Local Agenda 21 processes. Encouragement, expertise and other forms of support could have been offered to assist local governments across Australia (as has occurred in South Australia). Rewards in the form of financial benefits and recognition to councils that were performing well, and financial punishment in the form of ineligibility to apply for additional sustainability and infrastructure funding for those councils that were laggards, would have encouraged more local governments to adopt Local Agenda 21 processes and work towards sustainability. This can still happen, if national and state governments have an environmental ethic that favours sustainability. The problem at the local level, and at the international level given Australia's refusal to ratify the Kyoto Protocol on Greenhouse Gases and Climate Change ('Kyoto Protocol'), is that we have lost significant time and momentum in pursuing sustainability. This is one of the most troubling legacies of the Howard Government.

AUSTRALIA'S LARGEST CITIES: ISSUES, GOVERNANCE AND PLANNING

The example of Local Agenda 21 highlights the importance of governance at national, state and local levels, and particularly the interaction between each of these levels of government and the people who elect governments. While there are similarities between cities, and sometimes the same forces are operating in all cities, it is important to look at the particular issues, the structures and processes of governance, the responsibility for planning and the key documents being produced, in order to understand the current issues and planning of each Australian city. As the following discussion of each of the five largest Australian cities highlights, in the move towards sustainable cities, one size, shape or cut does not fit all.

SYDNEY

Sydney is, and is likely to remain for some time, Australia's largest city. In the 1990s, Sydney was internationally oriented, often being described as a second order city (or a beta rather than an alpha city) in various global city hierarchies, behind cities such as New York, London, Tokyo and Paris, and on a par with Toronto, Zurich and San Francisco (Beaverstock, Taylor and Smith, 1999). As has been noted in earlier chapters, Sydney is experiencing population growth and has limited capacity for expansion without major conflicts about environmental sites. The governance of Sydney is complex and unstable. In 2003, the New South Wales state land use planning agency underwent a series of structural and name changes as part of a major restructuring of various government departments. The former Department of Urban Affairs and Planning is currently known as the Department of Infrastructure, Planning and Natural Resources. Decision-making for subdivision and other development control is devolved to the local government level, but the state planning minister can, and does, call in major developments and other developments where there is a difference between state and local government perspectives. Developers often appeal to the Land and Environment Court if their development proposals are rejected. This court in its current form is seen by many environmental activists to be pro-development and therefore a major obstacle to achieving a sustainable city.

There is no metropolitan level of government in the Greater Metropolitan Region which stretches from Port Stephens in the north to south of Wollongong. If such an organisation did exist it would likely be very powerful and would be seen as a threat to the state level of planning. Within Sydney there are regional councils based on geographic area. For example, the Western Sydney Region of Councils comprises 11 councils, and over one and a half million residents in its 5851 square kilometres (Dollery and Marshall, 2003). One of its major roles is to act as a regional lobbyist, as evidenced in its opposition to the proposed Badgerys Creek airport in Western Sydney.

As of March 2004 there are 37 local governments in Sydney. Based on the 2001 Census data, these range in population from 256 364 in Blacktown to 12 692 in Hunters Hill. The local government scene in Sydney includes rumours of council mergers, takeovers and dismissals that regularly appear in newspapers. The local government boundaries are relics from early 20th-century urban growth. No major changes on the scale of local government restructuring as occurred in Melbourne in the 1990s (see below) have taken place in Sydney, although the Inner Sydney Inquiry covering eight local government areas was commissioned by the NSW government in October 2000 and chaired by Kevin Sproats (May, 2003). The Sproats Report was released in 2001, but to date no comprehensive changes have been made arising from the report. Recent council mergers that have occurred in Sydney include the local councils of Drummoyne and Concord amalgamating in December 2000 to form the new council of Canada Bay. There have been boundary changes involving councils such as Leichhardt, Sydney and South Sydney. In early 2004 the state government dismissed the Sydney and South Sydney councils. Tension results when a business-oriented (and -controlled) city council governs surrounding residential areas where voters often have a neighbourhood focus. This tension is now being brought into the city centre itself as a result of residential apartment development. From the sustainability perspective presented in this book, it appears that very little of this restructuring is likely to lead to improved sustainability outcomes.

In terms of planning focus, in the late 1990s Sydney was preparing for the 2000 Olympic Games. This meant the redevelopment of the former abattoir site at Homebush into the major Olympic venue. Planning for the Olympic Games was supposedly based on Sydney 2000 being the 'Green Games', but various authors have highlighted how the reality fell somewhat short of the rhetoric (Owen, 2002; McManus, in press). The Olympic Games does, however, offer many useful lessons for sustainable cities, particularly in the areas of solar design, water treatment, the benefits of heavy rail transit, green architecture, site remediation, the need for openness and accountability in planning and the ability to use an event like the Olympics as a catalyst for funding wider environmental improvement.

While Sydney was becoming the Olympic city, the two major metro-politan-level planning documents released in this period were *A Framework for Managing Growth* (1997) and *Shaping Our Cities* (1998). The 1997 document supported the compact city approach, but incorporated some of the corridor/node thinking of earlier plans by establishing four subregions, namely, Sydney, Newcastle, Wollongong and the Central Coast. The 1998 document has a strong emphasis on sustainability, but there is a tension in the document in that it is maintaining and encouraging conventional economic growth and attempting to manage it in a way that is considered ecologically sustainable. As Gleeson and Low (2000, 222–3) have recognised, 'planning as "growth management" will never achieve ecological sustainability if current economic dynamics are not rethought and reformulated'.

The recent experience in Sydney appears to validate the concerns of Gleeson and Low. Although Sydney's environment was cleaned for the Olympics, and while developing a clean and attractive environment is a strategy to encourage business investment, Sydney's environmental quality and management of growth have contributed to the development of new roads and private motorways that are contributing to greenhouse gas emissions, are consuming inordinately large amounts of urban space and in some cases are luring people off the public transport system. Sydney in the early 21st century is a city that is experiencing rapid population growth (in relation to other Australian cities and its own history), partly because of the economic growth that the city is experiencing. As long as growth is being encouraged and attempted management is occurring, ecological sustainability looks a remote prospect for the biggest vortex in the Australian urban system.

MELBOURNE

Melbourne is clearly the second largest city in Australia and is continuing to grow and prosper, as these terms are conventionally understood. The current Bracks Labor Government inherited the mega-project legacy of the Kennett era. Melbourne has its casino, Formula One car race, Southbank redevelopment, Docklands redevelopment, and so on. The most significant changes at the local government level in Melbourne occurred during 1994, when the number of local councils in Melbourne was reduced from 56 to 31. The council boundaries were significantly redrawn and the council names were changed so that vestiges of the previous local government structure would not remain. These changes were accompanied by appointed administrators and the practice of compulsory competitive tendering. The Bracks Government also inherited the corporatised planning structures of the Kennett era, including the Docklands Authority which in August 2003 was merged with the Urban Regional Land Corporation to form Vic Urban.

The major changes initiated by the Bracks Labor Government are greater public participation in planning, especially through the Melbourne Metropolitan Strategy process which lasted for three years, cost $5 million and involved approximately 5500 people, and the release in October 2002 of the document *Melbourne 2030: Planning for Sustainable Growth* (Mees, 2003). While many people have been supportive of the consultation process, Mees argues that the planning documents produced contained almost all of the same content as the Kennett Government's *Living Suburbs* document that was released in 1995. The major difference was the strengthening of protection for the 'green wedges' between the urban growth corridors, but even on this point Mees (2003, 12) notes that 'each of the major freeways proposed runs through one or more of the green wedges, which are supposedly to be preserved from urban development'.

There has been much activity at the local government level across the metropolitan region. In the city centre, the Melbourne City Council has been active with its 'triple bottom line' decision-making processes (that is, decisions are to be made with consideration of economic, social and ecological impacts), and with the preparation of City Plan 2010. This planning strategy is intended to make Melbourne a 'thriving and sustainable city' (City of Melbourne, 2004). This is but one example of a shift in discourse and, for the most part, action. While it is too early to appreciate the significance of change, it does appear that some of the inner local government areas in Melbourne are beginning to take sustainability more seriously than they have in the past, and more seriously than most other local governments around Australia.

BRISBANE

Brisbane is the heart of a rapidly growing region known as South-East Queensland. In 1925 the Brisbane City Council emerged as a unitary government (similar to what occurred in Newcastle) after the amalgamation of 20 smaller local governments. By the late 1990s it was apparent that even this large and powerful council was not able to address the sustainability and other issues of the expanded region.

The priority for Brisbane and regional planning in South-East Queensland has become growth management. At the local government level, there has been stability in the Brisbane City Council under the leadership of Jim Soorley who was Mayor of Brisbane from 1991 to 2003. This enabled relationships to be built with the state to ensure at least some compatibility in local/metropolitan and metropolitan/regional planning between the powerful Brisbane City Council and the South-East Queensland planners.

Planning in Brisbane, like Sydney, is using a discourse of growth management and a geography of distinct urban areas within a greater regional setting. The plan set out in the 1998 *Regional Framework for Growth Management* document seeks to manage growth while preserving the identity of Brisbane, the Gold Coast, the Sunshine Coast and Toowoomba (Hamnett, 2000). The planning timeframe is to 2011, by when it has been assumed that the population of the South-East Queensland region will exceed three million, with the region absorbing 29 per cent of Australia's population growth between 1991 and 2011 (Hamnett, 2000).

This planning is complemented by the Brisbane City Council's *Brisbane 2011: The Livable City for the Future* which was also released in 1998. This document employs a similar discourse to that used in Melbourne, that is, the notion of livability (Stimson and Taylor, 1999).

Livability is one of the positive outputs in the Extended Metabolism Model of Human Settlements (see Newman, et al, 1996; Newton, 2001). *Brisbane 2011* calls for transit-oriented development and other sustainability initiatives, but as Hamnett (2000) has noted, the most significant challenge appears to be the generation of a shared vision around infrastructure development and compatibility in implementation between the Brisbane City Council and the Queensland state government.

PERTH

Perth is a city that continues to grow rapidly in population and, despite high-profile inner-city redevelopments in East Perth and to the west of the city centre, continues to expand on the Swan Coastal Plain. The major planning issues for Perth include water supply, the protection of groundwater reserves and the provision of more sustainable transport infrastructure.

The election of the Liberal–National Coalition Government led by Richard Court in 1993 resulted in little initial change to previous metropolitan planning in Perth. It was not until 1997 that the State Planning Strategy was released. This strategy highlights the shift in Western Australia from statutory and strategic planning to statutory planning (as manifested by the 1963 Metropolitan Region Scheme) and strategic policy-making. Metropolitan planning in Perth is conducted by linking state planning policies with a statutory zoning map.

The major change during the period of the Court Government (1993–2001), compared to the previous Labor governments, was the completion of many road projects contained in the 1963 Metropolitan Region Scheme that Main Roads WA had been seeking to implement for a number of years. These projects included the 6.5 kilometres long Graham Farmer Freeway, as well as the duplication of the Narrows Bridge and the extension of the Mitchell and Kwinana Freeways (see McManus, 2002b).

The election of the Gallop Labor Government in 2001 has seen a renewed emphasis on public transport planning and sustainability. The establishment of the Sustainability Policy Unit, as one of eight units within the Policy Division of the Office of the Premier and Cabinet, means that transport and sustainability issues potentially have good access to the major decision-makers in the government. The Sustainability Policy Unit was initially headed by a transport specialist, Professor Peter Newman, who was seconded from Murdoch University to assume the position. One early tangible outcome of this focus on sustainability was the release of the WA State Sustainability Strategy in September 2003. The strategy aims to embed sustainability at various scales, and in different sectors, particularly in the planning system.

In the area of transport, the major new rail development being planned is a line from Perth to the rapidly growing southern city of Mandurah. This is an important link because none of Perth's existing rail lines serve the southern suburbs of Perth (the Armadale line does serve the south-eastern suburbs and the Fremantle line runs along the north side of the Swan River to terminate in the port city of Fremantle, which is the modal interchange for buses to the south-west corridor suburbs). Two of the most rapidly growing local authorities in Western Australia are the southern cities of Rockingham, up 4800 people between June 2001 and June 2003, and Mandurah which experienced a population increase of 5600 over the same period (Australian Bureau of Statistics 2003d, 2004a). These locations are served by bus transport, but the major transport infrastructure that has been provided to date has been the Kwinana Freeway.

At the local government level, Perth, and Western Australia generally, has not experienced the major restructuring of the type exemplified by the Kennett Government in 1993 in Victoria or by the gradual amalgamation of local authorities as seen in South Australia since 1996 and the current amalgamation of mostly rural local authorities in New South Wales. Western Australia is the only state to have increased its number of local councils between 1991 and 2001 from 138 to 142 local authorities, in stark contrast to most other states (May, 2003). The new councils include a smaller City of Perth, the new authorities of Cambridge, Vincent and Victoria Park, and the division of the rapidly growing northern council of Wanneroo into Joondalup and Wanneroo.

ADELAIDE

In contrast with the rapid growth of the other four major cities and their regions Adelaide has experienced slower population growth since the mid-1970s. New areas for land release beyond the existing urban area were not identified by either the 1994 Metropolitan Adelaide Planning Strategy or the more thorough planning review published in January 1998 (Hamnett, 2000). Unlike Brisbane, which is focused on growth management and maintaining the identity of individual centres within the strengthening regional framework of South-East Queensland, the planning of Adelaide has focused on urban consolidation (particularly in the middle-ring suburbs) and protecting the water catchments for Adelaide (see chapter 6).

The current focus in metropolitan planning in Adelaide is called 'Re-Vision', the intention of which is to 'create a refreshed Planning Strategy to guide future development in Metropolitan Adelaide' (Planning SA, Department of Transport and Urban Planning, 2003, 4). In addition to the Metropolitan Regional Planning Strategies that are being updated from earlier, 1996 versions, the Inner Regional Planning Strategy area has been created. This is the area that surrounds Metropolitan Adelaide, and experiences many of the development pressures and spill-over impacts from Adelaide.

At the local level, there have been significant changes in the numbers of local government authorities in South Australia, down from 122 in 1991 to 68 in 2001 (May, 2003). In the metropolitan area of Adelaide the number of councils has been reduced from 30 to 19. Unlike the 'fell swoop' in Victoria, the process in South Australia was gradual and largely voluntary, although there was obviously an agenda for amalgamation. Some high-profile metropolitan council mergers included Port Adelaide–Enfield (in March 1996) and Elizabeth and Munno Para merging to form the City of Playford (in May 1997) (both in the north of Adelaide), and the local authorities of Happy Valley, Noarlunga and part of Willunga to form the city of Onkaparinga (in July 1997) (in Adelaide's south). The outcome of these mergers includes a reduced number of local councils, but also the formation of councils with the resources to move beyond a 'roads, rates and rubbish' agenda and address major sustainability issues.

It can be seen that the five major Australian cities are unique. They experience different challenges, and while there are similarities between cities, they have evolved to differ from each other in character, form and size. When considering important issues such as sustainability, it is apparent that even if all five of Australia's major cities made concerted efforts to be more sustainable, this would manifest differently in each city. Bearing this in mind, the following section of the chapter introduces three planning-related ideas to improve sustainability, in the knowledge that these ideas may be translated in particular ways in Australia's major cities.

IDEAS FOR THE 21ST CENTURY?

There are many possible ideas for change in the 21st century. Some of these ideas are discussed under issues such as waste and water in section 2 of this book. Three ideas discussed in this chapter are new urbanism, smart growth and bioregionalism. All three concepts attempt, sometimes in markedly different ways, to address the issues of urban expansion, sense of place and resource use. These ideas are bold experiments that to varying extents depart from the conventional approach to planning as development control, residential subdivision or the facilitation of investment. Godschalk (2004) classifies new urbanism and smart growth under the banner of 'livability' and argues that while economy and ecology are secondary values of smart growth, new urbanism primarily addresses a growth management conflict. Studies of new urbanism's contribution to sustainability through transport and water planning (Berke, et al, 2003; Lund, 2003) indicate that it is worthy of consideration as part of a sustainable city that is more than enhancing livability at the expense of the environment. The example of new urbanism highlights the importance that should be given to the interrogation of visionary ideas that build on the 19th- and 20th-century legacies of modernist planning, but are considered in conjunction with 21st-century agendas of sustainability, citizen empowerment and non-linear thinking in the development of sustainable cities. The consideration of these ideas should build on the history of planning ideas and implementation discussed in chapter 2 so that we can learn from the past without being a slave to it.

NEW URBANISM

It is important to consider the potential of new urbanism to contribute to sustainable cities in Australia because of the claims of its proponents about urban living, because its translation is currently happening in Australia and because it will be regarded as one of the significant urban experiments of the 21st century (Hebbert, 2003).

New urbanism is a concept that emerged in the United States in the 1980s. While it was called 'neotraditional design', it was criticised as 'backward-looking and nostalgic' (Southworth, 2003, 210). The label 'new urbanism', which suggests 'urbanity and innovation, rather than neo-historic suburbia' (Southworth, 2003, 211) was formally adopted by its proponents in 1993 (Thompson-Fawcett, 2003). The movement was incorporated as a non-profit organisation by six architects, and in 1996 the movement adopted a charter of 27 principles operating at three levels of development: region, metropolis, city and town; neighbourhood, district and corridor; and block, street and building (Godschalk, 2004).

New urbanism is an urban design movement that draws inspiration from the traditional architecture and layout of American towns. It rejects the modernist 'sprawl' of characterless suburbs in favour of more compact development, with a central focus around a public space and the ability to walk within a neighbourhood. These physical design elements are intended to foster a spirit of community, although this is challenged by authors who detect design determinism (De Villiers, 1997).

New urbanism has sometimes provided the layout and architectural designs for themed developments (such as Disney Corporation's development of Celebration, in Florida), and has been criticised for this simulation and fakery, perhaps even more stridently than was its earlier emphasis on neo-traditional design (Talen, 1999; Till, 2001; Marshall, 2003). New urbanism has also been challenged on these points: its 'newness' (De Villiers, 1997; Fulton, 2002; Southworth, 2003); whether it is urban or suburban (Zimmerman, 2001; Southworth, 2003); how it relates to transport issues (Lund, 2003; Crane and Schweitzer, 2003); its limited focus (De Villiers, 1997); its determinism (De Villiers, 1997; see Talen, 1999).

Despite these and other challenges, new urbanism, unlike some of the ideas discussed in chapter 2 of this book, has been implemented in the United States and Australia. As of 2002, according to a survey by *New Urbanism News*, there were 272 neighbourhood new urbanist projects that had been completed or were under construction in the United States. Another 200 projects were in the planning stages, which represented an increase of 97 projects from the previous year. Of the total of 472 projects, about half were greenfield (that is, there was no prior urban development), about one-third were infill projects and the remainder were greyfield/brownfield (that is, former industrial sites) (Southworth, 2003).

Implementation of new urbanism in Australia ranges from isolated coastal developments such as the Town of Seaside, located on the Sunshine Coast in Queensland and named after the new urbanist development of Seaside in Florida (made famous as the set in the 1998 movie *The Truman Show*), to inner-city redevelopments such as Honeysuckle Grove in the Newcastle suburb of Carrington. The former development is isolated, car-dependent and a conscious attempt to 'create a small seaside township of the past, complete with old-fashion neighbourhood values built into its infrastructure' (Town of Seaside, 2003). By way of contrast, the new urbanist agenda was linked with broader planning agendas (somewhat akin to smart growth) in Newcastle and was renamed and implemented as part of a redevelopment of former transport and industrial waterfront land in inner Newcastle.

> Newcastle Urbanism is a term used to embrace a range of urban design and town planning development philosophies which seek to produce a built environment which is diverse in use and population, scaled for the pedestrian and capable of accommodating the automobile and mass transit. (Newcastle City Council, 1997, 17)

There is potential for new urbanism to contribute to sustainable cities, but not if the emphasis of the approach is on isolated, car-dependent, greenfield sites or on neo-traditional housing and themed developments. Given that there is diversity within the new urbanism concept, it is possible that urban developments of increased density, reduced impervious surfaces, pedestrian orientation, and so on, can contribute to increased sustainability. By linking new urbanism with other small-scale initiatives, such as 'water sensitive urban design' (see chapter 6) and the restoration of urban waterways, and situating new urbanist design within a larger context of metropolitan transport networks, it is possible that the strengths of new urbanism may be enhanced and its limitations acknowledged. The concept has very little to offer on this last point about transport and the larger metropolitan scale, which is why it is necessary to consider a related concept of smart growth.

SMART GROWTH

Smart growth has been variously described as a 'sister movement' of new urbanism (Godschalk, 2004, 7) and, by inference, as a '"West-Coast" branch of New Urbanism' (Marshall, 2003, 236). New urbanism is sometimes seen to embrace all of the tenets of smart growth, given that its charter covers the scales identified in the preceding section. Still, Marshall (2003, 236, citing Kelbaugh, 1997) claims that the West Coast or 'Calthorpian' branch (named after Peter Calthorpe) has grown more out of the environmental movement than the East Coast or 'Duanyian' branch (named after Andres Duany), which is more focused on neighbourhood design and aesthetics, and, crucially, lacks an ecologically sound approach to mass transit and regional planning.

Whereas the East Coast branch of new urbanism may appeal more to designers, urban planners are more likely to be attracted by the West Coast branch which has otherwise become known as smart growth. The origins of this American movement are varied; they include being 'a response to the no-growth movement, which gained momentum in the 1990s in California and other US jurisdictions facing intense demographic pressures' (Filion, 2003, 50), and evolving 'from statewide growth management initiatives' in the US state of Maryland (Godschalk, 2004, 7). Maryland's role is important because the introduction of the Smart Growth and Neighborhood (sic) Conservation Initiative in 1997 meant that the idea of smart growth entered the arena of government policy. Rather than attempting to limit or direct growth through regulations about the use of land, fiscal policy and incentives were used to direct growth towards preferred locations (Tregoning, et al, 2002).

Smart growth is an umbrella concept that, like new urbanism, covers a range of actions designed to improve the quality of urban growth and, some people would argue, slow growth (Cervero, 2003). These actions include flexible design standards, density bonuses, transit-oriented development and moving towards more compact cities. The aims underlying smart growth include restricting the conversion of bushland and agricultural land to urban uses, reducing reliance on the private automobile, and improving the efficiency of infrastructure provision. Smart growth, like new urbanism, is opposed to 'sprawl', partly because it is ecologically destructive and partly because it is an inefficient form of urban growth (Tregoning, et al, 2002; Filion, 2003; Godschalk, 2004).

Smart growth differs from concepts such as no growth and ecological sustainability because it is focused on livability and basic quality of life issues and it accepts the notion of urban growth. The problem is seen as inappropriate growth, that is, sprawl, because of its ecological, economic and social costs. The answer, according to smart growth advocates, is not to stop growth, but to improve the quality of growth. In this sense, it is similar to new urbanism. It is also similar to the globalised notion of sustainable development (see World Commission on Environment and Development, 1987) which included growth but focused on the quality of growth (that is, development). In doing so, it marginalised anti-growth advocates whose position had been gaining momentum prior to 1987. The notion of smart growth appears to be having a similar impact on anti-growth and other more radical concepts such as bioregionalism.

BIOREGIONALISM

Bioregionalism is about living at home within the limits of nature. It is concerned with place-making, local ecological knowledge and ecological restoration of geographically defined regions. The concept is similar to new urbanism in its emphasis on home and belonging, but is radically different in its theoretical underpinnings on design, transportation issues, self-reliance and local democracy.

Bioregionalism emerged from the 1960s counter-culture in the United States. The term was coined by Van Newkirk in 1975, and the ideas have been developed by authors such as Callenbach (1975), Sale (1985) and Aberley (1999). Bioregionalism covers the establishment of bio-physically defined boundaries rather than the arbitrary administrative boundaries of modern government systems (think of state and local government boundaries in Australia and their general lack of alignment with physical regions such as water catchments). Importantly, bioregionalism is not simply about redrawing maps. It is about the transfer of decision-making and financial resources to the local and regional levels where local knowledge and the impacts of the decisions will be felt, rather than in distant locations such as Canberra. It is about self-governance.

Another emphasis within bioregionalism is on local self-reliance, rather than extending the vortex of resource acquisition and disposal functions. It is about learning to live within the limits of nature in a particular place by using the resources of that place in a sustainable manner. This requires intimate knowledge of the place and how it changes through the seasons.

Bioregionalists have made some large claims about this concept in relation to sustainability. Aberley, for example has stated:

> As the human race collective stumbles into a new millennium, bioregionalism offers the best hope we have for creating an interdependent web of self-reliant, sustainable cultures. (Aberley, 1999, 38)

By way of contrast, it has been vigorously attacked by geographers such as David Harvey who lambasted bioregionalism as a:

> return to an urbanization regulated by the metabolic constraints of a bioregional world as it supposedly existed in what were actually pestiferous and polluted medieval or ancient times, or a total dissolution of cities into communes or municipal entities in which, it is

believed, proximity to some fictional quality called 'nature' will predispose us to lines of conscious (as opposed to enforced) action that will respect the world around us (as if decanting everyone from large cities into the countrysides will somehow guarantee the preservation of biodiversity, water and air qualities, and the like). (Harvey, 1996, 427–8)

The concept has been used, or abused depending on your perspective, in a number of planning arenas. It is used at the national level in Australia for conservation planning, but this is largely an exercise in creating new maps along biophysical lines and does not include bioregionalist concerns of self-reliance and self-governance. The concept has also been used in New Zealand for resource management and the restructuring of government boundaries created under the *Resource Management Act 1991*, which was partly driven by neo-liberalist notions of decentralising power from large state authorities. The success of this radical restructuring of government and of resource management and planning is questionable because, as Jay (1999, 478) has identified, 'planners were unable to link environmental policies to the social and economic factors which drive them'. In an evaluation of planning at the local level, Miller (2003, 341) believes that 'there was insufficient guidance from central government, local authorities were under resourced, and many local authorities were too small to produce quality plans and planning outcomes'.

An example of the application of bioregional thought in Canada was the 1992 Royal Commission on the Future of the Toronto Waterfront, chaired by the former Toronto Mayor, David Crombie (Crombie, 1992). This study could easily have proceeded within narrow boundaries that focused on the nexus between Lake Ontario and the built-up area of Toronto. Instead, the study adopted bioregional boundaries that included the catchment area for the Toronto–Lake Ontario nexus, and adopted an ecological way of thinking about the linkages between water, topography, urban development, and so on. It did not embrace the self-reliance or self-governance elements of bioregionalism, and its implementation was severely impacted by a change in provincial government, but the study remains a visionary document that highlighted what could be done in a city of about four million people (see Hough, 1995; Cooper, 1999).

Bioregionalism has been advocated and critiqued in Australian cities. Urban Ecology Australia Inc in Adelaide refer to their home as

'Tandanya', which was the name given to the area by the Aboriginal people, the Kaurna, and means 'the place of the red kangaroo' (Gargett and Marsden, 1996). This example highlights the links between bioregionalism and Aboriginal cultures and boundaries. By way of contrast, Brennan (1998) recognises the existence of 'bioregional denial' (where people do not know how to adapt to and live in their environment), but he is critical of 'homely bioregionalism', which he identifies as being a misplaced project and not a solution to bioregional denial. The example he uses is Perth, which he describes as a 'schizoid city, with an artificial suburbia dominating the coastal plain, while people in the hills aspire to be dwellers in the land' (Brennan, 1998, 223).

Thus it appears that bioregionalism does offer insights for sustainable cities, but even in parts of the world that are well endowed with natural attributes, the benefits and likelihood of its application are questionable. Greater participatory democracy at the local level, increased local environmental knowledge, living within the constraints of the local region's water supplies and eating sustainably produced local food in season are all important elements of sustainability that are, I believe, achievable and desirable. In any move towards sustainable cities, people will have to see the advantages of these actions and, if they have not already done so, be willing to make the necessary lifestyle changes. This raises a tension between what may be considered ecologically necessary (that is, to reduce our exploitation of nature as soon as possible) and the benefits of social learning derived from a gradual adoption of bioregional practices by people who are willing to make changes in their lives.

SUMMARY

The contemporary governance and planning structures for Australia's largest cities are not geared towards sustainability. As can be seen from the discussion in this chapter, there are conflicting agendas of growth, international competitiveness, maintenance of power bases, livability, sustainability, and so on, each being driven by vested interest groups. This chapter has highlighted some of the recent governance and planning changes in Australia's major cities. We return to these themes of structures and processes in section 3 of the book.

The chapter has also highlighted some possible ideas for moving Australian cities towards sustainability. These ideas involve structures, processes of governance, planning and design and everyday lifestyle decisions by millions of people. Other ideas emerge in section 2 of the book where we look at crucial issues that must be addressed in the move towards sustainable cities in Australia. As with governance and planning, it is important to look at the ideas, the practice and the specific context of each city. Without this articulation, ideas for change remain ideas.

CHAPTER 4

TOWARDS SUSTAINABLE CITIES

INTRODUCTION

When many Australians think of environmental campaigns and sustainable development, they may think about the Franklin River campaign, the Fraser Island dispute, Jabiluka, the forests of Western Australia, the Great Barrier Reef, and so on. This fits the image many Australians have, or had, of themselves as being in a country of bushmen. The Australian environment that is marketed for tourism is the area outside of bustling, cosmopolitan cities. Our most high-profile and successful environmental campaigns (with one notable exception) have also been conducted away from the cities (see Frawley, 1999; Hutton and Connors, 1999). The exception is the Green Bans campaign conducted with community support by the NSW Builders Labourers' Federation in the 1970s.

Urban environmentalism is, however, at least as old as environmentalism outside of the cities. The origins of urban planning, the rise and decline of the Green Bans in Australia during the 1970s and the contemporary Environmental Justice Movement in the United States are examples of urban environmental action. These examples are important because they challenge environmentalists and other people to rethink notions of the environment and how we construct boundaries and define cities and nature.

The move from environmentalism to sustainable cities is an important step because it challenges the environmental side and it also challenges much of the planning and planning history in Australian cities that has been discussed in earlier chapters of this book. The concept of sustainable cities has generated a significant body of literature since the early 1990s. Early publications addressing urban planning and geographic issues in developed countries include those of Blowers (1993) and Haughton and Hunter (1994). More recent work on sustainable cities in developing countries has been produced by Burgess, Carmona and Kolstee (1997) and Pugh (2000). Other authors tend to emphasise a single aspect of sustainable cities, such as transport (Newman and Kenworthy, 1999), energy (Capello, Nijkamp and Pepping, 1999) and eco-partnerships (Inoguchi, Newman and Paoletto, 1999). Another approach which manifests an urban–environment link is the 'green urbanism' of Beatley (2000), which addresses numerous aspects of sustainable cities but concentrates on the potential to introduce ideas from Europe into the United States.

Having introduced the confluence of environmentalism and urbanism, it is now necessary to examine this movement in more detail for Australia. This chapter includes a brief history of environmentalism in Australia, focusing on those aspects of environmentalism that pertain to, or explain the move towards, urban environmental action. The chapter also includes an overview of the sustainable development concept, ways of ascertaining urban sustainability and the development of a model that considers the current Australian cities as being vortices (the Vortex City to Sustainable City Model). This model provides preliminary indications of what may be required to move towards making our cities more sustainable.

ENVIRONMENTALISM IN AUSTRALIA

There have been a number of histories written about Australian environmentalism and key figures in the various environmental campaigns (see, for example, Hutton and Connors, 1999; Mulligan and Hill, 2001). A tendency of most authors is to adopt a chronological approach, which understandably is useful for an overview. Hutton and Connors (1999) identify five phases – 1860s to World War I, World War II to 1972, 1973–83, 1983–1990 and the 1990s. Urban environmentalism tends to appear late in these chronologies.

As these histories demonstrate, in Australia we have developed, or followed, an approach to the environment that positions the environment outside of cities. This approach is theoretically flawed in that humans are part of the environment, our cities are constructed in and using the environment, and within urban areas nature abounds. The approach is also flawed in that designating land as 'wilderness' ignores connections to country of indigenous people. These connections have been maintained for thousands of years. Australia was not terra nullius. Aboriginal people lived here (usually concentrated in areas where Europeans have built their cities) and were living here when white explorers arrived. The history of settlement is important because Australia has generally followed the approach that is common in the so-called new world. That is, until recently, Australians have often seen the environment as being outside of cities. This did not change with the introduction of the notion of sustainable development, but over time there has been a greater emphasis on urban environments and the need to move towards sustainability.

SUSTAINABLE DEVELOPMENT

The term 'sustainable development' was first used in the 1980 World Conservation Strategy. However, like the attempt to promote 'eco-development' at the Habitat Conference in Stockholm in 1972, the 1980 initiative did not become very popular. This changed in 1987, when the World Commission on Environment and Development released its report, entitled *Our Common Future*. This report is also known as the Brundtland Report, after its Norwegian chairperson, Gro Harlem Brundtland. It was very important in promoting the idea of 'sustainable development'. The report defined sustainable development as 'development that meets the needs of the present without compromising the ability of future generations to meet their own needs' (World Commission on Environment and Development, 1987, 8). As Button has noted in a recent article in *Ecological Economics*, the emphasis in this definition is temporal rather than spatial or geographical (Button, 2002). This presents challenges when the implementation necessarily involves spatial and geographical considerations, including the unique context and character of Australia's major cities.

If we are to accept the idea of sustainability or sustainable development, then what do we mean by the term? Given that very few people these days are likely to say that they are acting in an unsustainable manner, this is a significant question. It is also no small challenge. To begin, there are different ways of conceptualising sustainable development vis-a-vis sustainability. Diesendorf (2000, 22) presents the relationship as 'sustainability' and 'sustainable futures' being the 'goals or endpoints of a process called "sustainable development"'. By contrast McManus (1996) presents sustainable development as more of a reformist approach, whereas an emphasis on sustainability and particularly ecological sustainability necessitates a fundamental change in the structures that perpetuate unsustainable practices.

In Australia, this contested conceptual terrain has resulted in the emergence of the term 'ecologically sustainable development'. This terminology is unique to Australia and was largely due to the power of major environmental groups in Australia in the early 1990s. In 1992, 'ecologically sustainable development' was defined as 'using, conserving and enhancing the community's resources so that ecological processes, on which life depends, are maintained, and the total quality of life, now and in the future, can be increased' (Ecologically Sustainable Development Steering Committee, 1992, 6). This definition incorporates economic, social and environmental considerations, but it also acknowledges that life depends on ecological processes and that these need to be maintained. In many cases these ecological processes are damaged and need to be repaired.

It should not be surprising then that many of the initial approaches to implement the idea of sustainable development often seemed to be an extension, or perhaps even a repackaging, of what used to be called 'environmental management'. 'Environment' was often equated with 'natural environment' or 'nature'. Sustainable development appeared to have a lot to do with trees, mountains, rivers and oceans, but less to do with cities. If the concept did include cities, it was often thought of in terms of the environmental quality or the environmental assets of cities. The concept that appears to have been most successful in drawing this link between cities and their hinterlands and other parts of the planet is the notion of an ecological footprint (see below). Once it became increasingly accepted that in order to achieve sustainable development of rural, marine and bush areas it was necessary to limit or modify the impacts of cities, the focus shifted to thinking about sustainable cities.

SUSTAINABILITY

The language of sustainability emerged during the 1970s and became popularised in 1987 as 'sustainable development' by the Brundtland Report. There are numerous definitions of sustainability, but the key question to be asked is, what is to be sustained?

If we are attempting to sustain economic growth for its own sake, how is this reflected in our planning? If we are attempting to sustain the earth, in order for humans to survive into the future, how is this reflected in our planning? If we are attempting to preserve the existence of all life and ecosystems on earth, not just for what they can contribute to us, but for their own sake, how is this reflected in our planning?

It is impossible, given legislation, not to be planning for sustainability. However, there are various concepts of sustainability, and many of the differences between these can be attributed to the relative weight given to economic, social, cultural and environmental components of sustainability. The differences are also caused by the perception of how these components fit together. For example, are economic, socio-cultural and environmental factors going to be *balanced* as in the intersection of three circles of equal sizes, or is the economy a part of society which in turn is part of the environment?

Variations in the models of sustainability, or sustainable development, are generally variations on either a model of hierarchy or of balance. The hierarchy often includes ecology at its base, followed by society, because there would be no society without an environment, and then by the economy, represented by the smallest circle, because there would be no economy if there was no society. Variations may include a base of thermodynamic processes to support biochemical cycles which allow ecosystems to flourish, rising through a number of levels to eventually reach human societies and the needs of individuals, as in the Albrecht Model of Foundational Sustainability (Albrecht, 1998). In the case of models predicated on the notion of balance, the sense of balance may be maintained but there may be different terminology used or another circle of culture added.

These questions about how to visualise sustainability in a model are important because, like the transport and land use planning of the 1960s, our planning for sustainability is going to influence the lives of people and other living things both today and for many years into the future. This is obviously a significant challenge, but to not engage in this debate is to surrender to the type of planning that will most likely emphasise short-term economic gain in the name of efficiency.

It is also important to consider aspects of scale when discussing sustainability. Table 4.1 highlights the importance of scale when considering threats and opportunities in relation to sustainability. It is apparent that action on some scales is unlikely to prevent a threat from occurring, while action on other scales may result in environmental improvements and create an image conducive to business, but is unlikely to result in sustainability. This conceptualisation of sustainability on the basis of scale reinforces the notion that action at the scale of the city and its hinterland is likely to be most achievable and most effective in moving towards sustainability.

The remainder of this book will concentrate on the term 'sustainability'. The emphasis in this book is on what has been termed 'strong sustainability', derived from Daly and Cobb (1994). This version of sustainability, in contrast to the 'weak sustainability' often advocated by

Table 4.1 A conceptual framework of sustainability and cities

Scale	Threat or opportunity	Potential for human action	Importance for sustainability
Universe and galaxy	Black holes, large meteors, and so on.	Impossible to prevent.	Unsustainable. It will destroy all cities on earth if it happens.
Planet	Global warming, plus associated impacts such as fire, flood, disease and cyclones.	Possible to prevent, slow and/or mitigate the 'enhanced' global warming.	Unsustainable for the planet, but impacts will be unevenly distributed.
	Earthquake and tsunami	Impossible to prevent, but it is possible to ameliorate or mitigate the potential impacts.	Unsustainable for the cities affected.
Individual cities: urban wide sustainability issues	Increasing wastes, depleting and degrading available resources in the city and in surrounding regions.	Possible to prevent and/or change, but is challenging because it involves changing structures and values.	Unsustainable for the cities affected. Currently the impacts are often transferred to other locations.
Individual cities: urban environmental issues	Perceived clean environment, improves the market profile of cities.	Possible to achieve.	This is not necessarily threatening sustainability, but is important for city image. It may enhance sustainability, but not necessarily so.
Local environmental issues	Saving local environments, preventing inappropriate development, cleaning up dog waste on footpaths.	Possible to address, and is the source of many local environmental conflicts.	This is not important for sustainability, but is important for local environmental quality and it is important because it is the daily experience of many people.

planning authorities in Australia, has been represented by Palmer et al (1997, 92) in terms of futurity, environment, public participation and equity. The planning policies currently being pursued in the name of sustainable development are unlikely to move Australian cities from vortex cities to sustainable cities.

If we are prepared to accept the challenge of moving towards sustainable cities, this involves structural change, cultural change and the planning and design of cities to be as sustainable as possible. In planning for sustainability it is important to understand the legacy of previous attempts to plan for desired outcomes, be they environmental quality, economic efficiency, aesthetics or social equity. Critically examining the 'planning process' from idea to implementation and monitoring and incorporating feedback is important to understand the success, failure or translation of previous planning visions. Any attempt to move towards sustainable cities that does not interrogate urban and planning history is likely to be, at best, immodest, and at worse, to repeat the errors of previous generations.

ASCERTAINING THE SUSTAINABILITY OF CITIES

In recent years there has been an increasing awareness of the importance of cities in achieving sustainable development. For example, two transport planners in Australia, Peter Newman and Jeff Kenworthy, wrote that 'cities shape the world and we will never begin the sustainability process unless we can relate it to cities' (Newman and Kenworthy, 1999, 6).

It is one challenge to recognise the need for sustainability in cities, but quite another challenge to ascertain if cities are becoming more or less sustainable. Many people may answer this from their experience or observation, noting that aspects of social sustainability such as feeling secure in the city have declined since the 'good old days'. Others may

Figure 4.1 Urban sprawl

Photo: Gary Peel

point to the 'sprawl' of cities, especially the new suburbs at the urban fringe. 'Sprawl' is a significant factor to consider in relation to sustainable cities because it impacts on issues such as water, transport, and biodiversity (covered in chapters 6, 7 and 10 below respectively) and it is one of the most visible aspects of the relationship between cities and other physical environments. As Peiser (2001, 278) notes, the term 'sprawl' is used to mean different things, including 'the gluttonous use of land, uninterrupted monotonous development, leapfrog discontinuous development and inefficient use of land'. In terms of sustainability, each of these problems labelled 'sprawl' invokes different solutions in order to make cities more sustainable. One 'solution' is the repackaging of the notion of urban sprawl by developers, as seen in the advertising of a new land release in Melbourne (see figure 4.1).

There are a number of approaches that have been used to ascertain the sustainability of cities. A survey of various sustainability literature (particularly helpful was a study by Taplin, 1999) has highlighted the following approaches:

- State of the Environment reporting
- urban metabolism analysis (including ecodevice modelling)
- ecological footprint assessment
- environmental costing
- best practice assessment
- sustainability indicator projects
- comparative initiatives analysis
- sustainability metrics.

These approaches are not mutually exclusive. The history, use, strengths and weaknesses of each of these approaches are discussed below in order to improve our understanding of the approaches and consider how they may be useful in the Australian context.

STATE OF THE ENVIRONMENT REPORTING

State of the Environment reporting practice has developed at national, state and local government levels in Australia to report on the current state of the environment and on perceptions of the environment, and to monitor changes over time. This approach can identify problems and opportunities in a particular location, and has the potential to develop solutions that are appropriate in a specific area. The reports generally measure compliance with benchmarked standards (for example, maximum accepted pollution in parts per million). This may lead to satisfactory but not optimal outcomes if the standards are achieved and there is no pressure for further action towards sustainability.

URBAN METABOLISM ANALYSIS

The Metabolic Flow Model was introduced by Boyden et al (1981) in their important study of energy, water, waste and other flows in Hong Kong. This work identified the ecological inputs, throughputs and outputs of the city and built on the earlier ideas of Wolman (see Boyden, et al, 1981, 115). The model has since been developed by different authors. A modified version, the Extended Metabolism Model of Human Settlements, was used by Newman et al (1996) in the 'Human Settlements' section of the 1996 Australian State of the Environment Report. This model was praised and extended in the 2001 Australian State of the Environment Report (Newton, et al, 2001) and is shown in figure 4.2.

The 1996 model has also been used by Newman and Kenworthy (1999) and Yencken and Wilkinson (2000). These latter authors recognise the 'great strength' of the model as being its 'potential to analyse, measure and compare over time the flows of energy, water, food and materials into settlements and the waste outputs from them' (Yencken and Wilkinson, 2000, 122). The same authors note, however, that not all urban environmental issues relate to flows. They cite land and biodiversity as examples of stocks, rather than flows. Their chapter on 'the sustainability of settlements' recognises the need to create sustainability in settlements of all sizes. In recognition of the strengths and limitations of various models, this chapter incorporates a number of different ways of ascertaining sustainability, including the 1996 model and ecological footprint analysis (Yencken and Wilkinson, 2000).

A variation of the metabolism model is the Ecodevice Model, developed in the Netherlands. This model, which identifies flows and cycles, is an 'approach that analyses the contribution of city activities to environmental effects within and outside the city on the basis of flows entering and leaving the city' (Priemus, 1999, 224). It is useful in that it recognises the sustainability of cities is based on an 'ecological footprint' (see below) and that 'areas, material flows and actors' is a useful way of conceptualising the relationships between people, where they live and the flows that enable the relationships between people and places to continue.

Figure 4.2 2001 version of the Extended Metabolism Model of Human Settlements

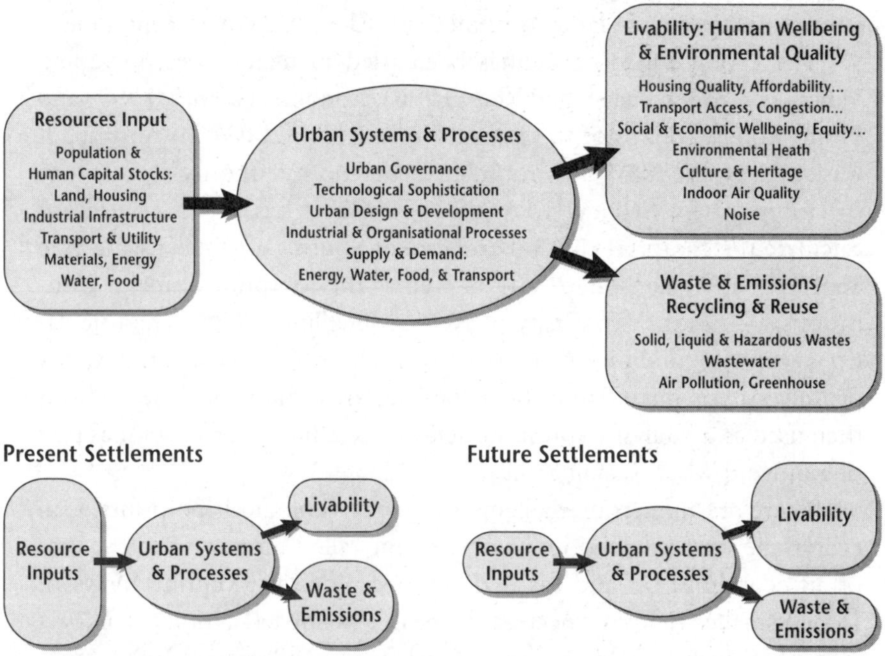

Source: Newton et al, 2001, 11

ECOLOGICAL FOOTPRINT ANALYSIS

The concept of the ecological footprint as a way of ascertaining sustainability was developed by Bill Rees and his students, particularly Mathias Wackernagel, at the University of British Columbia in Vancouver, Canada (Wackernagel and Rees, 1996). The approach is similar to the 'ghost acres' idea developed by the Swedish academic Georg Borgstrom in 1965 (Robins, 1995). It is also similar, as Moffatt (1999) has recognised, to the 'sustenance space of cities' concept that was conceived, but not explicitly named as such, by Mark Jefferson (1917) in his study of England's urban geography. A somewhat similar concept, which uses the weight of materials rather than land as the measurement, is the 'ecological rucksack' which was developed by Friedrich Schmidt-Bleek and refined with the assistance of Ernst Ulrich von Weizsaecker at the Wuppertal Institute in 1993 (Robins, 1995; Takeda Foundation, 2002).

The concept of the ecological footprint is a metaphor for ecological impact, regardless of where that impact occurs. The ecological footprint measures the impact by converting impact variables into the single unit of land. In the case of a city, the approach can be used to calculate the equivalent amount of land consumed in order for a city to function.

The ecological footprint has been used in many cities, including Vancouver (Wackernagel and Rees, 1996), London (Giradet, 1999) and Hong Kong (Friends of the Earth, Hong Kong, 2002). In Australia it was used by the NSW Environment Protection Authority to calculate the footprint for Sydney (EPA NSW, 1997). It has also been used to calculate the footprint of Canberra and of South-East Queensland (see Yencken and Wilkinson, 2000), as well as the footprint of major institutions such as the University of Newcastle (Flint, 1999). The calculations invariably indicate that the ecological footprint of a country, city or university is much larger than the land area that it occupies. This is then used as a catalyst to promote actions to reduce the footprint as part of a move towards sustainability.

There are numerous challenges in using ecological footprints. Can everything be converted into a single unit called money (as in the case of an economy) or land (as is done in ecological footprint analysis)? Does a smaller footprint necessarily mean less impact? Not if the impact is in a high-value ecological area. Yencken and Wilkinson (2000) highlight the need to include water, which is not always included in the calculations of affected 'land', especially in a dry country like Australia. There is also the problem of boundary definition. It is easy to achieve a smaller ecological footprint if the boundary around the city is drawn wide enough to include agricultural land (this explains some of the huge discrepancies in footprints between Sydney and South-East Queensland, for example). Finally there is the issue of representation. Given that the footprint of a city occurs '*wherever on Earth that land is located*' (Wackernagel and Rees, 1996, 52, emphasis in original), it is surprising to see the city and its hinterland being used to represent Sydney's ecological footprint (EPA NSW, 1997). This is an inaccurate representation and gives the impression that the 'region' of a city can be equated with its hinterland. This is in contrast to the important idea in ecological footprint analysis that cities consume parts of the planet far away from the city.

The strength of the ecological footprint as a way to ascertain the sustainability of cities is that it enables us to think about the resource flows to the city and the 'waste' flows beyond the city that currently perpetuate unsustainability. It is a concept that informs the model used in this book. Given the weaknesses in the concept, as discussed above, whenever the term 'ecological footprint' is used in the remainder of this book it refers to the notion of extending impact rather than the detailed measurement and calculation of a footprint.

ENVIRONMENTAL COSTING

This approach derives from environmental economics. It suggests that by assigning costs and values to various environmental items, or more accurately, to people's preferences regarding environmental items, it is possible to ascertain sustainability and costs of achieving it (see Pearce and Barbier, 2000). This approach has strengths in that it enables comparisons and accountable value judgements to be made. However, the tendency to assign costs to all environmental systems, the problems that occur with such practices (Burgess, et al, 1998) and the market-orientation of the suggested 'solutions' to environmental problems all reduce the usefulness of this approach to ascertaining sustainability.

BEST PRACTICE ASSESSMENT

'Best practice' designation is part of a management trend towards 'benchmarking' more and more aspects of life. It is also consistent with the idea of creating models and templates for imitation.

The use of models and templates is exemplified by Peter Newman and Jeff Kenworthy (see McManus, 1998). This approach to ascertaining sustainability or unsustainability through the trope of synecdoche, where the part comes to represent the whole (for example, Toronto equals sustainability because of the transit, while Los Angeles equals unsustainability because of the freeways), can be controversial. To extend the example, Toronto has been seen as the best practice of transit and land use integration among cities that Australian cities could realistically imitate, but there has been significant debate about the validity of the comparison and the explanation for Toronto's best practice (Kenworthy, 1991; Brindle, 1992; McManus, 1992; Kenworthy and Newman, 1994; Mees, 1994). The best practice approach has recently been used by Beatley (2000) in transferring ideas for urban sustainability from the European to the US context, although he stresses the need to consider the context of individual US cities.

The use of best practice is seen through awards such as the European Sustainable City Award. In Australia, there are various local government awards for councils that have implemented sustainability initiatives, in much the same way as there are awards for architecture, engineering, planning and design. In terms of ascertaining sustainabil-

ity, it could be argued that these awards are an extension of environmental quality awards (for example, tidy town competitions); however,
unless a critical perspective is taken it is possible that an award for
achievements in one aspect of sustainability can be translated by slick
public relations into an image of 'clean and green' for the entire city.
While not denigrating particular achievements, the sustainable city tag
can be both a motivator and a cover for some of the less sustainable
practices that support cities.

SUSTAINABILITY INDICATOR PROJECTS

The use of indicators for sustainability is an extension of the use of
economic and biological indicators (Bell and Morse, 1999). The most
well-known economic indicator is probably the GNP (gross national
product), which evolved from work done by the US Commerce
Department in 1934 and was then developed to measure the prepara-
tions of the war economy, before being published in 1947 (Daly and
Cobb, 1994). This indicator was never developed to measure welfare,
or long-term environmental quality. Even as an economic indicator it
has significant limitations, hence the rise of 'genuine progress indicators' and other forms of sustainability indicators.

The most famous use of sustainability indicators to ascertain the
sustainability of cities is the Sustainable Seattle Project (AtKisson,
1999). Many other cities have used indicators, including Australian
cities as part of the State of the Environment reporting process. The use
of indicators is premised on the idea that it is possible to gauge the overall picture by selecting a limited number of appropriate items to study.
This approach can take a lot of time, energy and money; there are also
concerns about attempting to measure the immeasurable. According to
Parker (1995, 51), 'the reduction of complex environmental systems to
a few simple indicators is argued to be a repeat of the attempt to find
quantitative social indicators to measure social well-being in the 1970s'.
Bell and Morse (2001, 292) also recognise the dangers in using indicators, but suggest that, while 'summarising complexity into simple
numbers can be dangerous, [it] does condense information into a form
that can be accessible to the non-specialist'. This potentially increases
public awareness of sustainability issues and enables greater public
participation in sustainability initiatives. Indicators have also been used
as educational tools, or as a way of benchmarking cities against other
cities in sustainability performance.

The use of indicators within a model such as Vortex City to

Sustainable City is appropriate. This is, however, different from a project that focuses on indicators as the main output, such that, despite denials by the proponents, they almost become an end in themselves.

COMPARATIVE INITIATIVES ANALYSIS

The comparative initiatives approach has been used by Portney (2002) to ascertain the sustainability of 24 cities in the United States. The approach compared 34 elements of sustainable cities, including indicators projects, smart growth activities such as eco-industrial development and eco-villages, and sound transport, land use, energy and pollution programs. The resulting composite index for a city can be used to compare cities, similar to the best practice approach to sustainability, but in this case incorporating a wide range of elements. Portney's findings were that some cities did take sustainability more seriously than others, but it was often the cities that needed it most that were unlikely to embrace the concept (Portney, 2002).

The strengths of this approach are that it is broad in its consideration of sustainability, the variables can be modified to suit the conditions of another country and it includes a mixture of plans and actions. The weaknesses are that it may lead to an assessment of sustainability leadership or best practice on the basis of the existence of certain elements, rather than the effectiveness of these elements.

SUSTAINABILITY METRICS

The sustainability metrics approach is demonstrated by Shane and Graedel (2000) in relation to Vancouver, Canada. This approach is based on a combination of best practice assessment and sustainability indicators, and at the same time attempts to universalise a set of metrics for the major sustainability concerns that the authors identify. The concept is designed to address a metropolitan region rather than the core of an urban area. The metrics are divided into high, medium and low, with each category representing a different degree of sustainability. As the authors note, 'a metrics set is at best ... a generic guideline to environmental performance, not a comprehensive local assessment' (Shane and Graedel, 2000, 660).

The strengths of this approach are that, similar to some sustainability indicators, it is possible to compare sustainability performance within a city over time and make comparisons between cities.

As has been shown here, the above approaches all have strengths and weaknesses in ascertaining the sustainability of cities. The following section of this chapter develops a model that builds on the above models and approaches, and can be used in conjunction with ideas such as State of the Environment reporting, comparative initiatives analysis and sustainability indicators.

TOWARDS A SUSTAINABLE CITY MODEL

The approach used in this book is based on 'situational thinking' which is context- specific, as opposed to 'homogenous thinking' which searches for a single best model and attempts to apply it in all contexts (Honadle, 1999). The approach also builds on the insights of actant network theory, particularly the work of Michel Callon on the process of translation (Callon, 1986). Traditional models of planning practice have worked on a principle of diffusion, where the idea or knowledge spreads from a particular point and is implemented in a variety of locations. As Callon (1986) has observed, and as has been demonstrated in the urban history chapter of this book, ideas are not diffused but are translated as they enter particular contexts. Another notion that is central to this book is the issue of scale. 'Sustainable cities' is a globalised idea that emerges from a discourse of sustainability, but the emphasis on situational thinking and linking various scales indicates that many ideas and models can move through a process of translation in both directions between local, national and international scales (see Wilbanks, et al, 2003). What is considered sustainable or unsustainable may vary depending on context, and the processes of achieving sustainability are also specific to the cultural, economic and political contexts of a city.

With all these concepts in mind, the Vortex City to Sustainable City Model shown in figure 4.3 has been developed to highlight generalised patterns of unsustainability and to indicate what needs to be done to reduce the vortex effect of cities. This is important because ecological sustainability is more than being 'clean and green' in one area; it is about reducing the impact of cities on other parts of the planet through reduced resource use and waste disposal. The model introduces a spatial aspect to the flows and stocks approach of many other models. It also highlights that sustainable cities are not necessarily 'clean and green'. Drawing on understandings of the ecological footprints and metabolism models, what is important in terms of sustainability is resource acquisition, the energy used for throughput and the 'waste' management practices of people living in cities (see figures 4.4 and 4.5 at the end of this section). This can be related to the earlier chapters of this book, where

Figure 4.3 Vortex City to Sustainable City Model

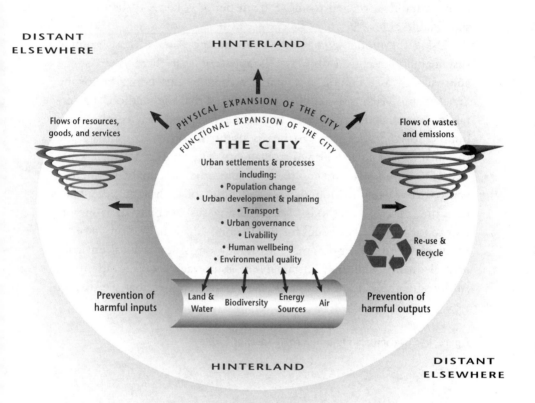

it was noted that different planning visions for cities all to varying extents had ecological sustainability impacts, yet the foci of these visions tended to be improved human wellbeing, environmental protection, efficiency, and so on. Unfortunately, as noted by authors such as Satterthwaite (1997), the question of scale is important because this was often achieved at the expense of sustainability in the surrounding region or other parts of the planet.

The Vortex City to Sustainable City Model builds on the work of Boyden et al (1981), Newman et al (1996), Satterthwaite (1997), Priemus (1999), Yencken and Wilkinson (2000), Shane and Graedel

(2000) and Newton (2001). The model differentiates between stocks and flows, allows for resource inputs and waste outputs from the surrounding region and from other parts of the planet, accommodates some of the key processes impacting on resource stocks and flows, and proves useful for demonstrating how cities can be planned, managed and governed to move from being vortices to being more sustainable cities.

Using the model, and building on the approaches to ascertaining sustainability discussed above, it is apparent that there is no single approach to ascertaining sustainability used in this book. Following Yencken and Wilkinson (2000), it is accepted that the method of ascertaining sustainability may vary between issues, and that combining a number of the above approaches is useful in order to estimate the sustainability of a particular Australian city. The attempt to universalise sustainability measurement (for example, the sustainability metrics approach) is likely to flounder on this point of each issue potentially requiring different methods of ascertaining sustainability. It is important to identify the key issues for sustainability in each location, in order to avoid wasting energy, time and money on issues of local environmental quality while key sustainability issues lack requisite attention. Addressing these key issues for sustainability requires that we do not

Figure 4.4: Transmission lines in urban areas of Sydney

Photo: Sonia Graham

Figure 4.5 A ship unloading cars at Glebe Island, Sydney

Photo: Sonia Graham

export unsustainable practices, either in space (to other locations) or in time (to future generations), which is the usefulness of ecological foot-prints and the metabolism-based models. The intent of the ecological footprint, rather than its conversion of ecological impact into a single value measured in hectares of land, is crucial. In other words, Australian cities are moving closer to sustainability if they can reduce consumption of non-renewable resources, reduce waste outputs, protect the most valuable ecosystems on which life depends, and do so without export-ing unsustainable practices to other locations or to future generations. How this is to be achieved will likely vary between cities and is the subject of sections 2 and 3 of this book.

SUMMARY

The previous three chapters have provided an overview of Australian cities and some of the key planning ideas and documents that have contributed to the present state of Australia's major cities. As has been demonstrated, ideas have often been incorporated in plans (albeit sometimes in a modified form), but the implementation of plans does not always proceed smoothly. This point should be obvious, but the history of urban planning and environmental management in Australia indicates that unless this point is borne in mind, mistakes are likely to be repeated.

Aspects of sustainability have been considered over a number of years, perhaps under different terminology, while other aspects are recent or have yet to be adequately addressed. Sustainability is often considered to be another function to be added to planning, but as the abbreviated history of planning presented in this book and the discussion on the transition from environmentalism to sustainability highlight, this way of thinking is flawed. Sustainability requires that we not simply add new categories or activities to planning, environmental management and governance, but rather it requires the review of why and how we are doing things. It necessitates that we think not of growth management, but interrogate the notion of growth and the kind of society we are developing. It requires a new ecological literacy that renders previous environmental management insufficient. It requires the implementation of new and sometimes well-established but neglected ideas. If we do not move in this direction, Australia's largest cities will continue to be vortices, potentially causing irreversible resource depletion and environmental degradation.

In this chapter a model of sustainable cities was developed. The model prioritises ecological sustainability, while recognising the importance of social, cultural and economic considerations. In the urban context, ecological sustainability does not mean a clean, green local environment. It requires a reduction of the ecological inputs and outputs of the city while simultaneously protecting biodiversity and other environmental attributes within the city. The Vortex City to Sustainable City Model highlights that the move from vortex cities towards sustainable cities requires careful consideration of the impacts of urban processes on environmental stocks and flows. It is to this task that we turn in section 2 of this book, which looks at six key issues for sustainability to suggest actions for the future. If these issues can be addressed in ways that are appropriate for each major Australian city, Australia's largest cities will be moving towards being world exemplars in sustainability. Section 3 of this book provides suggestions on the processes required to make Australian cities more sustainable.

SECTION 2

SUSTAINABILITY ISSUES

This section of the book focuses on a number of the issues that are important to address in order to move Australian cities towards sustainability. As Gleeson and Low (2000, 274) have recognised, 'issues such as sustainable development are irreducibly spatial'. This section builds on the spatial character of the earlier chapters in this book. It develops the convergence of urban planning and environmentalism and the move to sustainability, including urban sustainability, by looking at key issues for each Australian city.

Section 2 comprises six chapters which are based on the themes of population, water, transport, waste, climate change and biodiversity. Many of these and other issues overlap. For this reason, issues such as energy use are addressed in various chapters, including chapters 7 (transport) and 9 (climate change). Shortage of land has been discussed in section 1, and emerges in section 2 in chapters 5 (population) and 10 (biodiversity). Other issues such as food production are briefly discussed in chapter 6 (water).

The choice of the number of issues to address, and the manner in which they are categorised, is clearly a matter of judgement. It is possible to devise various formats to cover the many sustainability issues facing Australian cities. Similarly, it is possible to focus on one, or a limited number of issues, or to expand the study and attempt to incorporate all possible issues that may be important. For example, Troy (2001) nominated the three most important aspects of sustainability in the city as being: (1) energy consumption and its relationship to greenhouse gas production; (2) water consumption and its impacts; (3) waste production, minimisation and recycling. These issues, and others such as population, biodiversity and other air quality issues, are covered in the next six chapters. These chapters focus on providing enough depth on a number of key issues to highlight the manner in which Australian cities are currently unsustainable, to indicate positive actions being taken on all of the identified issues, and to suggest potential options for future implementation to move towards sustainability.

The structure of the chapters vary, depending on the nature of the issue. In each case, the chapter highlights that Australian cities are different from each other, perhaps in topography or history or maybe in the degree to which an issue is important relative to other issues in a particular city. In addition to the focus on the five largest Australian cities, the following chapters sometimes discuss new or recently emerged ideas that may be important as part of a sustainable future. In these cases, the ideas are often treated at a general level because, as section 3 of the book highlights, the processes of implementation may lead to the translation of these ideas to make them appropriate for the conditions of each Australian city.

CHAPTER 5

POPULATION

INTRODUCTION

Population is a major factor in any move towards sustainability. The important question to ask is, how significant is population growth relative to other factors in any consideration of sustainable cities in Australia? This leads to the development of a number of sub-questions that are necessary in order to construct a sophisticated understanding of the causes of unsustainability and the means of achieving sustainability. These sub-questions include the relationship between population and environmental damage, the possibility that population is a surrogate for other variables, and the possibility of change within other variables, for example, consumption patterns or technology.

This chapter looks at changes in population pressures, in housing occupation rates, and in the demand for new housing to establish the context for the expansion of urban areas. It also considers the importance of population relative to other factors in contributing to the unsustainability of Australia's cities. It does not explore the changing ethnicity of Australia, mortality by gender or many of the other crucial demographic questions that should be considered if we are considering the social sustainability of Australia. This chapter situates the population debate within a sustainability context and sets the foundation for the following chapters to explore the implications of urban growth, arising in part from population growth, for sustainability.

THE INTERNATIONAL CONTEXT

Population, and particularly the topic of population growth, is a very controversial issue that is often avoided by many commentators. This is partly because of the complexity of the issue and its manifestations at different scales. For example, each year about 80 million people (or four times the Australian population) is added to the global population. The global population exceeded 6.3 billion in 2003. The growth and projected growth of the world's population is shown in table 5.1. This table highlights the recent rapid growth in the world's population relative to human history on the earth, but it also points to the success of various population planning approaches (considered solely in gross population statistics), because despite people living longer, the rate of population growth has decreased.

While attention is often focused on the countries with the large populations such as China (1285 million in 2001 and projected to be 1462.1 million in 2050) and India (1025.1 million and 1572.1 million projected for 2050), there are smaller countries with rapid population growth. These include Bangladesh, with a population of 140.4 million in 2001 and a projected population of 265.4 million in 2050 (United Nations Population Fund, 2001). Many countries, especially in Africa, will continue to increase their population due to 'population momentum', whereby a youthful age structure combined with high fertility rates and falling death rates means that population increase is inevitable (O'Neill, et al, 2001).

Conversely, there are countries that are anticipated to decline in population, partly because of low fertility rates. According to McDonald (2003, 278), 'a fertility rate below 1.5 is likely to cause sustainability problems in any country'. While the notion of sustainability being used in this quote is not consistent with ecological sustainability, evidence suggests that some countries are already experiencing low fertility rates, low mortality rates, slow population growth rates, an ageing population and questions about the size, rate and type of immigration that is desired. In 1998 there were 16 countries with a population in excess of ten million people that could be considered to have stabilised their populations. All except for Japan were European countries (Brown, et al, 2000). Projections for 2050 indicate that countries such as Japan (127.3 million people in 2001 and projected 109.2 million people in 2050), Spain (39.9 million in 2001 and 31.3 million in 2050) and Italy (57.5 million in 2001 and 43 million in 2050) will have to deal with issues associated with a declining total population (United Nations Population Fund, 2001). This is largely because the fertility rates in 1995 were 1.42 for Japan (it was 1.76 in 1985), 1.18 for Spain (1.64 in 1985) and 1.17 for Italy (1.42 in 1985) (Carmichael and McDonald, 2003).

Table 5.1 World population milestones

World population reached	Year	Years since previous billion people reached
1 billion	1804	
2 billion	1927	123 years later
3 billion	1960	33 years later
4 billion	1974	14 years later
5 billion	1987	13 years later
6 billion	1999	12 years later
World population may reach		
7 billion	2013	14 years later
8 billion	2028	15 years later
9 billion	2054	26 years later

Source: Miller Jr, 2002, 5

One important point to note about population growth is its relationship to urbanisation. In 1800 London was the only city in the world with a population over one million people. By 1999 there were at least 326 cities in the world with a million or more residents (Brown, et al, 2000). Most of the very rapidly growing cities are in the developing countries. These cities currently face enormous challenges in terms of the provision of infrastructure, the impact on the surrounding countryside, social issues, governance and technological capacity. The rate of population increase means that these cities have little time to address the above challenges before they are exacerbated by the issue of accommodating more people.

THE AUSTRALIAN CONTEXT

The population debates in Australia range from national population figures to debates about the size of individual cities. In Australia, the fertility rate was 1.73 in 2001 (McDonald, 2003). The context for Australia may be summarised as a country with a lot of space that is not conducive to, sustaining a large population. In 2001, over 70 per cent of Australia was occupied by less than one per cent of the total population, at a population density of less than 0.1 persons per kilometre. By way of contrast, over 76 per cent of Australians lived on 0.33 per cent of land (Hugo, 2003), with 85 per cent of the population living within

50 kilometres of the coast in 2001 (Australian Bureau of Statistics, 2004b). The Australian population is increasing through net migration and, to a lesser extent, through a fall in mortality rates. After allowing for births, deaths and migration we are adding another person to our population every two minutes and forty-two seconds (Sustainable Population Australian, 2003).

Our population of 20 million is small relative to the world population, and large relative to our capacity to live sustainably in Australia. Our projected population is 26.5 million in 2050 (United Nations Population Fund, 2001). This can be viewed in many ways. It could be seen as an increase of about 33 per cent on the 2001 population in Australia. Alternatively, in 2050, for every additional Australian in the world, there are over 500 additional people in the rest of the world.

The population of Australian cities has grown rapidly since European settlement began, although the growth booms of particular cities have occurred at different times in the past two centuries. As noted in earlier chapters, while Sydney and Hobart were among the oldest European settlements, the early cosmopolitan character of Sydney was overtaken by 'Marvellous Melbourne' in the latter part of the 19th century. The late 20th century was notable for the rapid growth of Brisbane and Perth, especially relative to the older, more industrialised city of Adelaide. The most recent population statistics are shown in table 5.2, where it can be seen that not only are the other four major cities larger than Adelaide, but they are growing at a much faster rate. This trend is predicted to continue based on population projections: see table 5.3.

It is difficult to imagine that trend is destiny in the population projections. While Adelaide's population may remain relatively stable, it is unlikely that Hobart's population will decline by about one-eighth between 2021 and 2051, nor will Canberra's population be likely to decline given the growth of Sydney. Rising populations in Melbourne and Sydney are likely to widen differences in house prices between these cities and Hobart and Canberra, while improved transport infrastructure is likely to reduce commuting times between the larger and smaller cities. The latter will be a lifestyle attraction for some people. It is dangerous to ignore political, economic and cultural factors and base population projections on existing trends and demographic data. It is important to consider and relate political, economic and cultural factors to the processes of urbanisation and the spatial impacts of demographic change.

Table 5.2 Population change in Australia's five largest cities, 1996–2001

CITY	1996 Statistical Division, (000's)	2001 Statistical Division, (000's)	% change per annum, 1996–2001
Sydney	3881.1	4154.7	1.4
Melbourne	3283.3	3488.8	1.2
Brisbane	1520.0	1653.4	1.7
Perth	1295.1	1397.0	1.5
Adelaide	1078.4	1110.5	0.6

Source: Australian Bureau of Statistics, 2003a

Table 5.3 Projected population growth of Australia's capital cities

CITY	Projected population in 2021 (millions)	Projected population in 2051 (millions)
Sydney	4.9	5.6
Melbourne	4.1	4.7
Brisbane	2.2	3.0
Perth	1.8	2.2
Adelaide	1.1	1.1
Hobart	0.2	0.176
Canberra	0.4	0.39
Darwin	0.14	0.2

Source: Australian Bureau of Statistics, 2003d

POPULATION GROWTH AND ISSUES OF URBAN GROWTH

In Australia's largest cities, until recently, the dominant mode of accommodating population increase was to expand the built-up area at the periphery. Using Sydney as an example, compared to when Wills (1945) wrote about the urban-rural fringe in Mona Vale and Bankstown, or when Golledge (1960) noted its dynamic nature and expansion into Liverpool, Campbelltown, Windsor and Penrith, the Sydney Basin is now highly urbanised. There are virtually no remaining grainlands of the Hawkesbury–Nepean region to convert into intensive agriculture, which itself is under threat from urban expansion as the land prices increase. While many agriculturalists are keen to use their land as a form of superannuation, the pressure to accommodate more population on finite land is becoming acute. Current proposals to accommodate 300 000 people in the Bringelly area in south-west Sydney (near Campbelltown) show the desperation of planners attempting to accommodate an extra 50 000 people per year (about 1000 people per week or a city the size of Wagga Wagga each year) into the Sydney Basin. The Bringelly area, formerly known as South Creek Valley, has been earmarked for urban use since the 1980s, but is renowned for its poor air quality (Davies, 2003).

This vignette highlights one of the problems with debates that are focused on numbers, particularly in this case from the population boosterism side of the debate. It certainly is possible to accommodate more people within the existing urban boundaries of all five of our major cities (and within smaller cities such as Hobart, Canberra, Newcastle and Cairns). After all, Hong Kong and Manhattan show how it may be done using high-rise accommodation. It is also possible to achieve higher population figures at the existing urban densities by converting parkland (for example, Centennial Park in Sydney, Kings Park in Perth, the Adelaide Parklands) into residential accommodation. Of course, turning Kings Park into high-rise towers as in Hong Kong (which would incorporate the latest environmental technology as part of moves towards sustainability) would enable even more people to live within urban boundaries. The use of inner-city parkland areas for accommodation would also assist transport initiatives because, similar to redevelopments such as Pyrmont in Sydney, there would be more walking to work and less use of the private automobile.

Many people would, rightly, be horrified at the above suggestions. They are deliberately extreme, and they ignore compromise approaches such as medium-density housing, or low-rise high-density housing. This does not mean that the idea is technically impossible, allowing for legal considerations governing the said parks. In Hong Kong the concept of sustainability is premised on the perpetuation of a high-density city, which guides the development towards 'greening' high-rise buildings and making the new buildings more energy- and materials-efficient than the older housing structures. The purpose of this exercise has been to highlight the importance of value judgements in any consideration of settlement options. In summary, more people in a city require more accommodation and associated services, and there is a tangible, physical component that is often overlooked in debates that focus on population numbers.

POPULATION STUDIES AND DEBATES

There have been a number of important population studies in Australia. These studies have been motivated by various issues, ranging from ecological sustainability to generating economic growth through to a 'populate or perish' mentality based on the threat of a 'yellow peril'.

There have been government studies into what may constitute a sustainable population for Australia. In 1994 the House of Representatives Standing Committee for Long Term Strategies (referred to as the 'Jones Inquiry') considered six population scenarios for Australia. These scenarios were high population (50–100 million), high population, low resource use (30–50 million), modest (23–30 million), stable (17–23 million), reduced (5–17 million) and a return to 1788 population levels of 1–9 million people. It is apparent that the study authors did not really believe that some of the lower projections were possible or desirable (House of Representatives Standing Committee for Long Term Strategies, 1994). The study did recommend that a national population policy be developed for Australia. It concluded that through adjustments to the migration program, Australia could potentially support anywhere from a 'near-stable population' (defined at 15 per cent above the 1994 figure) to a population of over twice the size of the 1994 population (House of Representatives Standing Committee for Long Term Strategies, 1994). The committee did not nominate a specific upper limit of population, beyond which Australian society would be at threat (this is the concept of carrying capacity), but noted that the population level that can be supported in Australia 'for the longer term will depend upon whether people are prepared to modify their behaviour in resource use' (House of Representatives Standing Committee for Long Term Strategies, 1994, 125).

A more recent study by the CSIRO developed a model, the Australian Stocks and Flows Framework, to investigate the physical impacts of scenarios for Australia's future in 2050 (Foran and Poldy, 2002). This study contained a range of population projections, with the high-growth option based on a constant percentage (0.67 per cent of the total population) but an increased number of immigrants arriving in Australia annually. This high-growth calculation led to a projected population of 32 million in 2050 and a population of 50 million living in Australia by 2100. The authors concluded that their low-growth option would reduce ecological impacts, but expose Australia to the risks of an ageing population. The middle range option, which can be labelled the 'business as usual' approach, led to a population of 25 million in 2050. This option led to medium-level ecological impacts and potential for economic growth. The high-growth option is technically feasible and would likely generate economic growth, but would have significant energy and greenhouse emission implications. It would also require the establishment of 90 cities the current size of Canberra in order to accommodate this population growth.

The CSIRO study included scenarios of individual cities. As part of the high-growth scenario, Sydney would become a mega-city with a population exceeding ten million in 2100. Opportunities for economic growth would be increased in Sydney, but the risk of further disconnecting Sydney from its rural hinterland was also noted. The ecological impacts of increasing Sydney's population by approximately 150 per cent within the next 100 years also need to be considered carefully. Given the spatial limitations and other resource issues such as water supply and air quality, the desirability of a large population in Australia and its distribution in locations such as the Sydney Basin is debatable.

Issues of population are vigorously debated by various lobby groups. Advocates for lower population, zero population growth and sustainable population for Australia include the organisation Sustainable Population Australia. In opposition to this stance are population boosters, such as the Federal Member for North Sydney, Joe Hockey, who wants the population of Sydney to reach 6.5 million by 2021 and 8 million by 2050, and the Australian Population Institute which is seeking an annual migrant intake of one per cent of Australia's population (this would immediately raise the intake from its present level of about 125 000 people per year to 200 000 people per year). The Australian Population Institute is claimed to be 'a non-profit organisation formed by a group of Australian business people, supported by peak industry bodies including the Urban Development Institute of Australia' (Australian Population Institute, 2003). The polarity of positions, with significant variation between the range of outlying positions that have been identified here, means that any debate about population and sustainability for Australia, and Australian cities in particular, is going to be contentious.

HOUSEHOLD FORMATION RATES

While debates often focus on population numbers, the impacts of other factors cannot be ignored. These factors include cultural considerations such as the age when women are having children or if they are having children at all. These considerations, along with education policies, government welfare policy, and so on, influence the household formation rate. This rate is very important to consider because while it does not directly equate with population growth rates, it is a crucial factor that affects the relationship between the supply and demand of dwellings and the process of urbanisation. The emphasis on population growth is therefore somewhat misplaced.

Household formation rates are increasing faster than population growth. A study by the Australian Bureau of Statistics projected that the number of Australian households would increase from 6.9 million in 1996 to between 9.4 and 10 million in 2021, a rise of between 38 and 46 per cent. Population growth over the same period was projected to be 24 per cent (Australian Bureau of Statistics, 1999). Queensland, which includes the rapidly growing South-East Queensland region where many retirees are locating, is anticipated to have an increase of between 61 and 74 per cent in total households, or 800 000 to one million new households, over the period 1996–2021, with large rates of growth in the lone person household and couple families without children categories (Australian Bureau of Statistics, 1999).

While a rapidly growing population adds new households, and therefore new demands for housing and the associated commodities of contemporary urban life in Australia, it is also possible to have an increase in household formation in the absence of population growth. This may occur through separation and divorce, or young people moving away from home to share housing. Rapidly growing and expensive cities such as Sydney may actually contribute to a reduction in the household formation rate as students, lowly paid workers, and so on, may choose or be forced by economic conditions to stay at home and not create a new household.

Household formation rates are related to household size, but there are other variables to consider such as the decline in the number of children per family. The average household size in Australia has been declining, notably in cities such as Sydney where it fell from 2.9 persons per household in 1981 to 2.7 persons per household in 1996 (NSW Department of Infrastructure, Planning and Natural Resources, 2003). This is due to a number of factors, including less children in the traditional family structure, the increase in one-parent families (due to separation/divorce, death of a spouse or birth by a woman who is not living with a partner), more (possibly career-oriented) people choosing to live alone and the changing nature of care for the elderly (see Rowland, 2003). This means that new forms of housing are needed to ensure compatibility between household types, the aspirations of people and the location, size and form of their dwelling.

The declining household size is, however, sometimes counteracted by the increase in size of dwellings. Foran and Poldy (2002) note that between 1940 and 2000, the average area of a single detached residential dwelling in metropolitan areas increased from 100 to 150 square metres. In a submission to the Productivity Commission in 2003, AVJennings (2003) reproduced figures from BIS Shrapnel to demonstrate that the average floor area of new homes across Australia (including but not limited to cities) had increased by 28.4 per cent between 1992 and 2002. Of the four regions named, this change was greatest in New South Wales (up by over 41 per cent), then Queensland and Victoria (up by between 30 and 33 per cent each), and least in South Australia (up by 19.3 per cent) (AVJennings, 2003). The variations in increases, given that in 1992 the average floor area of new homes ranged from 176.2 square metres in Victoria to 191.2 square metres in New South Wales, has meant that as of 2002, the size of new homes varied from 213.2 square metres in South Australia to 269.9 square metres in New South Wales (AVJennings, 2003). At the same time, average lot sizes have decreased due to the subdivision of existing lots, or the creation of new lots of a smaller size than was previously created in so-called greenfields development. The spatial outcome of these trends is the 'McMansion' phenomenon, where a large dwelling is built on a small lot (see figure 5.1). The combination of demographic and building trends noted above is the creation of more McMansions occupied by fewer people. An analysis of demographics and urban planning that is narrowly based on population numbers is unlikely to identify this phenomenon.

The trend towards more multi-unit dwellings in major cities has partly been investor-driven, but it also reflects the changing demography of urban Australia and the recognition that continuations of previous settlement patterns were unsustainable. For example, Sydney does not have the land for all new households to live in detached residences, even if people wanted this housing type. The forecast for the period 2002–07 is that 66 per cent of all new dwellings built in Sydney will be multi-unit dwellings, and that 86 per cent of dwellings built in the established urban area will be multi-unit dwellings (NSW Department of Infrastructure, Planning and Natural Resources, 2003). Most of these dwellings are anticipated to be built in the middle-ring local authorities (28 per cent, up from 22 per cent in the period 1997–98 to 2001–02), with a proportionate decrease of new, mostly detached dwellings being built on greenfield sites at the edge of the city from 27 to 25 per cent of all new dwellings over the same periods (NSW

Figure 5.1 McMansions at Glenwood, Sydney

Photo: Sonia Graham

Department of Infrastructure, Planning and Natural Resources, 2003).

The creation of new households, the ageing of existing households and the existence of support for residents to maintain independent living as long as possible are all factors that influence the number of dwellings required and type of dwelling required. An important point to consider is that these dwellings may meet the needs of their initial residents for a short period of time, but the process of subdivision of the land, the issuing of separate titles (both for detached houses and units), and the physical construction of the dwelling lead to the creation of long-term products. Using the population scenarios of the CSIRO study (Foran and Poldy, 2002), it is very likely that the majority of the dwellings that will accommodate even the high-population scenario (and certainly the low- and medium-population scenarios) have already been built or will be built in the next few years. It is therefore worth looking at how government actions can improve the sustainability of Australia's housing stock using population growth and household formation rates as a catalyst for this aspect of sustainability, or how government actions can perpetuate unsustainable urban growth. The recent federal government scheme to subsidise first home owners is an excellent example of lost opportunities that is leading to the perpetuation of unsustainable urbanisation.

THE FIRST HOME OWNERS SCHEME

The Federal Government of John Howard has been riding the wave of housing price increases since the late 1990s. This has enabled many existing home owners to borrow against the rising value of their house, thereby fuelling economic growth. State governments have also bene-fited from this situation because they have routinely collected more stamp duty than they envisaged in their budgets. Unfortunately, the rapid rise in housing prices in the late 1990s and early 21st century has meant that first home buyers cannot enter the market easily, and in places such as Sydney they are often forced to areas such as the Central Coast in order to be able to afford mortgage costs.

The First Home Owners Scheme was a federal government subsidy to first-time owners that was introduced in order to offset the impact of the Goods and Services Tax (GST). The scheme was introduced in July 2000 and provided eligible applicants with a one-off payment of $7000. The scheme was amended in March 2001 to include an additional $7000 for eligible applicants who built a new home or purchased a new, but previously unoccupied home. From January 2002 this additional grant was reduced from $7000 to $3000.

The impact of the scheme on the sustainability of Australian cities has been detrimental. While the initial grant could be justified as a compensatory measure for the GST, and therefore, arguably, should not be subject to environmental or other conditions, it is clear that the subsequent, additional grants were designed to boost the demand for new housing. The scheme helped fuel a housing construction boom, which was very significant in allowing Australia to avoid the worst of the world economic stagnation from 2001 to early 2003. There were, however, no environmental conditions or incentives attached to the additional finance provided for new dwelling construction. This failure to improve the ecological sustainability of the housing stock is appalling, given that the outcomes of a short-lived government scheme will very likely become the housing stock of Australia for at least the next 50 years.

THE SIGNIFICANCE OF POPULATION GROWTH

It is now worth revisiting the question about the significance of popula-tion in debates about sustainability, and particularly about sustainable cities in Australia. If there was no population growth in Australia, from a sustainability perspective we would have to reduce our ecological impact. There appears to be little doubt that Australia's population is steadily growing, which means that even to maintain the current unsustainable level of total environmental impact, we have to reduce our absolute and per capita impact on the environment. A rapidly growing population necessitates even greater reductions in environmental impact.

On the other hand, the question of population distribution also needs to be considered. While concentrating people in large cities may increase the impact of cities on air pollution, studies indicate that spreading the population over a large area (as in exurbia hobby farm development and coastal settlement) is likely to have a far greater ecological impact (Newman and Kenworthy, 1999). This is particularly the case when we consider transport, energy use and biodiversity conservation issues. The challenge facing leaders and planners in Australian cities such as Sydney, where population is growing rapidly and there is limited available land for development, is to address this issue in a way that promotes sustainability without impinging on other values such as respect for fellow humans and democratic processes.

The argument being put in this chapter is that while population boosterism should be opposed, there is a need to plan for an increasing population in Australian cities. This requires that we restructure laws, values, infrastructure and processes in order to reduce the impact of consumption on urban sustainability. To some extent this has been happening (think of those fuel-guzzling cars of the 1960s and 1970s), but there have been countertrends such as the increase in total fuel consumption as people are driving further, sitting in traffic longer, or in some cases choosing to drive fuel-inefficient four-wheel drive vehicles. The economic savings generated by positive environmental actions must be reused for further environmental benefit or else there is simply greater economic capacity to create unsustainability. That, unfortunately, is a summary of the current situation.

The impact of consumption means that factors other than population warrant significant attention. A heavily used, but flawed, formula is the I=PAT formula (where impact is equal to population multiplied by affluence multiplied by technology). Variations of this formula have been devised, but the basic formula is very useful for highlighting that population is only one factor that is creating an environmental impact. It is also necessary to recognise that affluence can to some degree be de-linked from resource use (or at least the resources can be used in a more sustainable manner), and to acknowledge that while the initial formula cast technology as a negative impact, technology can be environmentally beneficial. At the global level, a good indication of the importance of considering factors other than population can be seen with greenhouse gas emissions (see chapter 9), where the projected population increase of 71 million people in the United States between 2000 and 2050 will roughly equal the emissions of the 1 billion additional Africans added in the same period (Brown, et al, 2000).

Bearing this formula and example in mind, if we consider the environmental impact of Australians, then it is apparent that while our population is increasing by about 1.2 per cent per annum, our ecological impact is increasing at a much faster rate. For example, a decomposition of the parameters leading to changes in Australia's total greenhouse gas emissions over the period 1969–1997 indicates that while on average the emissions increased by 2.3 per cent per year, only 1.1 per cent (or under half) of this increase could be attributed to population increase (Wood, 2003). Other factors, particularly affluence (1.5 per cent), were more important, especially in times of economic growth (Wood, 2003). These modelling exercises are important because without them, it is too easy for some commentators and lobby groups to attribute the problems of unsustainability to a rising population, and thereby blame migrants and young people. This approach potentially absolves the current generation of Australians from addressing the ecological impacts of their lifestyles. Foran and Poldy (2002, 69) relate the size of the population, regardless of ethnicity or length of residence in Australia, to environmental impact and conclude that 'the size of the population will directly affect the size of the major capital cities, the domestic consumption of food, paper and plastic and the requirements of urban water supply'. Beyond these impacts, the influence of population is increasingly mitigated by affluence and other factors.

If we take this analysis further and consider a range of environmental problems and compare the effectiveness of acting on them, then Australia with a relatively low population and both a low rate of population growth and a low increase in population in absolute terms is doing poorly. The Environmental Sustainability Index produced by the World Economic Forum (2002) ranked 142 countries in key issues (many of which are addressed in the following chapters). On a number of key environmental aspects of sustainability Australia compared badly with countries of similar size and affluence levels (for example, Canada, Sweden, Norway), being ranked 115 of 142 countries for global stewardship. On specific issues, Australia was ranked 125 of 142 countries for conserving biodiversity, 125 for reducing waste and consumption pressures, 128 in reducing air pollution and 134 in reducing greenhouse gas emissions (World Economic Forum, 2002). While not all of this damage can be attributed to cities, it is apparent that neither can it be attributed to increases in population.

Clearly the causes of unsustainability do not primarily reside in the population growth of Australia. In order to move from our present vortex cities towards sustainable cities in Australia we need to seriously address the consumption issues that are causing environmental damage.

POPULATION AND SUSTAINABILITY

Given the above context, studies, debates and policies, what needs to be done in order to address the impacts of population change on sustainability?

First, there is a need for a population policy that extends beyond immigration issues. We do not have a national population policy, but as McDonald (2003, 267) has noted, 'no OECD country has a population policy expressed in terms of a target population size or a target rate of population growth'. Despite the challenges in devising such a policy, Australia should have one. The policy should not only consider numbers of people, but also factors such as their age and spatial issues such as the distribution and the ecological impact of the population. Such a policy, however, only makes sense if it is considered as part of sustainability, which is contingent on a thorough analysis of baseline environmental conditions and environmental trends and a sophisticated understanding of demographics, the 'affluence' and 'technology' of the IPAT formula and basic human rights.

Recently there have been a number of calls for national planning to consider both the number of people and their distribution (Gleeson 2001, McManus and Pritchard, 2001). Redistribution was attempted by the Whitlam Labor Government in the early 1970s through its decentralisation initiatives. I am not suggesting that a form of decentralisation simply be reintroduced, despite the appearance that currently the market is the de facto national population planner after immigration levels have been set. This is because Australia's major source of population growth is the net increase in migration, and most migrants move to the large cities, with approximately 40 per cent of new migrants settling in Sydney. This figure excludes migration from New Zealand, which could make the figure even higher. It is significantly higher than Sydney's proportion of the total population of

Australia, which is 21 per cent (Millett, 2002). Of particular concern to some commentators and authors is that the expansion of cities such as Sydney is occurring at a time when many small country towns are declining, some regional cities are expanding at the expense of their hinterlands (the so-called sponge cities) and most large cities and coastal locations are experiencing urban expansion pressures (Burnley and Murphy, 2004). A redistribution of population based on the attractiveness of inland centres with transport links, good educational and medical facilities, recreational opportunities and a lower cost of living than the large cities, is possible without the need for any coercive policies. One possibility to encourage the redistribution of population is differential taxation rates, or a rebate, for taxpayers living in particular zones, as currently happens through section 79A of the *Income Tax Assessment Act 1936* for residents who live in either Zone A (remote areas north of the 26th Parallel) or Zone B (remote areas south of the 26th Parallel) of Australia (Hicks, 2001). Given that the boundaries drawn up for these zones in 1945 have only been modified slightly since that time, it may be possible to change these boundaries or even to simply increase the rebate (which based on 1997–98 taxation claims was $180 million foregone due to the rebate) to increase the attractiveness of inland centres (Hicks, 2001). This issue does, however, require processes of coordination between Commonwealth and state governments in terms of expenditure, incentives, infrastructure provision and the alignment of discourses about the issue.

Second, on the issue of discourse, there needs to be a questioning of population growth as a desirable end in itself. The high-growth urban regions, particularly Sydney and South-East Queensland, are focused on growth management. In other words, many people desire the growth because it has connotations of success, it expands markets and it enables opportunities to introduce new technologies and ideas. It is, however, dangerous to perceive population growth as a competition between cities. Rather than being seen as a problem (as it is by commentators such as Bernard Salt and others who see population change as a race), the zero or slow growth of Adelaide provides an interesting opportunity to compare potential approaches to sustainability. Is a city likely to become more sustainable as it revalorises capital through rapid expansion, as is tending to happen in Brisbane and Perth, or does the slower rate of population increase projected for Adelaide allow time to develop plans and generate less pressure to service a rapidly growing population? Does the rapid growth of some Australian cities offer

opportunities to design and build many examples of new 'green architecture' (that is, dwellings and gardens that are oriented and designed
for energy efficiency, have low embodied energy in their construction,
generate low greenhouse emissions, incorporate the reuse of water, and
so on), or is the slower growth of cities such as Adelaide crucial for
reducing the consumption of resources and for preserving biodiversity?
Is it possible to derive all of these benefits with minimal ecological cost?
If so, how and where?

Third, if the rapid population growth of cities such as Sydney,
Brisbane and Perth does enable the development of green architecture,
there is no guarantee that it will be developed. This requires development control at the local level to prevent the perpetuation of unsustainable housing design and construction, but development control
cannot produce and disseminate innovation so that it becomes more
than a single showcase project. As the federal government's First Home
Owners Scheme demonstrated, without careful consideration of regulations and incentives, it is possible to build more unsustainable dwellings
and to miss the opportunity to link housing construction with sustainability. Therefore, what is required is the articulation between sustainable cities and other activities at all levels of government. Initiatives in
green architecture, biodiversity conservation, and so on, need to be
constantly incorporated into government spending programs, design
codes and approval processes. Further, staff who are working at
'customer counters' and inspectors in the field need to be educated
about the latest developments in sustainability design so that they can
advocate them and be agents of change, rather than barriers to change
as is sometimes the case.

SUMMARY

This chapter has demonstrated that population change is an important
issue that should be discussed and debated in Australia. A declining
and/or ageing population is likely to have implications for sustainability. This does not, however, make a policy of continued population
growth through the attraction of migrants to join the workforce the
best answer to the question of what is a sustainable population for
Australia. While the question is relevant, as the material in this chapter
indicates, it is not necessarily the best question to be asking.

With or without a national population policy, it is possible for
Australia's major cities to accommodate more people (given that this is
where most of the additional growth will occur), but in order to

become more sustainable we have to address issues of consumption. Increased migration, and indeed any increase in the Australian-born population, will only add to a problem of unsustainability because most migrants and young people will quickly learn to aspire to Australian standards of living and lifestyle choices. It may be an attraction for some migrants, and a source of pride for many Australians, but the evidence suggests that it is the major contributor to unsustainability in Australia. Our land and water resources, air quality and biodiversity cannot accommodate even the present number of Australians living unsustainable lifestyles.

The solution is not to aggressively limit the number of people living in Australia, but to significantly reduce our consumption and de-link our lifestyle from high-resource use and waste outputs. As the following chapters demonstrate, in order to be more sustainable we need to do this anyway, regardless of any changes in population.

CHAPTER 6

WATER

INTRODUCTION

Australia's urbanisation, particularly since the Second World War, has been predicated on the basis of ready access to cheap water of high quality. (Lloyd, 1995, 59)

This chapter considers the limited, and limiting, factor of water. Water is crucial for all forms of life. It is, arguably, the most vital issue facing the future of Australian cities.

The availability and accessibility of fresh water has been a major factor in the development of Australia's urban pattern. Fresh water was a key reason why Sydney Cove, rather than Botany Bay, became the site of first settlement. In Perth, the availability of fresh water at the base of Mount Eliza (now Kings Park) and the defensive protection of wetlands (since drained) were instrumental in the siting of the settlement. However, since the first settlers in Sydney Cove polluted the Tank Stream, the history of water in Australian cities is largely one of degradation and depletion, although not necessarily in that order.

In a continent as dry as Australia, it was important that settlements were established near sources of fresh water. Cities and towns that are located far from fresh water supplies, for example, Kalgoorlie–Boulder in Western Australia, have often developed because of mineral deposits. Kalgoorlie–Boulder was supplied with water by horses and camels, and since the early 20th century by water pumped from Mundaring Weir in the hills east of Perth. Changes in technology have increased the capacity to move water to supply Australian cities, but unless greater efforts are made at demand management then this technology merely enables the perpetuation of a frontier mentality to resource management and is therefore not sustainable. Any discussion of water should begin with the hydrological cycle because cities have literally tapped into this natural cycle and significantly altered it at local and regional levels.

The argument made in this chapter is that Australian cities are not doing enough to address the demand for water. This does not imply a lack of action or that significant reductions in water use, and particularly water use per capita, have been achieved. Rather, as with all other issues discussed in this section of the book, there is a lot more that can and needs to be done in order to be more sustainable. A senate committee reported in December 2002 that 'it is clear that urban centres in Australia are using water in ways, and quantities, that are unsustainable' (Senate Committee, 2002, xi).

The importance of water quality will also be considered in this chapter, because a focus on the quantity of water does not recognise the potential of humans to both deplete and degrade this precious resource. Maintaining and improving water quality requires an ecological perspective of the water cycle and a catchment scale approach to the issue of water. It also requires the allocation of water so that water quality and use are matched, rather than the current situation where the major household use of potable water is on gardens.

The latter part of this chapter focuses on the ability of planning and urban design to be part of the solution. This is possible through 'water sensitive urban design' practices. There are excellent examples of water sensitive design, but unfortunately there are far more examples of potable water being used in great quantities for unnecessary purposes. The future of Australian cities will be very closely linked to the way we manage water in the cities and in the hinterland where food is produced (for example, the Murray–Darling Basin) and in the way that water is managed by other people in the 'distant elsewhere' from which we import food and other items that embody water use.

A conventional way of writing this chapter would probably focus on technology and infrastructure. It would consider the processes of water capture and storage, the treatment of water through purification techniques, distribution systems and the issues of stormwater management and sewerage disposal. It is admitted that some of these important processes are given cursory treatment in this chapter, partly because new ways of thinking blur the distinctions between categories such as stormwater management and water distribution systems. The alternative structure presented in this chapter is more ecologically based, especially in advocating water sensitive urban design which blurs the boundaries between water storage, demand management, reuse of water and the use of 'infrastructure' that is not based on long systems of pipes.

THE HYDROLOGICAL CYCLE AND AUSTRALIAN CITIES

Despite being located in the driest continent apart from Antarctica, Australian cities are generally fortunate to be located in the higher-rainfall regions of the country, certainly compared to the 'cadillac desert' of the United States where cities such as Los Angeles import and consume large amounts of water from western rivers (Reisner, 1993). The hot, dry climate and the resulting lack of water is a major reason why inland centres did not grow in Australia, unlike in more temperate countries such as the United States where there are many major inland cities. Australia's largest cities are all on the coast, and with the exception of Perth they are in areas of relatively high rainfall. They are backed by either mountain ranges or hills that force the clouds upwards. As they rise above the mountains, the clouds drop their rain in areas that are suitable for damming, and are not too far to pipe water to the city, especially as the force of gravity can expedite the process.

The hydrological cycle, in its simplest form, contains three layers. Many people are aware of precipitation from the sky to the ground, and evaporation returning water to the sky. The storage of surface water in lakes, rivers and reservoirs is also visible. What is not seen is the infiltration of surface water to underground aquifers. Little is known about recharge rates, the impacts of extracting water from the deepest groundwater supplies, and how this may affect other aquifers and surface water. The science is being developed, but it is also very likely that as the science is producing greater understandings of the hydrological cycle, the cycle itself is changing.

One of the key issues to be addressed is the connection between water and climate change (see chapter 9). In its *Value of Water* report (2002, 41), the Australian Senate Environment, Communications, Information Technology and the Arts References Committee acknowledged the uncertainty about the effects of climate change on rainfall patterns, but logically concluded that 'urban planners must factor this uncertainty of the future water supply into their calculations' and that in order to plan for unpredictable changes we need to 'build in a larger margin for error'. Luketina and Bender (2002, 114) consider the impact of climate change on water supply on a global scale and state that 'the non-greenhouse processes of decadal climate change and El Nino and La Nina climate change will almost certainly be more significant than greenhouse induced climate change'. Whichever analysis is accurate in the long term, it appears that a precautionary approach, one of acting now to reduce the demand for water, and particularly for potable water, is necessary in the move towards sustainable cities.

WATER SUPPLY AND USE IN AUSTRALIAN CITIES

On a global scale, the supply of water was important in ancient cities. The earliest engineering achievements of the Roman Empire and the irrigation networks of early Asian and South American cities are examples highlighting the enormous importance attached to the provision of water. It continues to be a major issue in the development of megacities today.

Australian cities are similar to other cities in their reliance on accessible, clean water. There is, however, significant variation in the way that water is currently sourced for each Australian city. Sydney, Melbourne and Brisbane rely on damming rivers to create vast reservoirs. Perth is supplied by a combination of surface and groundwater in roughly equal quantities, while Adelaide is supplied by a combination of water from the Murray River and from catchments in the Mount Lofty Ranges (Senate Committee, 2002).

Lloyd (1995) noted that the earliest water supplies for Australian cities were generally located on the coastal plains of each city. The growth of the cities, often accompanied by the degradation of the initial water supplies, led to the construction of large, and then larger, dams further from the city. This was the vortex city model of urban development. It was a 'supply-side', engineering-based, growth-oriented mentality that aimed to create or meet a projected demand for water. It is a mentality that reached its zenith in the post–World War II era, exemplified in the Australian context by the Snowy Mountains Scheme. This engineering achievement is notable for its inter-basin transfer of water and the resulting deleterious impacts on the Snowy River. While the scheme is not focused on urban water use, the irrigation areas created by the inter-basin transfer of water are crucial for the production of food, much of which is consumed in Australia's largest East Coast cities.

The traditional engineering mentality of 'dam, store, purify, pump and pipe' has enabled Australian cities to grow as low-density, high–water consumption cities. The construction of large dams at some distance from the city has given Australian cities the capacity to maintain water supply. Foran and Poldy (2002) compare the storage levels of water in the four largest Australian cities and relate this amount to the use of water. They conclude that Sydney has 3.5 years of water stored in reservoirs, Melbourne has 2.9 years, Brisbane has 5.2 years and Perth has 2.8 years. The amount of water stored does not equate with storage capacity because of the need for flood mitigation measures. For example, 60 per cent of storage capacity at Somerset and Wivenhoe dams in the Brisbane catchment are left empty to accommodate flood flows (Cossins, 1990). Despite the existence of large dams in the hills behind all major Australian cities, it is now predicted that existing sources of water will soon be inadequate in some of the cities with rapid population growth. Information supplied to the Senate Environment, Communications, Information Technology and the Arts References Committee (2002) indicated that a new water source will likely be required for Perth between 2005 and 2007 and for Brisbane by 2015. By way of contrast, Melbourne appears to have sufficient capacity to store water until 2040, while Adelaide is not affected by water quantity concerns (Senate Committee, 2002).

In cities such as Sydney and Melbourne, in particular, it is the age of the distribution infrastructure that is the concern for capital investment. This infrastructure is often inappropriate, given that it was often simply added-on to existing systems as the cities expanded. The infrastructure is deteriorating and the consequent leaks and water contamination result in loss or degradation of water. The development of a new city would include modern technology and a more logical water distribution system, but the reality is that the infrastructure has been built up over many years and its redesign and replacement is a long and expensive process.

The need for new sources of water is dependent on factors such as rainfall, population growth and per capita use of water. This last variable is influenced by cultural attitudes towards gardens, household water use, and so on. It is also influenced by education and the pricing structures for water. These activities form part of what is known as 'demand management', which may be defined as 'any program that modifies (decreases) the level and/or timing of demand for a particular resource' (White and Fane, 2000). In recent years demand management has delivered significant (but still insufficient) reductions in the demand for water per person in various Australian cities, thereby extending the life of existing infrastructure.

Water use varies significantly from year to year, influenced mostly by the extent and duration of the summer heat. It is therefore more useful to look at changes by decade, rather than picking individual years within different decades, as was done in table 4 in the *Value of Water* report (Senate Committee, 2002, 29–30). The same report provides evidence from three Australian cities (Sydney, Melbourne and Newcastle) to demonstrate that the total amount of water used each decade has been increasing at a reduced rate, and was approximately stable in the decade 1990 to 2000. The amount of water used per person increased in the decade 1970 to 1980, but since that time there have been major reductions in the amount of water used per person (Senate Committee, 2002). This pattern is demonstrated by Sydney Water in the period March 1992 to March 2002 where water use has fallen from 506 to 412 litres per person per day, although it is acknowledged that additional improvements are required to meet the water use targets of 364 litres per person per day by 2004–05 and 329 litres per person per day by 2010–11 (Department of Environment and Conservation NSW, 2003).

Water used per capita is important, but it must be considered in conjunction with population change and the supply of water (that is, rainfall, evaporation, and so on) in the search for sustainability. As of 2002, water consumption in Sydney was 106 per cent of the yield, which is defined as 'the amount of water that can be withdrawn from a reservoir on an ongoing basis with an acceptably small risk of reducing the reservoir storage to zero' (Department of Environment and Conservation NSW, 2003, 18). Not surprisingly, water restrictions were introduced and then tightened for the 2003–04 summer season in Sydney.

Modelling by Foran and Poldy (2002, 99) suggests that if the existing water consumption rates, the existing storage capacity and the possible population growth projections discussed in chapter 5 of this book (the high-growth scenario that would see Sydney's population rise to ten million people by 2100) are considered together, then 'large investments in interbasin transfers or a considerable reduction in water use per household would be required'. As has been demonstrated in Newcastle and the Hunter Region, one way to achieve water reductions at the household level is through pricing structures. My concern is that if water is priced at a higher rate according to its use, this will make water a more precious commodity and may encourage interbasin transfers to the wealthy cities where many people will, perhaps begrudgingly, pay more for water to maintain unsustainable lifestyles.

We return to this issue when we consider an aspect of demand management, the implementation of water sensitive urban design, in the latter part of this chapter. Now we turn to the issue of water quality, threats to water quality and the mismatch between the quality of water and its use.

WATER QUALITY

The arrival of European settlers was quickly followed by a deterioration in the quality of water in Australian cities. The Tank Stream in Sydney was soon polluted, despite a proclamation from Governor Phillip that was intended to avoid the degradation of the settlement's main source of drinking water. When the Tank Stream was no longer able to supply potable water, the Lachlan Swamps in what is now Centennial Park were used as a water source, and the water was conveyed by a tunnel called Busby's Bore to the corner of Hyde Park (Warner, 2000). Other examples of water degradation include Sydney Harbour being used as a dump, and some of its tributaries being so polluted by slaughterhouses and other uses that they were reclaimed (for example, Blackwattle Creek was filled in to create Wentworth Park in Glebe). By the 19th century the Yarra River in Melbourne had effectively become a sewer for the slaughterhouses and factories that lined its banks. The degradation of water supply can, in the worst cases, mean the termination of that supply of water because it is no longer usable for certain purposes. This does not restrict it from all uses, but the pollution of high-quality drinking water has enormous environmental costs and it limits our capacity to live in a dry continent.

Modern Australian cities also face challenges in terms of water quality, both in urban waterways and in the location of water supplies. The issue of water quality is primarily related to the management of the catchment, or 'watershed' as it is known in North America. As will be demonstrated below, the quality of catchments varies significantly between Australia's largest cities.

According to the *Value of Water* report (2002), farm animals could access 38 per cent of all rivers in the Sydney catchment area and, by inference, only 30 per cent of the catchment was in excellent condition. This report cited 'threats and pressures from continuing urban, rural and industrial development' as problems for catchment management and water quality in Sydney (Senate Committee, 2002, 23). Lloyd (1995) identified the importance of water catchments in directing urban growth away from locations such as the Southern Highlands to other parts of the urban fringe and hinterland. The geographic impacts of an increased population, regardless of the density of the built-up area due to demands such as daytrips and food production, means that

protecting Sydney's water catchments is becoming an increasingly serious challenge.

In Melbourne, there is ample storage capacity in the Thomson Dam
in the Gippsland District. This reservoir supplies 60 per cent of
Melbourne's water (Senate Committee, 2002). About 90 per cent of
Melbourne's water comes from the mountains of the ash forests to the
north-east of the city (Griffiths, 2001). The catchment is largely unin-
habited by humans and is of a high quality. The major risk to
Melbourne's water quality is fire. This relationship between trees, water
and fire was highlighted at the 1939 Royal Commission following the
devastating Black Friday fires, and 'forged into public policy' (Griffiths,
2001, 90). The engineer of water supply, AE Kelso, explained to the
commission that 'to endanger the Mountain Ash forests on those watersheds is to actually endanger the supply of water' (Griffiths, 2001, 90).
Foran and Poldy (2002, 99) note that the old-growth forest ecosystems
has provided Melbourne with high-quality water for more than a
century, but if they were destroyed by bushfires 'the water yield falls by
50 per cent and the ecosystems require 150 years to return to the previous physical state that can deliver similar levels of ecosystem service'.
There is an ongoing risk of bushfire, and this risk is exacerbated by
climate change (see chapter 9).

Brisbane's water quality is compromised by grazing activity in half
of the Brisbane River catchment area. Forests and plantations account
for another 35 per cent of the catchment area (Senate Committee,
2002). This is a result of the history of agricultural and pastoral development in the catchment upstream of Mount Crosby. Razzell (1990,
213) has claimed that 'by 1893 it was impossible to reserve the catchment upstream of Mount Crosby or restrict access to the river'.

The intrusion of human activities that are largely incompatible with
high water quality is pronounced in the catchments serving Adelaide.
Sixty per cent of Adelaide's water comes from catchments in the
Mount Lofty Ranges, while 40 per cent comes from the Murray River.
The drinking water in Adelaide from both of these sources was
described as being of 'poor quality and poor taste ... [and] is probably
the primary reason that 20 per cent of Adelaide home owners use rainwater as their primary source of drinking water' (Senate Committee,
2002, 24). The Mount Lofty catchments have only 8 per cent of their
native vegetation, while 80 per cent of the catchment area is used for
primary production (Senate Committee, 2002). The extent of vegetation clearance substantially increases the risk of salinity, and it is

predicted that by 2050 water supplied to Adelaide from the Murray River will exceed the World Health Organisation standards for drinking water 50 per cent of the time (Senate Committee, 2002). Reducing transport energy used in food production is vital for sustainability, but the example of Adelaide highlights that this cannot be achieved at the expense of the sound catchment management that is required to deliver high water quality to a city.

Perth's water quality is better than Adelaide's, but there are concerns about water supply in Perth as the population grows and the threat of climate change means that the south-west of Australia is likely to experience higher temperatures and reduced precipitation. Perth's water is sourced from 11 dams in the Darling Ranges and from aquifers (Senate Committee, 2002; Foran and Poldy, 2002). The Gnangara mound to the north of Perth has largely been protected accidentally by an otherwise unprofitable pine plantation, while the Jandakot mound to the south has been less protected as the area has been used for semi-rural activities. These groundwater reserves are particularly vulnerable. The Senate Committee *Value of Water* inquiry was told that 'one fifth of Perth's 500 service stations had leaking underground tanks' and that 'one station had leaked 15 litres a day into the system for two years', which represented a level of pollution 1000 times higher than the National Health and Medical Research Council guidelines (Senate Committee, 2002, 52)

While it is apparent that each major Australian city faces different water supply and water quality issues, there are a number of common lessons. First, it is important to maintain the quality of the catchment. This not only makes ecological sense, it makes economic sense in that it reduces the need to install expensive treatment plants. Unfortunately in this instance, modern cities are very much influenced by not only their own history, but the history of activities in their hinterland. While it is possible to clean and redevelop individual industrial sites, or to restore channelised urban creeks into meandering watercourses with living wetlands, it is extremely difficult to remove agricultural, urban and industrial activities from large catchment areas once they have become established.

Second, maintaining water quality is not simply obtaining sufficient supplies of potable water. It is about demand management to reduce the unnecessary use of water, thereby alleviating the need to access water that is of marginal quality in order to maintain supplies. This consideration is important in areas of high population growth (Sydney,

Melbourne, Brisbane and Perth), and crucial in areas where high population growth and climate change in the form of hotter temperatures
and lower rainfall are likely to coincide (such as in Perth).

Third, maintaining water quality is about using the appropriate
quality of water for specific activities. In the 2003 NSW State of the
Environment Report it is claimed that 'potable standard water is essential for less than four per cent of total consumption, mainly for drinking
and personal hygiene' (Department of Conservation and Environment
NSW, 2003, 21). The recycling rate of sewage in Sydney is only about
two per cent (Department of Conservation and Environment NSW,
2003), partly because of the existing sewage infrastructure being
directed towards ocean outflows. This poor rate of recycling represents
an opportunity for future improvement. The good news is that there are
an increasing number of examples of water recycling (including the
Homebush Olympic site and the Rouse Hill development in Sydney)
where water quality and the purpose of its use are being matched. When
these activities are combined with water sensitive urban design, public
education and the threat of financial punishment for violating water
restrictions, there is significant potential to positively influence the
water supply and water quality of Australia's major cities.

WATER SENSITIVE URBAN DESIGN

Water sensitive urban design (WSUD) is a concept that aims to 'optimise and integrate urban planning and the management of the urban
water cycle', primarily by 'integrating urban planning and design with
water, wastewater and stormwater service provision across a range of
planning scales, from city-wide down to the site (or visa versa)'
(Mouritz, 2000, 7). Most of the focus to date has been on 'integrating
urban design and stormwater management' (Mouritz, 2000, 7).

The concept opposes the traditional approach taken to addressing
engineering and public health concerns about water management (see
figure 6.1). Admittedly, these concerns can also be seen as responding
to human suffering caused by the 'outbreak of water-borne infectious
diseases among urban populations' (Badcock, 2002, 209). The
responses have been to source water from a limited number of large
dams at an increasing distance from the city (as outlined in the above
two sections of this chapter), to prevent flooding in urban areas by
discharging water in large pipes so that it exited the site as soon as possible, and to remove sewage in pipes so that it could be treated and then
pumped into a large body of water. In short, the traditional model of

Figure 6.1 An engineering approach to stormwater management

Photo: Sonia Graham

water management is based on control of nature and of access by human beings, but it creates a vortex effect where the city is increasingly reliant on new sources of water supply and the supposedly free disposal capacity of nature.

WSUD is 'an holistic approach to the management of water in urban environments [that] views the urban water cycle as a whole rather than by its individual sectors such as wastewater, stormwater and water supply' (Senate Committee, 2002, 181). It is based on the principle of greater self-reliance within a city, thereby reducing the need to import water from outside the city, and particularly from interbasin transfers. As much as possible, water is sourced from 'harvesting' rainfall in the urban area and from seeing used water as a potential resource, rather than as waste to be discarded. Given that urban land uses such as roads, car parks and paved areas around houses have 'hardened' catchments, thereby reducing infiltration and creating increased surface run-off during periods of high rainfall, water harvesting is also a necessary flood management technique. If implemented, WSUD will reduce the vortex effect of Australian cities.

Early implementation of many of the principles of WSUD can be seen in the development of Village Homes, a 242-unit, mixed-use residential project that was developed in Davis, California in the early 1970s (Corbett and Corbett, 2000). Implementation within the

Australian urban context is, however, 'very much the exception rather than the rule, even in new developments, while it is even rarer in existing suburbs' (Senate Committee, 2002, 187). This is despite suggestions that it may be economically beneficial to implement WSUD because it can lower infrastructure costs and developers can receive a premium for higher amenity value (Senate Committee, 2002). Evidence from Village Homes in Davis, California indicated that not only did the natural drainage system work better than the engineering solution under heavy rainfall conditions, but it saved US$800 per lot in 1975, thereby funding the entire cost of landscaping the common areas of the development (Corbett and Corbett, 2000).

Examples of the implementation of WSUD principles in Australia include residential developments of Lynbrook Estate in Melbourne and Ascot Waters in Perth. Lynbrook Estate does not use conventional kerbs and gutters on local streets; instead, stormwater is directed into swales and then into wetlands for filtering and purification. Ascot Waters is divided into three zones for the purpose of run-off. Each zone relates to particular land uses. Pollutant traps and wetlands are used for areas of hard surface run-off that are likely to be more polluted, while a perforated pipe allows aeration of water as it travels from a residential area to swales, detention basins and a wetland (Senate Committee, 2002).

These Australian examples of WSUD may be classified as 'conventional' in many other aspects of urban planning. For this reason the example of Village Homes in Davis, California is important because it highlights the possibilities of linking WSUD with other ecological innovations that can improve the sustainability of cities. Village Homes incorporates the idea of an 'edible landscape' (sometimes known as a 'productive landscape') including fruit trees, almonds and other sources of food in the public spaces and along bike paths (Corbett and Corbett, 2000; see also Hough, 1995). There are other possible connections, for example, between WSUD and river restoration projects. It is also possible to link WSUD with concepts such as new urbanism (see chapter 3), especially given the potential of new urbanism to reduce the amount of impervious surface areas and to protect ecologically sensitive areas because of the emphasis on communal space. A study by Berke et al (2003) compared 50 new urbanist developments (32 greenfield sites and 18 infill sites) to 50 comparable conventional developments in five states of the United States and demonstrated that the new urbanist developments protected sensitive ecological areas and restored streams and floodplains, with some exceptions. If concepts such as new urbanism were closely linked with ideas such as WSUD, this is likely to provide demonstration projects which can become the basis to normalise this form of development.

Two other Australian examples of WSUD are interesting to note, as much for their process as for the physical aspects of the design. Mouritz (2000) has explained the process undertaken by his office in Kogarah Council in the southern suburbs of Sydney for the developments of Allawah and the Kogarah Town Square. The Allawah development is an old service station site that was owned by the Kogarah Council. Rather than selling the site to developers, the local government authority engaged an architectural firm to prepare a development application to incorporate elements of 'green architecture', such as solar passive design, natural ventilation, stormwater and flood control and the reuse of rainwater (designed to save 600 000 litres of potable water per year). A development application was approved and the site was sold to developers with this approval. It was recognised that the stormwater controls present in the Allawah site should be incorporated into the council's normal development controls (Mouritz, 2000). (This is similar to the situation with the Brisbane City Council, where WSUD is incorporated into the city's plan and the onus is on developers to demonstrate why they should not adopt WSUD in their practice (Senate Committee, 2002)).

The lessons from Allawah were transferred to a bigger site, namely, the Kogarah Town Square project. This process of experimentation, adaptation and learning from experience is an important part of developing water sensitive urban design and sustainable cities. The Kogarah Town Square site comprises retail and commercial functions, a public library, underground public car parking and 190 apartments. Eighty-five per cent of rainfall on the site is captured ('harvested') and used to flush toilets and irrigate gardens. Estimates of water-saving were in the order of 17 per cent of mains water compared to a conventional development of comparable size with a similar number of residential units (Mouritz, 2000). The development of this award-winning project, which included a grant of $629 000 from Environment Australia for the urban stormwater initiative, has resulted in a 42 per cent reduction in potable water use compared to a typical development of a similar size (Kogarah Council, 2004).

The ecological gains from water harvesting are clearly worthwhile in their own right. However, as with savings in energy use, innovations that enhance sustainability and provide financial gains should be considered in light of the subsequent use of these savings. While it is both undesirable and beyond the power of a local council to dictate how residents should spend the savings on their water bills, the savings only contribute to the bigger sustainability picture if they are not used to perpetuate unsustainable practices. This requires value changes and an ecological awareness that appears to be beyond many members of society at the moment. These actions are addressed in section 3 where we consider the processes that are necessary to make Australian cities more sustainable.

SUMMARY

Water is a crucial issue to be addressed if Australian cities are to be made more sustainable. The traditional approach to water management has emerged from human health and engineering mentalities that are dated, not because the issues that were being responded to have decreased in importance, but because there are new ways of thinking about and solving the (perceived) problems of water management. These new approaches include demand management rather than a water supply orientation, on-site capturing of water rather than sourcing supplies from increasingly distant locations, and the ability to clean and reuse water on-site rather than piping contaminated water to a larger water body as rapidly as possible.

While recognition of the importance of protecting surface catchment and groundwater sources is not new among water managers, the need to do so has probably become more apparent to ordinary people. The challenges of protecting the existing large supplies of water is becoming increasingly difficult as the built-up area of cities, and the area within the orbit of a city's activities, expands to threaten catchment management. The urban expansion generates opportunities for concepts such as WSUD to be developed as showcase projects and incorporated into existing development control processes so that they become normalised. If WSUD continues to perform well both financially and ecologically against the traditional engineering approach to water management, then the redevelopment of ageing water infrastructure also offers potential opportunities to incorporate WSUD into Australian cities. Concepts that promote sustainability should not be reliant on population growth and fringe development in order to be implemented.

In time, as with other planning issues discussed in this section of the book, technological improvements and new ideas will enhance water management for sustainability. It is important that in all of the issues we set the goalposts right. In the management of water, this means that we need to be planning for reduced water use and appropriate water standards relative to the purpose for which water is being used. If this can be achieved, Australian cities will be in a better position to adapt to changing climatic conditions and are likely to become internationally recognised as world leaders in the sustainable management of urban water ecosystems.

CHAPTER 7

TRANSPORT

INTRODUCTION

Transport of people and freight is important for the functioning of every major city in the world. Too often, however, the idea of transport can become an end in itself, with policies and plans designed to facilitate mobility and tending to devalue the reason for the use of transport, which is accessibility. Contemporary technology combined with outsourcing and management theory that emphasises workforce productivity rather than attendance has enabled many people to access their work from home. While this has sustainability implications (particularly for energy use), it reduces the need for transport, thereby effectively extending the capacity of existing transport systems to cater for passengers who do need to commute.

Urban transport is used for journeys to work and for access to medical and educational services and recreation opportunities, and so on. The ecological sustainability impacts of urban transport may be summarised as being the source of the energy used, the space and infrastructure used to provide the transportation service, the waste products emitted by the urban transport and the mutually constitutive impacts of transport and land use in shaping Australia's major cities. The social sustainability issues include equity issues of access to employment, recreation and community, as well as issues of health and safety. Economic sustainability issues include the ability to maintain the production and consumption of goods and services. It is acknowledged that some 'strong sustainability' advocates are likely to argue that maintaining the production and consumption of goods and services is unsustainable. In other words, we are more likely to achieve sustainability with a decline in the use of transport and a decline in the production and consumption of goods and services.

This chapter will concentrate on private and public urban passenger transport. In 1995 for Australia as a whole, passenger vehicles consumed 62 per cent of the fuel used (freight was 35 per cent) and accounted for 74 per cent of the kilometres travelled, compared to 24 per cent for freight (Australian Bureau of Statistics, 1997). The movement of freight is very important, but is beyond the scope of this chapter. Trends towards working from home, often for part of the week, are important, but again are beyond the scope of the chapter. The chapter begins by looking at recent trends and patterns in urban transport for Australia's largest cities. This is followed with a discussion about the major sustainability impacts of transport, beginning with energy use in transport. The section on energy looks at the location of the sources of energy and at comparisons of energy use between transport modes and between cities based on modal shifts. The third section of the chapter considers the space requirements of transport and the embodied energy in rolling stock and transport infrastructure. The fourth section considers waste products emitted by transport, although aspects of this issue are covered in more detail in chapter 9. The fifth section of the chapter covers a discussion on the relationship between transport and land use. While this structure does not do justice to all the sustainability issues that involve urban transport, it covers many of the key concerns and areas that need to be addressed in order for Australian cities to move towards sustainability.

RECENT TRENDS IN URBAN PASSENGER TRANSPORT

Australia's largest cities have experienced a number of important and sometimes conflicting changes in urban passenger transport structure, provision and use. While this section talks about trends, it is important to note that sometimes there has been no discernable trend (although the common denominator was the persuasion of the political party in office at the state level). For example, at various points during the 1990s, governments of Victoria and Western Australia were privatising their major metropolitan public transport providers, while at the same time in Sydney the State Transit Authority was extending the public bus system westward to Parramatta, which previously had only been serviced by private bus operators.

The first major trend to note is that total passenger vehicle numbers, total fuel consumption and total kilometres travelled by passenger vehicles increased in the three years to 31 October 2000 (Australian Bureau of Statistics, 2003d). While over time there have been increases in the fuel efficiency of motor vehicles, these gains have been insufficient to reduce total energy use. This is partly because on average more people are driving further, for longer periods (often in congested traffic) and more often. This continues the trend identified by Laird (2001, 179 – table A.2) of a continual rise in car passenger kilometres travelled in the period 1970–71 to 1994–95, although Newman, Kenworthy and Bachels (2001) note that car kilometres travelled per capita declined in Perth between 1991 and 1996, due mainly to the opening of the Northern Suburbs Rapid Transit System in 1993. The other factor contributing to additional fuel use is the increase in engine sizes of vehicles, particularly in the trend towards more four-wheel drive vehicles being used for urban transport (see Australian Bureau of Statistics, 1997). Overall, despite the increased use of public transport, the proportion of journeys being made by car is increasing. The private automobile is the dominant mode of urban transport in Australia's largest cities.

Taking the major modes of transport in turn, it is apparent that buses are important in the public transport systems of all five largest cities in Australia. They form the dominant mode of public transport in smaller cities such as Canberra and Hobart. Laird (2001) and the Australian Urban and Regional Development Review (1995) note that the number of bus kilometres travelled in Australian cities has remained relatively constant since the early 1970s. This observation is supported by data used by Lenzen (1999). The number of passengers in the two largest cities, Sydney and Melbourne, have fluctuated somewhat, with a trend towards more private bus company passengers because these services operate in the newer outer suburbs and because of the dispersal of employment. Patronage in Perth has remained relatively unchanged, there has been a decline in Adelaide, while Brisbane experienced a spike in patronage during World Expo '88 (Australian Urban and Regional Development Review, 1995; Lenzen, 1999). Interesting points about sustainability here include the ability to integrate transport and land use planning in new developments, and to integrate bus routes and timetables to support other transport modes, and the move towards energy efficiency and cleaner fuel sources for buses.

Two Australian cities have light rail transport facilities, while trams have been retained in Melbourne and one route remains in Adelaide. The ability of Melbourne to retain its trams when other cities were scrapping their tram systems during the 1950s and 1960s not only provides a well-serviced inner and middle suburban area, but it also provides a foundation for Melbourne's unique and strong identity as a city. The conversion of two rail lines to light rail in Melbourne in the 1990s was politically divisive, and not exactly the best advertisement to promote light rail because residents of the affected areas felt that their service was being downgraded. On the other hand, the development of light rail in Sydney represents a genuine addition to the transport infrastructure of the city, but unfortunately it is currently an expensive form of privately-operated mass transport that does not link well with a public transport system. This is somewhat ironic because in 1912 in the Legislative Assembly in Western Australia the then state premier admired the Sydney system of trams and trains for their integration and their lack of opposition to each other (see McManus, 2002b).

The major form of high-volume public transport service in the largest Australian cities is the rail network. Table 7.1 shows the changes in urban and non-urban rail patronage during the period 1997 to 2000–01. It is apparent that while there has been growth in urban rail patronage, the non-urban systems have grown very little in recent years. Table 7.2 shows some of the rail system characteristics and recent changes in rail patronage in Australia's five largest cities. The overall trend in recent years has been an increase in rail patronage, particularly in Perth from the early 1980s when the Perth–Fremantle line was reopened, the three existing rail lines were electrified and then in 1993 the Northern Suburbs Rapid Transit System was opened (see Alexander and Houghton, 1995; Newman, 1992; Newman and Kenworthy, 1999). Table 7.2 also indicates that, unlike Melbourne (and to a lesser extent Sydney and Brisbane), rail passenger numbers in Perth have stabilised, possibly indicating the limits to the catchment potential of the four railway lines without major changes in transport culture among the city's residents.

The performance of Perth can be contrasted with that of Adelaide in terms of attracting rail passengers (see table 7.2). Adelaide's rail service was heavily criticised by Bachels and Newman (2001, 150) who wrote that 'Adelaide's rail service is just a little better than that of Auckland, which means that it is one of the worst cities in the developed world'. Importantly, Perth transport planners are developing the long-awaited rail link to the southern suburbs and to the rapidly growing coastal city of Mandurah at the southern edge of the Perth Metropolitan Region. This will increase substantially Perth's rail patronage when the new line is eventually opened.

Competition between public transport modes (for example,

Table 7.1 Rail passengers numbers in Australia, 1997 to 2000–01

Passengers (millions)	1997	1998	1999	2000*	2001*
Urban rail	455.8	457.3	462.8	482.2	537.1
Non-urban rail	9.8	9.9	10.0	10.5	11.7

* Financial years 1999–2000 and 2000–01 respectively. Other cited years are calendar years.

Source: Derived from Australasian Railway Association Inc, 2002 yearbook

Table 7.2 Rail systems and patronage for Australia's largest cities, 1981–82 to 2001–02

CITY	Rail system (km) in 2002	Power in 2002	PASSENGERS (millions)						
			1981–82	1992–93	1997–98	1998–99	1999–2000	2000–01	2001–02
Sydney	1025	Electric	210	245	266.5	270.5	278.7	286	276.4
Melbourne	385	Electric	85	105	116.8	115	124.2	127.9	131.8
Brisbane	325	Electric	28	39	41.5	41.1	42.4	44.7	45.4
Perth	95	Electric	6.6	13.6	28.3	28.8	29.5	31.1	31
Adelaide	120	Diesel	12.5	9	8	7.4	7.4	7.9	8

Sources: Derived from Australian Urban and Regional Development Review, 1995, 74–7, Australasian Railway Association Inc, yearbooks for 1999 to 2003

between buses and rail) is generally not helpful, whereas coordination of services is crucial. Perth's rail patronage increased substantially in a short period of time without corresponding increases in residential density. This was due in part to the reorientation of many bus routes so that they became 'feeder services' for the rail network, thus developing a viable transport alternative to the use of the private car.

In contrast to this example, the opening of the M5 East motorway link in Sydney in late 2001 resulted in 53 329 fewer people in 2002 taking the train on the East Hills line than in 2001 (Kerr, 2003). The patronage on Sydney's rail system has increased from a low of under 200 million journeys in 1984–85 (it had been as high as almost 220 million in 1981–82) to 276.4 million in 2001–02, although there have been rises and falls in annual passenger numbers since 1980–81 (see Gunton, 2000; Australasian Rail Association, 2003). During the Olympic Games period in 2000–01, patronage on the Sydney rail system rose to 286 million passengers. Despite evidence of the Sydney system being able to cope with more passengers, there are concerns that the growth in rail transport in Sydney, especially in areas where urban consolidation has meant that more people are within walking distance of a rail station, means that the limits of capacity on key parts of the Sydney passenger rail network are likely to be experienced in the near future (Gunton, 2000).

Rail patronage in Melbourne remained relatively steady between 1980 and 1995 (Australian Urban and Regional Development Review, 1995; Lenzen, 1999). Since the mid-1990s, Melbourne's urban passenger railway system has been expanded with the St Albans–Sydenham extension, and passenger numbers have risen consistently each year. Figure 7.1 shows that Melbourne contributed 48 per cent of the 31.5 million additional passengers carried by urban railway systems in Australia in 2001–02, compared to 1997–98. This figure is a more accurate representation of the long-term trend because, unlike 1999–2000 and particularly 2000–01, Sydney's railway passenger numbers are not likely to be elevated by the Olympic Games.

The rail patronage in Brisbane rose from 28 million passengers in 1981 to 39 million in 1993 (it was up to 50 million during World Expo '88), but had declined to 37 million in 1995 (Australian Urban and Regional Development Review, 1995; Lenzen, 1999). Since the mid-1990s, Brisbane's urban rail network has also increased its patronage each year. Figure 7.1 shows that Brisbane contributed 12 per cent (or 3.9 million passengers) of the increase in urban rail passenger numbers in 2001–02 compared with 1997–98. This proportion of the growth in urban rail passenger numbers was greater than in Perth (8.6 per cent), and in Adelaide, where there was no increase in rail passenger numbers over the same period.

There are other forms of 'public' transport (increasingly known as 'mass transit' to reflect the involvement of private operators), including a monorail in Sydney, the O'Bahn system in Adelaide and ferries in a number of cities. While these may be important in particular cities, the major forms of transport yet to be discussed in this section are walking and cycling (skateboards, rollerskating, and so on, should also be considered in this discussion). These forms of transport are the most sustainable, but are not necessarily suited for long distance travel, for carrying heavy loads or for people (usually women) who are picking up children on the way home from work, via the shops and a dance class, for example.

Figure 7.1 Proportion of the growth in urban rail passengers by city, 1997–98 to 2001–02

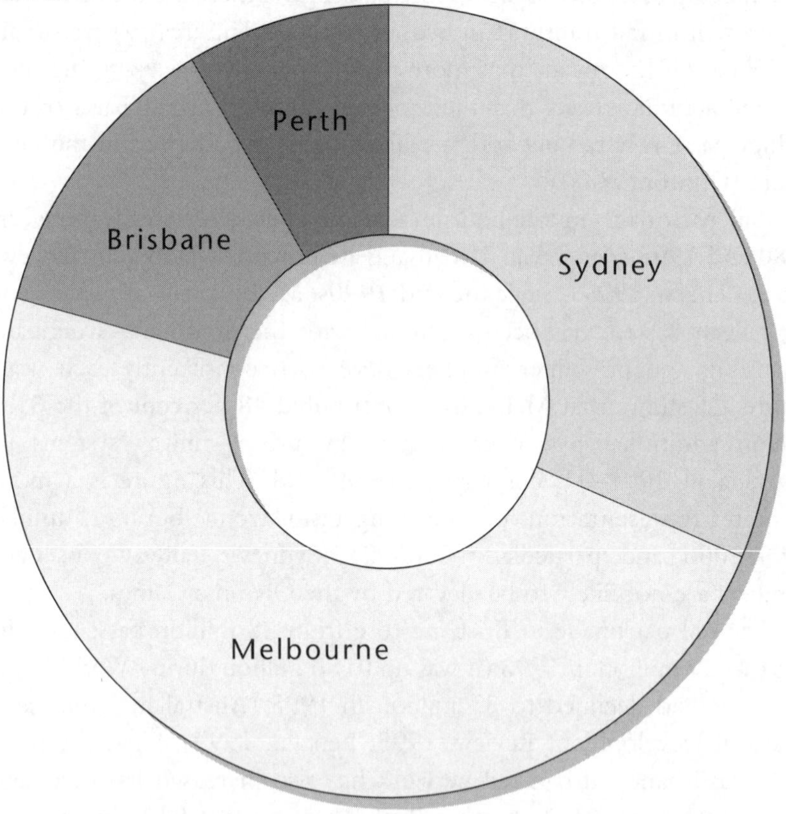

Source: Derived from Australasian Railway Association Inc, yearbooks for 1999 to 2003

The proportion of 'cycling and walking only' for the journey to work has been declining for a number of years. In 1991 this figure ranged from 5.6 per cent of workers in Sydney to 3.8 per cent of workers in Perth. In 1996 the corresponding figures were 4.8 per cent and 3.1 per cent, with other Australian cities between these two extremes (Forster, 1999). By 2001, the proportion of 'cycling and walking only' had risen to 5.5 per cent in Sydney and to 3.5 per cent in Perth (compiled from 2001 Census data). Interestingly, whereas the proportional split between cycling and walking was almost one-third cyclists and two-thirds walkers in Perth, in Sydney less than 12 per cent of this combined category were cyclists. This discrepancy is likely to be caused by the existence of more dwellings within easy walking distance of workplaces in Sydney, and by the increased danger of cycling in Sydney compared with other Australian cities.

Some Australian cities have excellent cycling facilities – Canberra is most notable, but Perth too has a good network of recreational cycleways along the rivers due to the Stephenson–Hepburn Plan of 1955 setting aside land. New inner-city residential apartments and the redevelopment of suburbs such as Pyrmont in Sydney and Northbridge and East Perth in Perth provide opportunities for more walking and cycling to work. There are significant issues about safety, particularly in Sydney where the lanes are narrower and there is more traffic, and about the integration between cycling and other modes (such as bicycle parking facilities and ability to transport a bicycle on a train).

These transport patterns, trends and problems all have significant impacts for sustainability. We begin the discussion by looking at the energy used in urban passenger transport in Australia's largest cities.

ENERGY USE IN TRANSPORT

The history of transport in Australian cities is necessarily a history about our reliance on nature to provide energy inputs for movement. The earliest form of transport in Australian cities was walking, which meant that the existence of food and water was necessary before propulsion could occur. Over time, the use of animal power (requiring hay and water) in Australian cities has been superceded by cable and steam trams, which gave way to electric trams, trolley buses, trains and the automobile. In 1995–96 transport consumed 1169 petajoules of energy, or 26 per cent of Australia's energy consumption (Australian Bureau of Statistics, 2003d).

The fuel sources of transport modes may vary. For example, urban passenger trains are electric in most major Australian cities, but are powered by diesel in Adelaide. Buses may be powered by diesel, petrol or natural gas. Automobiles could be powered by petrol, diesel, electric and hybrid power, and so on. Each of these sources of power has varying levels of efficiency, environmental impact and a dynamic political economy in terms of its location, price, reserves and cost of acquisition and distribution.

The unsustainability of energy use in urban passenger transport in Australia's major cities has been identified by numerous authors, including by Newman and Kenworthy (1999), Laird (2001) and the Australian Bureau of Statistics (2003). In this latter publication, it was acknowledged that 'the energy used and emissions caused by the consumption of almost 25 000 million litres of fuel by motor vehicles in 2000 are considerable' and that 'energy is sourced primarily from non-renewable fossil fuels, an environmentally unfriendly source of energy' (Australian Bureau of Statistics, 2003d, 735).

The levels of energy consumption (disregarding at this stage discussion of factors such as the source and whether it is renewable) vary between modes of urban transport. Lenzen (1999, 287) notes that 'on average, urban buses, trams and trains cause only about two thirds of the energy consumption and greenhouse gas emissions associated with passenger vehicles for every pkm [passenger kilometre travelled]'. He continues with an important caveat, that 'these average values change considerably between peak and off-peak periods' (Lenzen, 1999, 287). The explanation is that passenger loads on public transport such as trains can be very low at off-peak periods, while car occupancy rates tend to be higher outside of peak working hours. During peak periods, public transport is often carrying its full capacity while the average occupancy of private vehicles in congested peak-period traffic is 1.1 persons per vehicle. This means that the energy intensity of public transport at this period is 1–2 megajoules per passenger kilometre, compared with private cars at about 6.5 megajoules per passenger kilometre (Lenzen, 1999).

SPACE, ROLLING STOCK AND INFRASTRUCTURE ISSUES

An important sustainability consideration is the amount of space that each mode of transport consumes in the city. Any determination of space must account for shared space (for example, buses and cars on roads) and for the problems created by the sharing of space (for example, buses are slowed by competing for road space with cars, hence the adoption of dedicated bus lanes and the busway in Western Sydney – see figure 7.2). The total space requirements of the automobile includes roads, parking areas at workplaces and shops, the areas used for parking around the house, and the necessary service stations and tyre distributors.

The space requirements of automobiles compared to public transport has been known for many years. In Perth in 1966, a full Metropolitan Transport Trust bus vehicle with 72 passengers could transport the equivalent of 45 cars, based on the then occupancy rate of vehicles. If these numbers were translated into actual road space, an average family size car in 1966 occupied at least 30 times more space per passenger compared to the bus (Wayne, 1966). Beatley (2000) shows how the German city of Munster has communicated this same

Figure 7.2 The Sydney busway

Photo: Sonia Graham

message by comparing the amount of space used by bicycles, automobiles and a bus to transport a given number of commuters. Hill (2001) and the Australasian Railway Association Inc (2000) have claimed that today a suburban train with 1000 passengers has effectively kept 20 buses or 800 additional cars off the road, which is the equivalent of a line of cars stretching for five kilometres.

In terms of capacity, a double track railway, which can transport 20 000 people per hour, uses 2.5 hectares of land per kilometre of its length. By way of contrast, a six-lane freeway or motorway can only move about 5000 people per hour, and requires 10 hectares of land per kilometre of its length (Australasian Railway Association Inc, 2000). Assuming that the railway is being used by people, it is apparent that a well-planned heavy rail spine, to be fed by a coordinated bus and/or tram system and higher residential densities within walking distance of railway stations, is a major investment in saving land in a city.

These statistics are referring to the road space, not the total space, consumed by various modes of transport. While it is necessary to park buses, trams and trains when they are not being used, public transport can be used by different people throughout the day whereas a car driven to work is often parked all day before being driven home. In Australian cities, approximately one-third of the metropolitan land area is consumed by roads and car parks (Australasian Railway Association,

2000). Australian cities exhibit similarities to some automobile-dependent US cities in their provision of road space and central business area car parking space (see table 7.3). This devotion of space to the private automobile is excessive given the availability of other transport options.

There is another perspective on space that is important for sustainability. This is the relationship between transport and land use. Commentators such as Pund (2003) maintain that it is not necessary to undertake an urban consolidation program in order to increase transport patronage. He maintains that this can be achieved by thorough, integrated planning of bus routes and their relationship to other modes of transport. The high initial patronage and then the rapid increase in patronage once the Northern Suburbs Rapid Transit System opened in 1993 in Perth adds credibility to Pund's (2003) claim. Another perspective is that a high-speed rail network will lead to an intensification of land use patterns near stations, thereby reducing the need to expand at the fringe of the city (Newman and Kenworthy, 1999). This perspective is supported by data in Gunton (2000) which indicates that the growth in passengers on Sydney's rail network between 1991 and 1996 was mainly due to urban consolidation around existing rail stations such as Sutherland, Kogarah, Hurstville, Westmead and Wentworthville.

Table 7.3 Road supply and central business area parking provision in Australia's largest cities compared to five large US cities, 1980–1990

CITY	Road supply, 1980 (metres per person)	Road supply, 1990 (metres per person)	CBD car parking, 1980 (spaces per 1000 CBD jobs)	CBD car parking, 1990 (spaces per 1000 CBD jobs)
Sydney	6.2	6.2	156	489
Melbourne	7.9	7.7	270	337
Brisbane	6.9	8.2	268	322
Perth	13.3	10.7	562	631
Adelaide	9.1	8.0	380	580
New York	4.7	4.6	75	60
Los Angeles	4.5	3.8	524	520
Chicago	5.0	4.6	91	128
Houston	10.6	11.7	370	612
Phoenix	10.4	9.6	1033	906

Source: Extracted from Newman and Kenworthy, 1999, 82–3, and Newman, Kenworthy and Vintilla, 1992, appendix 1

The rolling stock sustainability impacts of urban transport relate to the embodied energy in the automobile and the rolling stock of public transport. The average age of passenger automobiles in Australia as of 31 March 2001 is 10.1 years (Australian Bureau of Statistics, 2003d). This age varies between urban and rural areas and between states due to motor vehicle licensing requirements. The sustainability trade-off is between reducing the embodied energy in new vehicles by extending the lifetime of a vehicle and reducing the number of new vehicles registered each year, and reducing fuel consumption and waste emissions by ensuring that newer, well-maintained vehicles are being driven (although if the new vehicles are large four-wheel drives on urban roads, this is not reducing fuel consumption). There is an alternative to this choice, which is to have older vehicles well-maintained, and all vehicles driven less. It is not the ownership of a vehicle that causes energy consumption and greenhouse and other emissions, but the driving of the vehicle.

The responsibility for the disposal of automobiles and the ability to recycle some of the embodied energy are aspects of sustainability that warrant serious consideration. A study by Environment Australia (2002) on the environmental impacts of 'end-of-life vehicles' (ELVs) found that each year over 500 000 of the 12.5 million vehicles in Australia reach the end of their life, that this number is increasing each year and that it could reach 750 000 million vehicles by 2010. The study found that the environmental impacts of ELVs are significant, particularly given fluids and batteries may not be removed from these vehicles. While the trend towards producer-responsibility has been led by German automobile manufacturers, partly due to landfill restrictions, the limitation in Australia has been said to be the lack of economic markets for the disassembly and recycling of ELV materials (Environment Australia, 2002).

Producer-responsibility, or the lack of it, is an important sustainability issue in Australia. In relation to a whole range of items, including soft-drink and beer bottles, producers are actively opposing any suggestion that they should be held responsible for the disposal of product packaging after use. The producer-responsibility for automobiles is an important and necessary change to enhance sustainability, but it must come as part of a larger cultural shift towards producer-responsibility across all industries.

The infrastructure requirements of urban passenger transport vary significantly, and are often in competition. This is not new. When horses were the dominant form of transport (admittedly often for freight), they required roads that were not too smooth in order to avoid slipping. The introduction of bicycles and later cars was accompanied by the emergence of lobby groups such as the Good Roads Association, formed in Perth in 1920 and based on the Roads Improvement Association which was formed in the United Kingdom in 1886 and the National League for Good Roads which was formed in the United States in 1892 (Lay, 1992; International Press Service Association, 1929). These lobby groups campaigned for smoother roads.

There is compatibility between some modes of transport – buses and automobiles, for example, can both use roads. For many years this was one of the attractions for state governments to fund bus services in preference to rail networks. The attraction was intensified by federal government funding assistance for new road construction which the states did not want to miss out on. A problem with any transport infrastructure system is that it has a finite capacity. This includes roads, railways and airports. There is potential to extend capacity, by encouraging non-essential peak travel to occur in off-peak periods or by sequencing traffic lights, establishing clearways, and so on, to smooth the flow. This is akin to the gains in distance made in marching an army, rather than letting them walk along at their own leisure. These actions do not resolve the problem, but they do enable more efficient use of infrastructure.

In the case of streets, this approach has turned streets into roads. This reduces the potential for social interaction and means that the road becomes single-purpose, existing for the smooth and rapid movement of automobiles. There are energy and greenhouse gains to be made by ensuring that traffic flows smoothly, but these gains are soon overwhelmed by more and more vehicles being driven, and then by another round of congestion on the road. The solution in the past has often been to widen roads or to build a bypass road some distance beyond the congested location.

The full cost of road infrastructure includes the provision and maintenance of car parking facilities, which are important in contributing to the expansion of the urban area. If transport issues are not addressed, it becomes necessary, to avoid urban expansion, to consolidate residential development and/or acquire space from other activities (for example, selling public land). According to Newman and Kenworthy (1999), in 1990 Australian cities were second only to the most automobile-dependent US cities in the provision of road space per person and the number of car parking spaces per 1000 central business area jobs. While these figures fluctuate with population change and central business area employment change, Newman and Kenworthy (1999) note that Australian cities are closer to the newer, automobile-dependent cities of the United States than the larger, older cities of New York and Chicago. These older cities have long-established public transport systems and make extensive use of taxi services (an efficient use of automobiles because it alleviates the need for parking).

Public transport is most efficient (in terms of speed and reliability) when it has its own dedicated right of way. This has been an advantage of trains over tram systems in Australian cities. The new light rail line in Sydney combines sections of running with vehicular traffic and sections of dedicated right of way by using an old freight rail line. Adelaide's O'Bahn, the world's longest guided busway, integrates a dedicated right of way that can only be used by buses, with the same buses then entering the shared traffic flow on roads. Perth's Northern Suburbs Rapid Transit System is largely built in the middle of a freeway, which was widened at the time of the railway's construction and as such relies on feeder bus services. This railway system has very few stops for its length, compared to the other three railway lines in Perth.

GREENHOUSE EMISSIONS AND WASTE OUTPUTS

In 2000, transport contributed 14.3 per cent of Australia's greenhouse gas emissions (see table 7.4 for a breakdown by transport mode). The bulk of these emissions were from cars (62.4 per cent)

Table 7.4 Estimated greenhouse gas emissions (CO_2 equivalent) by transport mode, 2000

Gas source	CO_2	CH_4	N_2O	Total	% of Australian total
Road	64 300	446	4 073	68 819	12.9
Rail	1 571	1	14	1 586	0.3
Civil aviation	4 308	5	42	4 354	0.8
Domestic naval	1 473	52	9	1 533	0.3
Other	41	0	0	42	0
All domestic	71 693	504	4 138	76 335	14.3

Notes: CO_2 carbon dioxide; CH_4 methane; N_2O nitrous oxide. Components may not sum to totals due to rounding.

Source: Derived from Australian Greenhouse Office, 2002, table 21

and trucks and light commercial vehicles (35.3 per cent) (Australian Bureau of Statistics, 2003). These figures are, however, a slight underestimation of the total greenhouse contribution of transport because they do not include the electricity generation component of electric train and tram systems.

It is significant that the greenhouse contribution of transport is growing rather than decreasing as would be expected under international measures such as the Kyoto Protocol. Australia's transport contribution in 2000 was an increase of 3.3 per cent on 1999 levels, and an increase of 24.2 per cent on 1990 levels, 1990 being the base year used for the Kyoto process. Between 1990 and 2000, emissions from passenger cars have increased by 22.2 per cent and those of other road transport by 32.8 per cent (Australian Bureau of Statistics, 2003d). In terms of sustainability, these figures indicate why Australia is going to have difficulty genuinely meeting its very lax target of an 8 per cent increase in greenhouse emissions by 2008–12.

There are outputs and emissions other than greenhouse gases from urban passenger transport. These include local air pollution, and the spillage of oils and rubber on roads which is then washed into the waterways after rain. Abandoned and dumped cars and vehicle parts such as tyres and car batteries are also a problem. These problems are being addressed to some degree by campaigns to prevent dumping. The problem of disposal, however, extends to legitimate actions. For example, in 1989–1990, 66 per cent of 14.4 million replaced tyres in Australia were consigned to landfill (Australian Bureau of Statistics, 1997). While this reduces the illegal dumping of tyres, it also limits the life of existing landfill sites and adds pressure for cities to locate new sources for the disposal of waste. It is also possible to address some of these issues through the development of environmentally friendly automobiles and through greater emphasis on the reuse of products. For example, old tyres can be shredded and used in the manufacture of playground equipment and sports courts.

While the problem of emissions, wastes and disposal is more significant and harder to address in relation to private automobile owners, it is also relevant to public transport operators. The life of trains is often extended by their use on less popular lines, and buses are often sold to private operators when they leave the public transport system. The issue of final disposal is often one that is not faced by the public transport agency.

RECOMMENDATIONS FOR TRANSPORTATION AND SUSTAINABLE CITIES

The preceding discussion of transport trends in Australian cities and the ecological impacts of urban transportation leads to making a number of recommendations on how to plan Australian cities to be more sustainable for urban transport.

The first of these recommendations is to focus on accessibility, not mobility, and to encourage the use of contemporary technology to reduce unnecessary demand for transport. This approach is likely to be especially effective because it addresses the travelling of more educated workers who are also the ones likely to be using corporate cars. If these workers are driving or using public transport to get to work, then their working from home for part of the week will most likely reduce the peak-period congestion in our major cities.

The second recommendation is to encourage the use of sustainable modes of transport, particularly walking and cycling. This is achievable by spending money on widening footpaths, making these paths safe and making them interesting so that the perception of time spent walking or cycling is reduced. Urban planning and building development regulations could be amended to encourage developers to include showers and/or changing rooms and locker and bike storage facilities in all new buildings and major refurbishments. Building cycleways where there is a demand for safe cycling will also encourage more people to ride bikes. Where there are no cycleways on major roads and little space in which to build a new cycleway, it is easy for transport planners to move the cars waiting at traffic lights back by ten metres so that cyclists can move to the front of the queue. This would encourage cycling because it improves safety.

Third, the placement of facilities has a major impact on the ability to use particular modes of transport. This is the case for major sporting venues, for example, the Docklands stadium in Melbourne, or everyday trips such as collecting children from school and picking up milk and bread in the same journey. Drawing on studies of the existing transport patterns of people, there is enormous potential for integration, but the key points to make here are the need to recognise this opportunity, and to avoid siting frequently used facilities so they can only be realistically accessed by private automobiles.

Fourth, despite earlier comments about reducing unnecessary travel, it is apparent that public transport is more sustainable than the automobile only if it is being used by passengers. The strategy may appear to be simple – have more people on public transport during the peak periods. This does present problems, however, given the limited capacity of some fixed rail networks, the need for additional rolling stock and drivers to service the peak periods but to be idle at off-peak times, and the increasing dispersal of workplaces based on the premise of car travel to work. Despite these valid concerns, the recent experience of Perth highlights the potential for improved public transport provision and the likelihood of increasing patronage of the service. Trains, light rail, trams and buses operating at or near capacity for long periods of a day provide a viable alternative for passengers who may otherwise travel by car. This is reducing the consumption of non-renewable fossil fuel, particularly oil, which is increasingly being imported into Australia from regions of the world that are politically unstable.

Apart from walking and cycling, the evidence presented earlier in this chapter is that the most sustainable form of mass transport for large cities like the five major cities in Australia is an electric rail system that is well patronised throughout the day and night, including on weekends. Ideally this system is fed by light rail, trams, buses and ferries, with integrated ticketing, transport pricing and timetabling so that transitions between modes of transport are seamless. This may require the reorientation of existing public transport to become feeder services, or the design of new transport systems with this feeder strategy in mind. The use of modern technology, such as the Octopus Card in Hong Kong (which, incidentally, was developed by an Australian) links transport ticketing with banking facilities and enables passengers to board various modes of transport quickly. Too often public transport services, particularly buses, are delayed by passengers and drivers fumbling for change, thereby reducing the attractiveness of public transport for other potential users.

The sustainability of a public transport system based on a rail spine still varies between cities because of variations in patronage and in the ecological sustainability of the electricity generation and distribution process. Australia generates 84 per cent of its electricity from coal (Diesendorf, 2003). This non-renewable fossil fuel is a major greenhouse gas contributor to climate change (see chapter 9). The sustainability of electricity generation is important when we consider the benefits of urban transportation, but currently the major rival (the private automobile) is also dependent on supplies of cheap fossil fuel, mostly imported, in the form of petrol. This means that when we are considering issues of transportation, we need to keep in mind the sustainability impacts of that transport wherever in the world these impacts occur.

SUMMARY

The sustainability of cities is highly influenced by transport, and particularly by the relationships between transport and land use, and between transport and energy sources. Australian cities vary in their transport history, and particularly in their recent transport planning. Regardless of the mode of transport used, its energy source or its environmental impacts, it is apparent that all transport is dependent in some form on nature. It is impossible not to have some environmental impacts as a result of transportation, but it is possible to reduce negative environmental impacts by focusing on accessibility rather than mobility, and by encouraging a hierarchy in transport choice that favours walking and cycling for short trips, and a heavy rail network, fed by buses, trams and light rail, for longer urban journeys. These public transport modes are more sustainable than the use of automobiles, but only if they are carrying enough passengers. Their use, particularly in non-peak periods to spread the commuting load, should be encouraged. In the push to move Australian cities towards sustainability, the use of the private automobile should be made a last-resort transport option.

CHAPTER 8

WASTE, INDUSTRIAL ECOLOGY AND ECOLOGICAL MODERNISATION

INTRODUCTION

The issue of waste is crucial for urban sustainability. The inappropriate disposal of waste may threaten human health, lead to resource degradation, and generally reduce the amenity of cities. Improvements in the way that we conceptualise and handle the issue of waste are likely to have a positive impact on land area used by cities, transport of waste materials, conservation of biodiversity, and air and water quality.

The economic costs of not properly disposing of waste are high. These costs include the opportunity cost of degraded environments, fines for pollution and impacts on tourism. The economic costs are not limited to improper disposal. Landfill sites are one of the traditional, and until recently most widely accepted, methods of disposal. Landfill operators are competing with other potential land uses, and the siting of this activity is now more strenuously opposed by local community groups than in previous years.

There are, however, concerns about the concept of waste that go beyond technical issues of how to dispose of it or of the economic costs of disposal. These issues include the discursive construction of the idea of 'waste', as if this is a normal and expected outcome of production and consumption practices. An uncritical acceptance of the notion of waste justifies the perpetuation and expansion of a linear economic process that constructs nature as resources, accepts the notion of 'throughput' and sees waste as an inherent part of the production and consumption process. In the past this approach has generally led to attempts to conceal the waste (out of sight, out of mind), or to end-of-pipe solutions that focus on the waste but ignore a holistic perspective on production and consumption relations.

This chapter considers the problem of waste for Australian cities, beginning with a discussion on the discourse before briefly considering the sectoral generation of waste. The chapter then looks at some issues for waste disposal, including limitations of landfill capacity. The argument presented is that limited landfill capacity, like an inability to obtain new surface water and ground water reserves, is a benefit in the move towards sustainable cities because it restricts the 'frontier' mentality of resource management. The frontier mentality is one in which activities are simply moved from one location to another once the initial location has been exhausted. Given the breadth of the issue and the availability of literature on recycling and other waste minimisation strategies, the remainder of the chapter focuses on industry (which is itself a broad topic). This part of the chapter explores the potential of two concepts, industrial ecology and ecological modernisation, to address the issue of 'waste'. It is important to note what this chapter does not address in detail. The concept of waste is too broad to give sufficient depth of treatment to each sector and each approach here. Important issues such as the generation and transport of nuclear waste from Lucas Heights in Sydney are not discussed, nor is the issue of hazardous waste, which in Sydney increased from 170 000 tonnes in 1992 to 422 000 tonnes in 1996 (Australian State of the Environment Committee, 2001).

FROM WASTE TO RESOURCE?

In the past, the idea of waste usually meant that if people did anything about waste, they devoted energy and money to disposing of it. This was largely due to limited environmental awareness (compared to today) and concerns about health and technological limitations. Questioning the concept of 'waste' was not prevalent.

In fact, the notion of 'waste' has always been important and useful for environmental management, and it still is. The distaste of 'wasting' something is a catalyst to mobilise interests which may otherwise have little in common. This idea appears in the writings of Gifford Pinchot, who set out the scope and justification for conservation (Pinchot, 1901, in Wall, 1994). In the Australian context, Frawley (1999) notes that the roots of Australian environmentalism were identifiable in the latter half of the 19th century, and that the two influences were nationalism and 'a growing concern about reckless exploitation and waste of resources' (Frawley, 1999, 279). While not always the case, people who grew up in the era of the Depression or who come from backgrounds where resources were scarce are likely to be appalled by squandering either money or the earth. Waste is a useful concept to mobilise people for environmental action because many people oppose the idea of wasting something.

The notion of waste has become unpopular in recent times, for good reason. The idea of 'closing the loop' on linear production and consumption systems means that what was called 'waste' should be an input into something useful. In other words, there has been a linguistic transition from 'waste' to 'resource'. This was reflected in the naming of the new government body, Resource NSW, which replaced regionally based waste boards, and was itself restructured in September 2003 as part of a new super-department called the Department of Environment and Conservation. The logic of closing the loop to reduce waste is sound, but are we losing, in modifying our language, a motivation for environmental awareness and action? This concern is exacerbated by the belief that the change in material practices are much slower than the changes in terminology. We may have created a new language, but the same old unsustainable practices exist, and continue to exist partly because the new language has removed an impetus for environmental action. In the language of government departments and consultants, we are in the era of 'transition' (Wright, 2000).

Before considering two potential ways to address the problem of waste in industrial production and consumption, we will look at waste generation in Australia and then at how Australian cities have addressed the issue of waste over time and the problems that particular cities face.

WASTE GENERATION BY SECTOR

Australia's current waste management practices are inadequate, but there are some small signs of improvement. The targets set in 1992 when the *National Waste Minimisation Act* was introduced were not met by 2000. In 1999 our municipal waste disposal levels per capita were second only to the United States among the developed countries. What is particularly concerning is that the disposal rates per person generally increased in most states in the late 1990s before marginally declining at the end of the decade, but appeared to be on a steep upward trend in Western Australia (Australian State of the Environment Committee, 2001). A recent report produced in Western Australia may explain this apparent trend. It noted that waste data for the period 1991–97 'are inaccurate since weighbridges and reporting mechanisms were not in place at all landfills' (Western Australia Department of Environment, 2003a, 32). It appears that the *total* waste going to landfill in the Perth Metropolitan Region per annum declined marginally during 1999–2002. There is still cause for concern, however, as recent statistics indicate that although household recycling rates increased from 17 to 21 per cent of total waste, and green waste recycling increased by 78 per cent during 1998–2002, the household waste generated in the Perth Metropolitan Region grew by 33 per cent from 461 441 tonnes in 1998 to 616 764 tonnes in 2002. Even allowing for population growth, this represents an increase from 0.9 kilograms per person in 1998 to 1.2 kilograms per person in 2002 (Western Australia Department of Environment, 2004).

The success in diverting waste from landfill sites varies between states, with the per capita waste disposal rate in New South Wales declining by 16 per cent between 1990 and 2001, although this decline was not uniform throughout the period (Department of Environment and Conservation NSW, 2003). Given that Australia is one of the few OECD countries with a rising population, this means that unless there is a significant drop in the per capita waste disposal, it is likely that the total waste disposal per annum is increasing.

The composition of the waste varies in relation to location and economic growth. The combined categories of construction and demolition and commercial and industrial comprised 68 per cent of the waste in New South Wales and almost 70 per cent of the waste in Perth for 2002 (Department of Environment and Conservation NSW, 2003; Western Australia Department of Environment, 2003a). Using Sydney as an example, while there have been increases in the rates of kerbside recycling per capita and reductions in the rates of municipal waste per capita, the source of waste that fluctuates most is industrial waste. This is related in part to economic conditions (EPA NSW, 2000; Department of Environment and Conservation NSW, 2003).

ATTEMPTS AT WASTE REDUCTION AND MANAGEMENT

There are various waste reduction and management programs being operated throughout Australia. The focus of these programs, the scale on which they operate, their objectives and their source of funding are diverse. Most programs are funded by a state government levy on disposal costs at landfills. In New South Wales there is a three-tier levy based on distance from Sydney, with an annual increase in the top two tiers of $1 to a maximum of $25 per tonne. Levies in other states range from between $4 and $5 per tonne in Victoria and South Australia in the metropolitan areas, to $3 per tonne in metropolitan Perth and no levy in Brisbane (Western Australia Department of Environment, 2003b).

This section of the chapter highlights a few key programs, with examples of specific actions to show what is possible in the move towards sustainable cities. It is not intended to be comprehensive, but rather to indicate the possibilities for future action.

The issue of construction and demolition waste, which is very significant in central and inner Sydney, is being addressed through initiatives such as the WasteWise Construction Program which began in 1995. Examples of waste recovery and reuse through this program include Bovis Lend Lease in 1997 recycling 98 per cent of material from the State Office Block in Sydney (Environment Australia, 2003). Examples of excellent practice outside the program include the restoration and additional construction of the 60L Green Building in Carlton, Victoria, which has won a number of awards including the Premier's Sustainability Award and the Banksia Awards (Category 10, Leadership in Sustainable Buildings) since it was completed in late 2002. The 60L Green Building incorporates numerous sustainability initiatives in water, air management, energy use, cycling facilities, tenant education, ongoing commitment to sustainability, and so on. In the area of 'waste', the bricks, glazed partitions, timber floor joists and planking wood from the old building were reused in the new building. The concrete used in the 60L Green Building comprised 60 per cent crushed concrete that was reused from other buildings (60L Green Building, 2004).

Many urban local councils across Australia now have programs that encourage the kerbside separation of materials. In addition to glass, can and paper recycling, these programs may include 'green waste' (vegetation) and household items – a practice that often results in reuse as these items are frequently reclaimed by other people before council collection.

Unfortunately, with the exception of South Australia's five cent deposit system on soft-drink bottles, the brunt of recycling effort is borne by local government. Efforts to amend this situation by moving towards producer-responsibility in New South Wales and the Northern Territory have encountered substantial resistance from the representatives of soft-drink manufacturers and their allies. The notion of producer-responsibility, exemplified by the responsibility of car manufacturers in Germany for the disposal of automobiles at the end of their working life, is challenged in Australia.

One recent campaign to reduce waste and litter was the plastic bags legislation introduced into the Australian Senate by Greens Senator Bob

Brown in October 2002. The findings of the Environment, Communications, Information Technology and the Arts References Committee were staggering. Australians use 6.9 billion plastic bags per year, of which somewhere between 50 and 80 million plastic bags become litter. Less than three per cent of plastic bags are recycled, and plastic bags were identified as 'Australia's highest volume "add-on" packaging designed as a single use or disposable product and are not necessarily essential to product integrity' (National Plastic Bags Working Group, 2002, 4). One of the points that emerged from the inquiry was how the plastic bag 'epitomises an image of a wasteful society' (Senate Environment, Communications, Information Technology and the Arts References Committee, 2003, 9).

ISSUES FOR AUSTRALIAN CITIES IN RELATION TO WASTE

Today the idea of a waste hierarchy along the lines of 'avoidance, minimisation, (resource) recovery and disposal' (with recovery including reuse, reprocessing, recycling and energy recovery) is generally accepted by waste management specialists. This hierarchy may be framed in slightly different terminology between jurisdictions, but as a concept it is appropriate and is not being challenged in this chapter. The problem until recently is that most emphasis has been on disposal. This has often been in the form of a 'frontier mentality' where good waste planning meant the appropriate siting of a new landfill site, away from the city, and preferably downwind with consideration of water contamination issues. A contemporary version of this mentality is the proposal to transport Sydney's waste to abandoned mines at Woodlawn (about 35 kilometres south of Goulburn) and to locations in the Hunter Valley. These proposals effectively extend Sydney's ecological footprint because Sydney requires the resources of areas outside of its boundaries in order to function. Despite the findings of a commission of inquiry, the transportation of waste to a 'distant elsewhere' will not stimulate waste minimisation behaviour in Sydney (see Cleland, 2000).

It is still very important to consider landfills for a number of reasons. First, given their existence, their management is vital. A recent NSW study identified concerns of inadequate covering of wastes, inadequate dust suppression and water pollution issues at a number of landfill sites (EPA NSW, 2000). This is crucial because, as noted by Tammemagi (1999), landfills are not as dormant as they may appear to the casual eye, and activity within the landfill can result in groundwater pollution that is usually irreversible. This is very important in Perth, where 'the sensitivity of Perth's groundwater to possible pollution, which currently accounts for 60 per cent of the metropolitan drinking water [sic], is making it difficult to justify new landfills above these aquifers' (Western Australia Department of Environment, 2003a, 33). Second, the capacity and rate of uptake in Australian cities is crucial in minimising waste creation and disposing of waste appropriately. Third, while it may not be the most sustainable form of disposal (which is itself the lowest rung on the waste minimisation hierarchy), landfill 'accounts for over 95 per cent of solid waste disposal in some states and territories' (Newton, et al, 2001, 124).

The limitations of available landfill capacity, combined with the resistance to the siting of new landfills, is likely to be one of the biggest drivers of more sustainable practices. This occurs through pricing (for example, the discrepancy between landfill fees in Sydney, which are high and have commenced rising since 2002, and other cities) and through the move towards alternative actions such as recycling. With the possible exception of Darwin, where the life expectancy of landfill sites extends to 2026, Australian cities are now experiencing many of the waste disposal issues that have already been encountered in Europe and parts of North America (Australian Bureau of Statistics, 1997). The situation is rapidly approaching a crisis point in Sydney, where estimates of putrescible waste landfill capacity undertaken in 2000 (Wright, 2000) and updated in 2002 (Wright, 2002) demonstrate that the capacity of about 17–18 million tonnes as at July 2002 will be 'drawn down' at a rate of about 2 million tonnes per year. While the emphasis in these documents and in the 2003 State of the Environment Report (Department of Environment and Conservation NSW, 2003) is on the total capacity and the year it will be filled, consideration also needs to be given to the distribution of this capacity. While approximately 60 per cent of Sydney's putrescible waste was estimated to be sent to the landfill site at Lucas Heights in Sydney's southern suburbs in January 2001, other facilities such as Eastern Creek were available in the western suburbs (Wright, 2000). The scenario of a landfill crisis includes transporting waste even greater distances across Sydney unless new facilities are created, or more importantly, the amount of waste going to landfill is significantly reduced.

A similar scenario exists in Perth, where there are seven landfill sites that can take non-inert waste, but this will reduce to four sites by 2006 (Western Australia Department of Environment, 2003a). The waste issue highlights the links between population, packaging technology, cultural perceptions of waste and effective environmental management strategies to divert 'waste' from landfill sites. It has been noted that 'with expected population growth and current disposal practices, it is estimated that the overall life expectancy of the remaining putrescible landfills is less than ten years' (Western Australia Department of Environment, 2003a, 32).

A sustainable city is one in which there are high rates of resource recovery in all three sectors of waste management. In Sydney, the rates are 25 per cent for the municipal sector, 24 per cent for the commercial and industry sector and 60 per cent for construction and demolition (Wright, 2002). The comparison between Sydney and some European countries and progressive American cities highlights the need for concerted action on the issue of waste. According to Wright (2000), Sydney's rate of composting and recycling was 24 per cent of rubbish volume, compared to the European average of 30 per cent. This latter average disguised significant variations between countries, with those countries that had little landfill space and high charges having much higher rates than countries that had low landfill charges. The variation ranged from rates of 48 per cent in Austria, 46 per cent in the Netherlands and 42 per cent in Switzerland, to lows of 9 per cent in the United Kingdom, 12 per cent in France and 13 per cent in Italy (Wright, 2000). The US West Coast cities of Portland (53 per cent in 1998) and Seattle (44 per cent in 1998) highlight the possibility of increasing the rates of composting and recycling in Australian cities. Importantly, a landfill crisis in 1987 was the catalyst for Seattle increasing its rate from 28 per cent in 1988 to 44 per cent in 1995 (Wright, 2000).

Another approach that has been attempted, particularly in the United States where it was used in various forms in more than 3400 locations, is the concept of 'unit pricing' (Miranda and Aldy, 1998). This approach requires householders to pay per unit of waste generated, rather than paying a flat council rate. As such, it is similar to water and electricity provision or paying for the number of telephone calls made. Its application to the issue of waste in Australian cities is probably unnecessary because one study in the United States noted that unit pricing encouraged a transferal of waste into recycling before it encouraged source reduction behaviour (Miranda and Aldy, 1998). In Australian cities, we have implemented some of the measures that accompany the more successful unit pricing programs, notably a reduction in the size of the 'normal' rubbish bin, and an increase in kerbside recycling programs and education campaigns about waste and the environment. Reducing municipal waste is important, but concentrating on pricing the waste is not the panacea to alter source behaviour.

This section of the chapter has concentrated on the existing waste situation in Australian cities. It is grounded in the programs and statistics of today. The strategies that have been implemented in recent years to reduce the amount of waste going to landfill (such as raising landfill fees, expanding kerbside recycling programs and reducing packaging) are likely to play an important part in making Australian cities more sustainable on the issue of waste. They are, however, insufficient in the move towards making Australia's major cities more sustainable.

The next two sections of this chapter explore approaches that in the future may enable us to move towards an industrial economy befitting a progressive environmental consciousness. These ideas are still being tested and developed, but it is possible that they may have a significant impact on the use of energy, materials, water and waste in our cities. In terms of a waste hierarchy, ecological modernisation focuses on avoidance and minimisation of waste, with resource recovery also playing an important part as a catalyst for the development of new industries. Industrial ecology tends to focus on the resource recovery (including reuse, reprocessing, recycling and energy recovery) level of waste. Both concepts represent a potentially progressive way of addressing production issues that is not about creating new production frontier economies in countries where cheap labour and lax environmental regulations and enforcement abound, and where there is enormous fossil fuel use in the export of these products to countries such as Australia.

INDUSTRIAL ECOLOGY

Industrial ecology is a concept that has potential to convert 'waste outputs' into 'resource inputs', thereby reducing the economic, social and environmental costs of waste disposal while simultaneously preventing the need to take more raw materials for use in production. While some authors have traced the roots of industrial ecology to the mid-1950s (for example, Erkman, 1997), the idea is agreed to be more recent in origin. Some authors claim that it came from the work of Barry Commoner (1971), while others trace it to the West German government of the early 1970s. Others say that it originated with the Japanese Ministry of International Trade and Industry in 1971 (see O'Rourke, et al, 1996).

There are numerous debates about industrial ecology, including the (selective) use of nature as a metaphor (Allen, 1999; Andrews, 1999), and what the concept actually means. For the purposes of this book, two definitions are as follows.

> Industrial Ecology takes a systems view of the use and environmental impacts of materials and energy in industrial societies. It employs the ecological analogy in several ways, including analysis of materials flows. (Andrews, 1999, 366)

> Industrial Ecology ... is a systems view in which one seeks to optimize the total materials cycle from virgin material, to finished material, to component, to product, to obsolete product, and to ultimate disposal. Factors to be optimized include resources, energy, and capital. (Graedel and Allenby, 1995, 9)

These definitions are based on the idea that the traditional model of industrial activity should be changed to an integrated industrial ecosystem. This approach applies the ecosystem metaphor and model to restructure industrial systems in order to make them compatible with the way natural ecosystems function. This means that they should optimise the consumption of energy and materials, minimise waste generation and use the effluents of one process as the raw material for another process.

For some authors industrial ecology is a technical exercise at the scale of the individual corporation, while for others the term evokes images of linkages between firms in a geographic area. This latter vision is known as an 'eco-industrial park'. Korhonen (2002) summarised what he called the 'product' (that is, the technical exercise within a corporation) and 'geographical' approaches, and noted that while these two approaches are compatible in some ways, there are also tensions between them. The technical approach within a corporation is, arguably, easier to implement because it does not require external negotiations of the sort necessary to develop eco-industrial parks or the like (that is, the geographic approach to industrial ecology).

While both approaches are potentially useful, in terms of sustainable cities the geographical approach appears to have more potential because it socialises many of the benefits and because if suitable role models could be developed, they would transform not only corporations, but also land use and transport patterns. The challenge has been to develop suitable role models of eco-industrial parks (see Grant, 2000; Lambert and Boons, 2002). This is not easy, especially given the emphasis in the literature on one model (for example, the town of Kalundborg in Denmark), and the fact that this model has developed around a coal-fired power station. In 1994 in the United States, the President's Council on Sustainable Development initiated an eco-industrial park project. The results of this project appear to have been mixed, especially as some of the flagship eco-industrial park projects may be languishing (Gibbs, Deutze and Proctor, 2002). It appears that Gibbs, Deutze and Proctor (2002, 2) are accurate in their assessment that 'in an ideal-type industrial system, there would be complete or nearly complete internal recycling of materials ... [I]n reality most commentators realise that this is probably unattainable, but neverthe-less worth pursuing as a goal'.

The experience in Australia appears to confirm this assessment. The main examples of this type of thinking appear to be the now defunct Steel River eco-industrial development in Newcastle and the work done on the heavy industrial site in Cockburn, south of Perth. In the late 1990s the 107-hectare Steel River site in Mayfield West (a suburb of Newcastle) was proposed to become Australia's first eco-industrial park. The joint venture to develop the site dissolved in 2000, partly because of the failure to secure anchor tenants who would trade with each other. (This factor can be partly attributed to the availability of other indus-trial sites, with less costs because they were not developed to the same environmental standards, in the region.)

An example of industrial ecology in practice is the Kwinana Industrial Area, sometimes referred to as the 'Cockburn example' because it is located alongside Cockburn Sound, south-west of Perth in Western Australia. There were examples of industrial integration in this complex in 1990, when the Wesfarmers CSBP Plant, the Tiwest Pigment Plant and the WMC Nickel Refinery were all major players among 13 core process industries, with 27 interactions between these core process industries (Van Berkel, 2003). By 2000, there were 21 core process industries, and the number of interactions was 68, with another 55 potential interactions between the core process industries (Van Berkel, 2003).

The potential for this concept to reduce certain types of waste appears enormous. A waste output is transformed into a resource input for another industry. The danger, however, is that even where it is possi-ble to establish such linkages, these linkages become permanent and there is a reliance on the creation of 'waste' as a resource when the tech-nology may become available to eliminate such waste altogether

(Korhonen, 2002). The risk of becoming addicted to waste products as inputs when technological change makes the production of such wastes unnecessary is a genuine risk and should be considered carefully. This risk arises because industrial ecology is focused on the resource recovery level of the waste hierarchy. However, given the significant amounts of 'waste' to be recovered as a resource, attention to this level of the waste hierarchy is crucial.

ECOLOGICAL MODERNISATION

The idea of ecological modernisation originated in the corporate sector in the United States in the 1980s and spread to Europe following the publication of *Our Common Future* (World Commission on Environment and Development, 1987), having a significant impact on national environmental planning in countries such as the Netherlands (Kronsell, 2000; Young, 2000). The term 'ecological modernisation' is socially constructed and debatable. Christoff (2000, 209) notes that the term's 'growing popularity derives in part from the suggestive power of its combined appeal to notions of development and modernity and to ecological critique'.

There are three main ways in which ecological modernisation has been used. These are somewhat similar to differences in the use of the term 'industrial ecology'. The three normative dimensions of the term 'ecological modernisation' are as a technical adjustment, a policy discourse and a belief system (Christoff, 2000).

The technical adjustment approach is often restricted to those sectors of the economy where such a change is profitable. Importantly, unless the economic gains from technical improvements in pollution control or energy use, for example, are reinvested in ecological modernisation processes, then what has been created is greater capacity to impact on the planet. This version of ecological modernisation is similar to the corporate approach to industrial ecology, in that one of the ways environmental improvement (and hence economic gain in most cases) is achieved is through the adoption of a systems approach to resources, energy and waste.

The policy discourse version of ecological modernisation is most clearly represented in the writings of Weale (1992) and Hajer (1995). Similar to the corporate perspective, the key ideas of this version of ecological modernisation are that economic growth and environmental responsibility are not irreconcilable, and in fact they make good economic sense for three reasons. First, using waste as an example, savings in end-of-pipe 'solutions' to waste disposal problems are economic gains for a corporation, but also for an urban area, entire state, country or the world. Second, governments that enforce more stringent environmental regulations and encourage technological development to meet these regulations become the leaders in this field and can establish valuable new industries which are capable of earning export income. Third, there is a public relations spin-off as these countries are able to project themselves as being environmentally responsible global citizens.

A more radical approach is the concept of ecological modernisation as a belief system. In this approach, rather than being a policy discourse to maintain existing economic relationships and at the same time make them 'greener', ecological modernisation is a challenge to the market-based emphasis on efficiency. It is part of what Christoff (2000, 222) identifies as being 'strong' ecological modernisation, which he sees as being part of the solution to our ecological crisis. In contrast, the 'weak' version of ecological modernisation identified by Christoff (2000) perpetuates existing relationships and narrow, technological-oriented thinking, and therefore is part of the problem. In this strong version of ecological modernisation, the emphasis is on the 'avoid' and 'minimise' levels of the waste hierarchy. From an ecological perspective, if this approach is effective it will likely generate the greatest ecological benefits. From cultural and economic perspectives, the implementation of a strong version of ecological modernisation is fraught with challenges because it requires genuine, meaningful and lasting change.

APPLICATION TO AUSTRALIAN CITIES

There is potential for both industrial ecology and ecological modernisation to contribute to greater sustainability in Australian cities. Industrial modernisation, commencing at the national level with the signing of the Kyoto Protocol, would send market signals that the government wanted the Australian economy to move away from what Krockenberger (2003) has labelled a 'hot, heavy and wet' economy, that is, an economy that uses lots of energy, materials and water, to an economy that is 'cooler, lighter and drier'. More stringent environmental targets at all levels of government, supported by effective regulation and incentives to encourage positive environmental change, would have a significant impact in Australia's largest cities.

Industrial ecology has a limited focus relative to ecological modernisation, but the potential to develop new industrial estates based on this principle is exciting. The relocation of industry from older sites (often due to enhanced land values for residential development) means that if we are to continue to maintain something approximating our current standard of living, we need new industrial areas in Australia or we import more from overseas (and hence increase our ecological footprint).

The creation of a modern industrial economy with less inputs per unit of output, less environmental impact per unit of input and a closing of resource loops with minimal additional energy expenditure is essential if we are to maintain high standards of living. This economy cannot be achieved by technical processes alone and, as a number of authors have noted, one of the limitations of industrial ecology is a relative lack of emphasis on social systems (O'Rourke, et al, 1996; Hoffman, 2003).

This modern industrial economy, when linked with 'green architecture' and sustainable transportation, has the potential not only to reduce waste, but also to reduce land requirements, water use and the environmental costs of commuting. The reduction in all forms of waste is something that is economically and ecologically beneficial for Australian cities. It is also a necessity, rather than an option that we may choose to pursue, to make Australian cities more sustainable.

SUMMARY

The concept of waste is a potential motivating force for environmental action, especially when it is clear that the waste could be avoided. The notion of waste is, however, an idea that enables the perpetuation of unsustainable practices that go far beyond the disposal of the waste itself. These include new resource exploitation and expansion in throughput, which means that there is often more waste to dispose of in the future.

It is important to reduce the amount and worst types of waste, but how to do this in an energy-efficient manner while maintaining quality of life (not necessarily standard of living, although this is politically challenging) is a significant issue. The latter part of this chapter has focused on industrial production processes and suggested that Australian cities could be made more sustainable by the adoption of industrial ecology and ecological modernisation principles. It has been noted, however, that both of these terms are socially constructed and have been interpreted in different ways. While some environmental improvements are possible within narrow concepts of these terms, it appears that unless the more comprehensive visions are pursued (what Christoff, 2000, labelled 'strong'), the environmental improvements are unlikely to contribute to greater sustainability in Australian cities and may actually reduce sustainability because they enhance the capacity to be unsustainable.

CHAPTER 9

CLIMATE CHANGE, OZONE DEPLETION AND URBAN AIR QUALITY

INTRODUCTION

Improving the quality of air in Australian cities is vital for urban sustainability. This is, however, insufficient because we need to consider the impacts of activities in Australian cities on the global climate, and of activities that are located outside the designated metropolitan regions of Australian cities but are conducted primarily to maintain these cities. Two global issues are crucial: ozone depletion and climate change.

This chapter begins with a brief discussion of urban air quality and the changes in air quality in each of the five largest cities in Australia. We then look at the global environmental issues of ozone depletion and climate change. The chapter highlights the differences between these two phenomena and briefly discusses recent changes in the ozone layer. The bulk of the chapter is devoted to the issue of climate change. The science and the politics of climate change are discussed before we focus on Australia's contribution to climate change. The following section investigates the potential impacts of climate change on each of the five largest cities in Australia. The last part of the chapter looks at the contribution that cities can make to resolving climate change issues by focusing on the role of local governments and their involvement in the Cities for Climate Protection™ Program.

URBAN AIR QUALITY

The heading of urban air quality covers a variety of concerns about pollution, smog, urban heat islands and health. It covers indoor air quality, which is important for sustainability but is beyond the scope of this chapter to address, and outdoor air quality. It also covers point source (for example, power stations, industrial sites) and mobile source (for example, automobiles) pollution.

Local air quality varies widely in cities throughout the world, and has changed in individual cities over time. Certain cities, due to their climate, topography, stage of economic development and the accompanying mix of activities, are more prone to particular forms of pollution than other cities. While most political and media attention in the overdeveloped world is focused on the issue of climate change, and this chapter is mostly devoted to it because of Australia's contribution to climate change, there are many cities in the world where local air quality is a far more immediate and important concern.

Air pollution may be defined simply as the process of altering the constituents of the atmosphere (Graham-Taylor, 2002). This definition makes an allowance for the absorption of these constituent chemicals, but does not discuss impacts. Other definitions consider the impact of chemicals, where air pollution is defined as 'the presence of one or more chemicals in the atmosphere in sufficient quantities and duration to cause harm to humans, other forms of life, and materials' (Miller Jr, 2002, 274).

Air pollution in cities is not new. Ancient cities on the Mesopotanian Plain were dense cities with poor air quality resulting from fires used in baking and industry. Air pollution in Ancient Rome, caused by potters kilns, baking ovens and burning wood to heat the baths, obscured the sun. In London, the burning of coal caused local air pollution, such that in 1272 King Edward I decreed that the burning or selling of sea coal (that is, surface coal that is generally high in bitumin and sulfur) was punishable by death. The first offender caught was executed, but it was not a deterrent because few people could afford to pay the high price of wood (Urbinato, 1994). Air pollution may cause significant health problems, sometimes resulting in death. Examples of major air pollution episodes include the infamous London smog (a mixture of coal-smoke and fog) which hung like a pall over London and killed about 1150 people in 1911 (Haughton and Hunter, 1994) and 4700 people in 1952 (Cutter and Renwick, 2004). On a global scale, the major cities with the worst air quality are Mexico City, Beijing, Shanghai and Delhi (Cutter and Renwick, 2004). There are major efforts being made in China to improve the environment of the largest cities, particularly in Beijing which will host the 2008 Olympic Games.

Improvements in local air quality, particularly in the wealthier cities of the world, are largely due to a combination of legislative change arising from disasters such as occurred in London in 1952, the substitution of fuels such as coal by 'cleaner' sources such as natural gas and the removal of lead in petrol. In Australian cities the major air quality problems are dependent on the size of the city, topography, climate and other factors that influence the creation and dispersal of pollution. Some cities are particularly prone to photochemical smog while cities with colder climates are more likely to experience particulate matter pollution (for example, Launceston in Tasmania, as a result of burning firewood (Todd, 2002)). This problem can even occur in cities renowned for warm weather and beaches, such as Perth, where wood smoke has 'unequivocally contributed to episodes of poor air quality in the Perth metropolitan region in cool weather during recent years' (Tubby, 1998, 53).

While in developed countries today there are significantly less problems of industrial or sulphurous smog (the type that killed people in London), the incidence of photochemical smog that is synonymous with Los Angeles and the automobile-dependent city is rising in many cities, including some cities in Australia. Australia's five largest cities are similar to Los Angeles in terms of automobile dependence, although McManus (2002b) has noted the nuances in the history and extent of this phenomenon through a study of transport history in Perth. Most of the major Australian cities are also similar to Los Angeles in climate (having warm, sunny days in summer) and in topography, in that they are coastal basins rimmed by a range of hills which prevent the air pollution from being dispersed inland (Australian State of the Environment Committee, 2001). Brisbane has been identified as the Australian city with the highest potential for photochemical smog problems due to climatic and geographic factors, which includes being surrounded by mountain ranges on three sides and having Moreton and Stradbroke Islands as barriers to wind circulation off the coast (Australian Academy of Technological Sciences and Engineering, 1997; Foran and Poldy, 2002).

The process of photochemical smog development may be summarised as follows. In summer, as traffic increases in the morning, emissions of nitrogen oxides and unburned hydrocarbons increase. Sunlight causes nitrogen dioxide (NO_2) to break down into nitrogen oxide (NO) and a single atom of oxygen. This monatomic oxygen atom combines with the oxygen in the atmosphere to produce ozone (O_3). Photochemical smog is usually worse on hot days when there is no wind (Miller Jr, 2002). Conditions conducive to photochemical smog build-up vary between Australian cities, but it is often the sea breeze, for example, the Fremantle Doctor in Perth, that pushes the smog inland.

This smog circulates at the base of the hills or mountain range before drifting back across the city and out to sea at night. Photochemical smog causes respiratory tract problems and eye irritations, which in Australian cities has a greater impact in generally low-income suburbs that are located at the base of the ranges.

The air quality of Australia's major cities has generally improved over time; however, there are concerns about photochemical smog (Australian State of the Environment Committee, 2001). The 'maximum four-hour ozone concentrations' in Australian cities between 1979 and 1999 showed no consistent improvement trend (see Australian State of the Environment Committee, 2001). While allowances need to be made for variations in weather conditions between each year, there are discernable trends for two of the five largest Australian cities.

Melbourne exceeded the standard for ozone concentration of 0.08 parts per million less often in the 1990s than it did in the 1980s. In the 1980s it exceeded this standard on more than 20 days in seven of the ten years under consideration (including five years of 25 days or more, and in 1982 on over 40 days), while during the 1990s there were no years when Melbourne exceeded the standard on more than 20 days (Australian State of the Environment Committee, 2001).

By way of contrast, Perth with a smaller population had no days when the 0.08 standard was exceeded prior to 1990, but in the 1990s the standard was exceeded at least once every year, and in four of the last five years of the decade the number of days when it was exceeded was greater in Perth than in Melbourne (Australian State of the Environment Committee, 2001). While there are significant variations in temperature and topography between Perth and Melbourne that make Perth more susceptible to photochemical smog problems, it is apparent that there are clear trends in both cities relative to their own history, and the need for careful and effective airshed management in Perth cannot be understated.

Models of the three urban airsheds that are most susceptible to photochemical smog, that is, Sydney, Brisbane and Perth, indicate that the transport emissions of nitrogen oxides and volatile organic compounds are projected to rise in the future (Foran and Poldy, 2002). The projected increases vary, but the total kilotonnes of these compounds emitted per year may almost double in Brisbane and Perth during the period 1991–2021 (Foran and Poldy, 2002). If these emissions occur on hot, sunny days when little or no wind is present (as invariably they will), then there are likely to be more problems of photochemical smog in these cities in the future.

An understanding of air quality in Australian cities should involve consideration of the metaphor of an ecological footprint. How may the demands of Australia's major cities affect the air quality of other locations? To cite one example, a study by CSIRO Atmospheric Research rated the 44 major point sources of sulphur dioxide emitters by impact. Ten of these sources were located in the Hunter Region. They comprised five power stations and five industries. The major power stations, particularly Bayswater and Liddell, are important in the national grid that supplies cities such as Sydney with electricity. There is a loss at all stages of all forms of electricity generation, transmission and distribution. In the black coal fields of the Upper Hunter Valley of New South Wales (between Singleton and Muswellbrook), about 68 per cent of the energy in the fuel is lost or consumed at the power station and, in addition, about 10 per cent of the electricity sent out from the power stations is lost in transmission and distribution (Diesendorf, 2003). Sydney gets its power and the Upper Hunter Valley gets the heat loss and the sulphur dioxide, nitrogen oxide and other toxic emissions from the coal-fired power station.

OZONE DEPLETION

The ozone layer is a layer of ozone in the lower stratosphere (approximately 17 to 26 kilometres above sea level) that prevents about 95 per cent of the sun's ultraviolet radiation from reaching the surface of the earth. Ultraviolet radiation is harmful to almost all living things. Australia is particularly vulnerable to the effects of ozone depletion, which in humans include skin cancer, eye cataracts and possible damage to the immune system.

In 1974 chemists at the University of California–Irvine (Paul Crutzen, Sherwood Rowland and Mario Molina) calculated that chlorofluorocarbons (CFCs), a grouping of artificial chemical compounds which had only been manufactured since 1930, were causing a reduction in the amount of ozone in the stratosphere (Miller Jr, 2002; Cutter and Renwick, 2004). CFCs were widely used as refrigerants, propellants in spray-cans, blowers in foam-making and solvents. The theory was confirmed by satellite data in 1984, which indicated that there was significant ozone thinning (popularly but incorrectly referred to as an ozone hole) over Antarctica between September and December of that year. Research in 1988 indicated that a similar, but smaller, thinning was occurring during the Arctic spring and early summer. More recent research indicates that ozone thinning has worsened in both locations. Predictions by NASA indicate that ozone depletion over both the Antarctic and the Arctic will be at its worst in the years between 2010 and 2019 (Miller Jr, 2002).

These predictions are based on the lifetime of CFCs in the stratosphere, which range from 65 to 385 years, with the most widely used CFCs lasting between 75 and 111 years (Miller Jr, 2002). The addition of CFCs to the natural depletion of ozone, caused through activities such as volcanic eruptions (Haughton and Hunter, 1994), has resulted in more ultraviolet light reaching the earth's surface.

The measures introduced in the 1990s to address the problem of ozone depletion highlight the potential for environmental cooperation in the face of a very significant threat. These measures, however, have generally been successful because there were few corporations in a limited number of countries producing CFCs, and because there are readily available alternatives to the use of CFCs, namely, hydrocarbons (HCs), hydroflurocarbons (HFCs) and hydrochlorofluorocarbons (HCFCs). Unfortunately, these first two categories of alternatives, which are the main ones still being used, are greenhouse gases, although they are not ozone-depleting.

The Vienna Convention for the Protection of the Ozone Layer was adopted in 1985. This was later developed as the Montreal Protocol, which was signed by 25 countries in 1987. The Montreal targets were strengthened in 1990 at the meeting in London, where it was agreed to achieve a 50 per cent reduction of CFC emissions from 1986 levels by 1996 (rather than the earlier target of 1998) and to phase out CFCs by 2000 and all other ozone depleting chemicals by 2005 (Haughton and Hunter, 1994). Similar levels of cooperation and urgency are required to address the issue of climate change, but this is unlikely to be achieved because of the multitude of parties involved, the number of causes of climate change, the major contribution of fossil fuel combustion to the emission of greenhouse gases, the costs of substituting or eliminating the causes of climate change, and the discrepancies between who pays the costs and who receives the benefits of action to address climate change.

CLIMATE CHANGE

'Climate change is perhaps the most serious environmental threat facing humanity in the twenty-first century,' wrote Hamilton (2001, xi). He is not alone in this view, because the world's business leaders at a meeting in Davos, Switzerland, in 2000 also declared that climate change was the greatest threat that the world faced (Hamilton, 2001).

As a national entity, Australia's current position on the issue of climate change is very disappointing, but it must be acknowledged that various state and local governments are making important contributions to reducing the causes of climate change. The potential impacts of climate change are still being debated, but there appears to be a growing consensus that climate change is already happening and that it is having impacts on temperatures, weather patterns, agricultural productivity and biodiversity. This section of the chapter explores the science and politics of climate change before considering the potential impacts of climate change on each of Australia's largest cities, and highlighting the leading role played by some local governments in Australia on this issue.

CLIMATE CHANGE: THE SCIENCE

There is a naturally occurring greenhouse effect that means the Earth's surface temperature is 33 degrees Celsius higher than could otherwise be expected given the distance of the Earth from the sun (Yencken and Wilkinson, 2000; O'Neill, et al, 2001). Without this naturally occurring greenhouse effect there would be no life as we know it on this planet. The atmosphere acts as a transparent blanket that allows solar energy in the form of visible light to reach the Earth, but impedes the heat radiation re-radiated from the Earth from escaping into space. This property is due to the presence of greenhouse gases in the troposphere (the layer of the atmosphere that is closest to the surface of the Earth). These greenhouse gases include water vapour, carbon dioxide, methane and nitrous oxide. The greenhouse effect is different from the issue of ozone depletion that was discussed above (Miller Jr, 2002; Cutter and Renwick, 2004).

The 'enhanced' greenhouse effect is a cruel misnomer. It refers to the anthropogenic contributions to climate change. The term 'enhanced' generally has qualitative connotations meaning to improve, but in this instance the term 'increased' is probably more appropriate. In fact, it could be argued that the term 'exacerbated' may more accurately reflect that human-generated greenhouse gas emissions are responsible for human-induced climate change, which constitutes a problem.

While the greenhouse effect and the major greenhouse gases were identified in the 19th century, it was not until 1896 that the Swedish chemist Svante Arrhenius drew the link between the combustion of coal and the possibility of changing the climate (O'Neill, et al, 2001). Studies were conducted through the early and mid-20th century, but interest in climate change increased from the late 1970s as global temperatures began to rise. In 1988 the World Meteorological Organisation and the United Nations Environment Program established the Intergovernmental Panel on Climate Change (IPCC). This is a network of about 2500 climate experts from approximately 70 countries. The mandate of the IPCC was 'to assess the scientific basis for climate change and its potential impacts, and to evaluate potential response strategies' (O'Neill, et al, 2001, 32). It first reported in 1990. In its 1995 report the IPPC noted that 'the balance of evidence suggests a discernible human influence on global climate (IPCC, 1996, 4). By the time of its 2000 report the IPCC had strengthened its position to say that 'there is new and stronger evidence that most of the warming observed over the last fifty years is attributable to human activity' (IPCC, 2001, 10). The IPCC's projections of global warming were increased from between 1.0 and 3.5 degrees Celsius by 2100 to between 1.4 and 5.8 degrees Celsius by 2100 (IPCC, 2001).

Not only did the IPCC study climate change, but in 1990 they also made recommendations about the reduction in emissions of major greenhouse gases that would be required to stabilise the climate. The IPCC recommended reductions in greenhouse gas emissions of greater than 60 per cent for carbon dioxide, between 75 and 85 per cent for CFCs, 15 and 20 per cent for methane and 70 and 80 per cent for nitrous oxide (Houghton, et al, 1990).

The largest greenhouse gas emitters by total of carbon dioxide equivalent (CO_2-e, the common unit for measuring greenhouse gases) are the United States, Russia and Japan. In 1990 the countries with the highest greenhouse gas emissions per capita were Luxembourg (34.4 CO_2-e per capita), Australia (28.9 CO_2-e per capita) and the United States (20.0 CO_2-e per capita). By 1999 Australia was the world's worst greenhouse gas emitter per capita (27.9 CO_2-e per capita), followed by Canada (22.2 CO_2-e per capita) and the United States (20.7 CO_2-e per capita) (Turton and Hamilton, 2002).

Using the Kyoto accounting rules (see below for a discussion on Kyoto), and using revised estimates provided by the Australian Greenhouse Office (2003) of greenhouse gas emissions as millions of tonnes of carbon dioxide equivalent, for the period 1990–2000, Australia's greenhouse gas emissions increased by 16.9 per cent (Australian State of the Environment Committee, 2001). As a country we are one of the worst performing countries in the world in our approach to greenhouse policy and our contribution to change, being ranked 134th of 142 countries by the World Economic Forum (2002).

CLIMATE CHANGE: THE POLITICS AND POSSIBLE ACTIONS

Concern about the possibility of climate change arose in the late 1970s. At that time the major concern was global warming and accompanying sea-level rise. Since then the scientific community has recognised that the enhanced greenhouse effect will generate significant warming across the world in the 21st century. Much of this warming will occur during the winter months, but it is now recognised that the impacts of climate change will vary depending on location.

The first major scientific evaluation of the magnitude of climate change emerged from a conference in Villach, Austria, in 1985 (Hamilton, 2001). The 1987 report of the World Commission on Environment and Development built on the Villach conference and identified climate change as a major threat for future generations, acknowledged the scientific uncertainty about the rate of change, and stressed the need to follow the 'precautionary principle' and not wait for scientific certainty before taking action to reduce greenhouse gas emissions (World Commission on Environment and Development, 1987). A meeting of over 300 scientists and policy-makers in Toronto, Canada, in June 1988 created an initial target of a 20 per cent reduction in greenhouse gas emissions by 2005, from a base year of 1988 (Wood, 2003). In Australia this target was adopted in mid-1989 by New South Wales, Victoria and Western Australia 'as an interim objective for planning purposes', before the issue of climate change moved into the national arena (Hamilton, 2001, 32).

The creation of the Intergovernmental Panel on Climate Change in 1988 was followed by the release of its first report in 1990 which consolidated climate change on the international sustainability agenda. The United Nations Framework Convention on Climate Change, signed by 155 countries, was one of five major documents that emerged from the United Nations Conference on Environment and Development (the 'Earth Summit') in Rio de Janeiro in 1992. In December 1992, Australia became the eighth country to ratify this Convention (Bulkeley, 2000).

Following the Earth Summit, a number of Conferences of the Parties (COP) have been held to develop and implement the framework agreed on in Rio de Janeiro. The most significant of these was COP3 in Kyoto, Japan, in 1997. This meeting received enormous media coverage in Australia (McManus, 2000). At COP3, the Annex One (or 'developed') countries agreed to an average reduction of 5.2 per cent of greenhouse gas emissions from a base year of 1990 by 2008–12. Australia signed up to an 8 per cent increase in emissions over the same period, but significantly managed to insert a clause into Article 3.7 of the Kyoto Protocol to allow the emissions from land clearing to be included in the total emissions by Australia in 1990 (Yencken and Wilkinson, 2000; Hamilton, 2001). Given that land clearing had already decreased between 1990 and 1997, this example of 'baseline inflation' enables the expansion of other sources of greenhouse gas emissions within the 108 per cent target (Hamilton, 2001), or if Australia has managed to contain emissions in other sectors, an opportunity to trade emissions credits with other developed countries (Hamilton, 2000).

Australia's greenhouse gas emissions in 2002 were mainly generated by stationary energy production (47.6 per cent), agriculture (19.2 per cent) and transport (14.5 per cent) (Australian Greenhouse Office, 2003). Industrial processes contributed only 4.8 per cent of the total emissions in 2002. These aggregate figures can, however, be misleading. A study by Wood (2003) identified that in 1997 the three most significant greenhouse emitting sectors were electricity supply (46.6 per cent), road transport (19.6 per cent) and iron and steel (5.5 per cent), but when the final demand for production is taken into consideration, the three most significant sectors were electricity supply (15 per cent), road transport (6.2 per cent) and basic non-ferrous metal and products, that is, aluminium smelting (5.5 per cent). These figures also highlight the importance of urban areas in Australia's greenhouse gas emissions, especially as Hamilton (2001) has noted that 62 per cent of all fuel used for land travel in Australia, and about 70 per cent of fuel used by passenger cars in Australia, is used in urban areas. Taplin and Yu (2000) estimate that about half of Australia's greenhouse gas emissions can be attributed directly or indirectly to urban activities, including urban energy use. The relationship between location, density and energy use is relatively simple. Households would use much the same stationary energy, whether they are congregated in cities or spread out over the country. In the latter case they would use much more transport energy.

The figures also highlight Australia's reliance on fossil fuels. Our transport energy is predominantly petroleum (which contributes to photochemical smog in cities) and 84 per cent of our electricity is generated from coal (Diesendorf, 2003). Unlike countries such as Germany, China and the United Kingdom (where nuclear power and/or natural gas is used), Australia's use of coal increased by almost 40 per cent during the 1990s (derived from Diesendorf, 2003).

Our rising amount of coal burning contributes significantly to Australia's inability to reduce greenhouse gas emissions. This is one reason that this country has not ratified the Kyoto Protocol. A second, and very important reason, is the unwillingness of the present George W Bush Administration in the United States to ratify the Protocol. Australia's stance is largely symbolic because, at the time of writing, the politics of the Kyoto Protocol are very tight and Australia could not influence them directly. To come into force, the Protocol must be ratified by 55 industrialised countries that represent at least 55 per cent of greenhouse gas emissions. As of December 2003, 120 countries have ratified the Protocol. The problem is that these countries only represent 44 per cent of emissions, and the only way in which ratification is likely to occur is if Russia (with just over 17 per cent of emissions) agrees to ratify the Protocol (Hodge, 2003; Saunders, 2003).

Australia's dependence on fossil fuels could be dramatically changed at low cost, given the political will. A study by Saddler, Diesendorf and Dennis (2004) has shown that Australia could reduce its carbon dioxide emissions from stationary (that is, non-transport) energy by 50 per cent by 2040, based on small improvements to existing technologies, while maintaining a high rate of economic growth. The study develops scenarios that reduce the growth in energy demand through improved efficiency in energy use in residential, commercial and industrial sectors. It then envisages a shift in energy supply from coal to a combination of natural gas and renewable sources of energy, mainly electricity from tree plantations and crop residues, wind power and solar hot water. The policy recommendations to implement this scenario are inexpensive. The study suggests that they could be funded by the economic savings achieved from energy efficiency together with the transfer of a small fraction of the existing subsidies for the production and use of fossil fuels (Riedy and Diesendorf, 2003) to energy efficiency and renewable energy.

LIKELY IMPACTS OF CLIMATE CHANGE ON AUSTRALIA'S LARGEST CITIES

The impacts of climate change will vary throughout Australia (see Australian State of the Environment Committee, 2001). In a study of regional vulnerability to climate change, Watson et al (1997) noted that Australia is very vulnerable to drought, the ecosystems and biodiversity are very prone to climate change in the long term, fire occurrence and insect outbreaks may be increased, and coastal settlements (where most Australians live) are prone to flooding and erosion caused by sea-level rise. By 2050 cities in northern Australia, such as Cairns, are likely to experience more intense tropical cyclones, with wind speeds likely to increase by 10 to 15 per cent and the associated rainfall likely to increase by 20 to 30 per cent. This means that the area of Cairns that is inundated by storm surges is likely to double from its present level (CSIRO, 2001; Apps, 2003).

The large Australian cities are likely to be impacted directly and indirectly (for example, through food supplies from agricultural regions affected by drought, or through deteriorating winter snow conditions for skiers from the major cities). Inland temperatures are anticipated to rise more than temperatures in coastal locations, thereby making Australia very vulnerable to water shortages, threatening the health of our rivers, biodiversity and potential for irrigation and food production, and making our country even more prone to bushfires.

The projections for initial temperature increases in Australia's major cities, measured as the average number of summer days when the temperature is anticipated to exceed 35 degrees Celsius, are shown in table 9.1.

Table 9.1 Projections of the average number of summer days above 35°C in Australian cities

CITY	No. of days above 35°C now	Projected no. of days above 35°C in 2030	Projected no. of days above 35°C in 2070
Coastal cities			
Sydney	2	2–4	3–11
Melbourne	8	9–12	10–20
Brisbane	3	3–6	4–35
Perth	15	16–22	18–39
Adelaide	10	11–16	13–28
Hobart	1	1–2	1–4
Inland city			
Canberra	4	6–10	7–30

Source: Derived from Australian Greenhouse Office, 2003

These projections are important, but they need to be considered in relation to cumulative ecological impacts, and changes in population and ecological impacts of lifestyles. For example, while table 9.1 shows that inland centres such as Canberra are anticipated to have more hot days in summer, the cumulative impacts of many more hot and dry days, accompanied by lower annual rainfall, means that high-risk bushfire conditions last longer and the window of opportunity for fuel reduction (that is, 'burning off' vegetation) to starve any potential bushfires is reduced. To understand the increased risk generated by climate change, it is important that we can predict not only the number of days when the temperature exceeds 35 degrees Celsius but also the number of late winter/early spring days when the temperature is likely to exceed 25 degrees Celsius and the winds are too high for fuel reduction work. This level of knowledge is currently beyond the predictability of climate change models.

Temperatures are anticipated to rise in Sydney, particularly by 2070. In contrast with Canberra, there is a moderating effect from the coast. This effect, however, needs to be considered along with the urban heat island effect (which is important and can be significantly reduced by the introduction of vegetation in the city, especially on rooftops – see Johnson, 2003) and the cumulative impacts of climate change. For example, higher rainfall in intensive storms is likely to result in greater flooding, especially considering the greater amount of hard surfaces due to the urban consolidation of the city (see chapter 5) and the paving of private household space. In 2051, when Sydney's population is anticipated to reach 5.6 million, the impact of hotter days combined with more automobile transport (based on current rates of car ownership and vehicle kilometres travelled) mean that without strong measures to improve air quality, Sydney is likely to experience more days of photo-chemical smog. Sydney is also prone to bushfire because urban development is often located on flat ridges above steep, vegetated slopes and valley bottoms, and because the type of vegetation tends to result in a rapid accumulation of fuel (in Bradstock, et al, 1998). Sydney will be more prone to bushfire resulting from climate change because there will be hotter days and higher rates of evaporation and because the possible addition of about another two million people by 2070 will expand the urban-bush interface. Even allowing for high levels of urban consolidation, say about 15–25 per cent of new development in the future to be on the fringe of the city, this means that up to another half a million people will be living in areas that are currently rural or bush. The

urban-bush interface will necessarily increase, thus making it more difficult to patrol and exposing more people to the risk on bushfire.

Melbourne is already experiencing a change in that the peak electricity season was formerly winter, due to heating, but the increased use
of air conditioners has made summer the peak electricity consumption
time in Melbourne. The impact of more days where the temperature
exceeds 35 degrees Celsius is likely to be exacerbated by the heat island
effect of cities (Jones, et al, 2000). This is likely to continue in
Melbourne, where the number of very hot days may double by 2070
(see table 9.1).

Other cities are anticipated to have significant variations in their
impact. Brisbane, by virtue of being further north, is likely to experience
some of the impacts discussed for Cairns, but is also expected to experience higher temperatures (especially by 2070, although the range
shown in table 9.1 is very large) and possibly less annual rainfall. This is
particularly significant given the rapid growth projected for Brisbane
and South-East Queensland (see chapter 5). Hobart may have a few
more very hot days, but the impacts are likely to be less severe – the
initial conditions do not make Hobart as vulnerable to other Australian
cities and the city is not anticipated to grow like other cities. The
increased risk of bushfire is, like in all Australian cities, a major concern
in Hobart. The likely scenarios for Adelaide include increased temperatures and reduced rainfall, which is likely to be a major concern given
Adelaide's existing poor quality drinking water and the likelihood of
greater temperature increases, less rainfall and higher rates of evaporation in the inland areas of Australia. There is 51 per cent diversion of
water from the Murray–Darling Basin, mostly for irrigation, which
means that unless more water is returned to this basin, climate change
is likely to have a profound impact on Adelaide (National Land and
Water Resources Audit, 2002). Having said this, it is important to note
that the uncertainties in the modelling are very significant, and further
research is required (see Australian State of the Environment
Committee, 2001)

The one city where there appears to be more agreement about the
likely impacts of climate change is Perth, which is particularly vulnerable to climate change. Predictions for south-west Western Australia are
for a significantly warmer and drier climate than at present, which is
coming on top of a decline in rainfall of between 5 and 10 per cent
during the period 1910–1999 (Australian State of the Environment
Committee, 2001). The average annual temperature is anticipated to

rise by 0.4 to 2.0 degrees Celsius by 2030, and by 1 to 6 degrees Celsius by 2070, with only slightly less warming along the coast. Perth currently has an average of 15 days per year where the maximum temperature exceeds 35 degrees Celsius, but this is anticipated to increase to between 16 and 22 days by 2030 and between 18 and 39 days by 2070. While these high maximums are generally summer temperatures, the warming is expected to be greatest in the spring months, with autumn and winter rainfall to each decline by 20 per cent and evaporation rates expected to increase with temperature rises (Foster, 2002). This scenario is daunting for a city where surface water supplies in the hills zone east of Perth are already extensively developed and there has been an increase of 205 per cent in groundwater use in Western Australia (including irrigation areas) between 1983–84 and 1996–97 (National Land and Water Resources Audit, 2002). Extensive mining of groundwater for short-term use is unsustainable and risky given that the cumulative effects of groundwater depletion are not fully known. The anticipated growth in population, combined with more hot days, higher evaporation rates, increased risk of bushfire, more people exposed to the risk of bushfire and the probability of severe water shortages make Perth very vulnerable to the impacts of climate change.

THE CITIES FOR CLIMATE PROTECTION™ PROGRAM

Given the severity of the threat, what is being done to address it? There are a number of programs in government and business that are being run to address issues of climate change in various sectors of the economy. They include the Mandatory Renewable Energy Target which aims to achieve an additional 9500 gigawatt hours (the equivalent of 1000 million watts being used for an hour) of electricity generation from (mostly) new renewable energy sources by 2010, and the excise exemption for ethanol fuel. At the time of writing, the first of these schemes is under threat and the phase-out of the second is scheduled to commence in 2008. Some programs – such as Challenge and the various Green Power schemes run by energy retailers – are voluntary. Most greenhouse response programs are under-funded and of varying levels of effectiveness, especially given Australia's rising levels of greenhouse emissions.

One program worth exploring in greater depth is Cities for Climate Protection™ (CCPTM), which is coordinated and supported by the Australian Greenhouse Office and the International Council for Local Environmental Initiatives (ICLEI). CCPTM has been operating in

Australia since 1998. As of December 2002, the program included 164 councils representing 65 per cent of Australia's population. The program is very advanced in Australia, where there is about 30 per cent of the total world participation in CCPTM and more councils at Milestone 5 (implementation and monitoring) than in any other country (Australian Greenhouse Office and ICLEI, 2003). Australia also leads the way in the creation of a new category (see table 9.2), beyond the Milestone 5 category, for those councils willing to extend their commitment to addressing climate change issues beyond the best practice currently identified at the international level. The important contribution and leadership of urban councils in this program can also be seen in table 9.2, particularly in the coverage of population where the urban councils generally contain larger populations than the rural councils in each state.

The effectiveness of CCPTM is open to some question, but only in terms of its total impact within Australia's total greenhouse gas emission scenarios. Local councils working through the program have reduced their carbon dioxide equivalent emissions by 225 500 tonnes in 1999–2000, by 343 000 tonnes in 2000–01 and by 664 600 tonnes in 2001–02 (Australian Greenhouse Office and ICLEI, 2003). This reduction is significant and worthwhile, but must be kept in perspective rela-

Table 9.2 The state of the Cities for Climate Protection™ Program in Australia as of 2002

STATE/TERRITORY	NSW	Vic	Qld	WA	SA	Tas	ACT	NT
% of population in CCP council areas	61	75	69	74	69	23	100	25
No. of CCP councils	48	41	21	32	16	3	1	2
No. of rural councils	19	16	13	5	1	2	0	1
No. of urban councils	29	25	8	27	15	1	1	1
% rural	39.6	39	61.9	15.6	6.3	66.7	0	50
% urban	60.4	61	38.1	84.4	93.8	33.3	100	50
M4 councils	6	3	0	5	9	1	1	0
M5 councils	3	7	3	2	2	0	0	0
CCP Plus councils	3	6	3	2	1	1	0	0

Notes: M4: Implement the action plan. M5: Monitor and report on greenhouse gas emissions savings. CCP Plus: Promote community involvement in greenhouse emissions savings.
Source: Compiled from Australian Greenhouse Office, 2003

tive to Australia's total emissions, which vary depending on the accounting system used and particularly if land clearing is included. Measuring greenhouse gas emissions as millions of tonnes of carbon dioxide equivalent, for the period 1990–2000, Australia's greenhouse gas emissions increased by 16.9 per cent (Australian State of the Environment Committee, 2001).This means that urgent and major improvements are needed, particularly in relation to energy policies, and the CCPTM model is potentially a useful one for other sectors to follow.

SUMMARY

There are a number of atmospheric issues that are important for the sustainability of Australian cities. These issues are often generated by activities in urban areas which, given their impacts, must be considered unsustainable. This chapter has explored outdoor air quality issues, the occurrence of ozone depletion and the causes, impacts and a few actions being taken to address the issue of climate change. Australian cities have, for the most part, moved away from an image of the 'dirty old town' of the early Industrial Revolution, but they are increasingly reliant on coal-fired power sourced from outside of their boundaries. This may contribute to the city appearing to be clean, but the environmental impacts are felt elsewhere and the use of coal is a major contributor to climate change. Unfortunately, as Graham-Taylor (2002) has identified in relation to Perth, issues of air quality are often the subject of myths designed to promote tourism to our 'clean and green' country. It is sometimes hard to appreciate the extent of photochemical smog affecting our cities if we are standing in Rundle Street Mall in Adelaide or Murray Street Mall in Perth, but anybody viewing the city from the Adelaide Hills or Greenmount in Perth early on a summer afternoon should need little convincing that Australian cities have growing air quality problems. In terms of sustainable cities, it is our invisible impacts on levels of stratospheric ozone and the combination of greenhouse gases in the troposphere that undermine myths about Australian cities. Our activities are unsustainable. The projected increased frequency of hot days and the likelihood of more energy use through air conditioning (thereby creating more greenhouse gas emissions under current energy scenarios) is a cycle of unsustainability. Fortunately, there are meaningful actions being taken today, but more urgent and significant changes are needed.

CHAPTER 10

BIODIVERSITY

INTRODUCTION

The term 'biodiversity', also expressed as 'biological diversity', refers to
the stock and variety of all life forms, including species, genetic material and ecosystems. As such, biodiversity is an all encompassing concept
that privileges a scientific (that is, biological and ecological) perspective
of nature over other possible perspectives, such as spiritual, aesthetic or
resource ones. This scientific perspective is often extended into a
resource perspective, as in the idea of conserving the biodiversity of
rainforests because they may provide medicines for human health, and
of course corporate profit. As noted in the 1998 WA State of the
Environment Report, 'biodiversity underpins the economy and ecological processes that are vital to human health and survival and the continued evolution of life on Earth' (Western Australia Department of
Environment, 1998, 19).

Biodiversity is important because it is the basis of life support
systems. Without biodiversity, natural processes would not operate as
they do now. As the NSW National Parks and Wildlife Service has
noted, 'maintaining biodiversity is ... an essential part of ecologically
sustainable development' (National Parks and Wildlife Service NSW,
2001, 7). It is one of the three core objectives of the National Strategy
for Ecologically Sustainable Development (Ecologically Sustainable
Development Steering Committee, 1992).

This chapter explores the important relationship between biodiversity and science, before looking at the history of biodiversity policy
making in Australia. This is followed by an overview of biodiversity
issues and approaches to biodiversity conservation in each of Australia's
largest cities. The chapter concludes by investigating some possible
actions that may contribute to both the retention and restoration of
biodiversity in Australian cities.

BIODIVERSITY AND SCIENCE

There are various claims about the extent of biodiversity loss, and the significance of any loss. Yencken and Wilkinson (2000) and Healey (2001) identify the biodiversity of Australia and the actual and potential losses. The statistics are staggering: 618 endangered species, 824 vulnerable species and 118 extinct species (Healey, 2001, 5).

One of the problems, however, of the biodiversity research is the inadequacy of the science. While not disputing the above statistics, which mainly comprise the larger species that have been studied in more detail, in Australia this limitation is most apparent when we move beyond mammals, reptiles and birds to consider fungi (5 per cent of an estimated 160 000 species have been described) and bacteria (0.1 per cent of an estimated 40 000 species have been described) (cited in Yencken and Wilkinson, 2000). If nature was a series of compartments, the loss of large numbers of species may be a loss in diversity, and it may include a loss of species that we favour. There would, however, be no interconnections and therefore no cumulative impacts in ecosystems of any loss. Nature does not work this way.

The inadequacy of our science is a cause for concern. Despite research, we still often do not know what we are losing and at what rate compared to the normal background rate of species extinction. The 1996 Australian State of the Environment Report suggested that 'the loss of biodiversity is perhaps our most serious environmental problem' (State of the Environment Advisory Council, 1996a, 8 (executive summary)). This scientific and policy analysis is somewhat at odds with popular perception of environmental and sustainability issues in Australia. Using Australian Bureau of Statistics surveys, Lothian (2002) has traced the environmental concerns of Australians from 1992 to 1999. 'Biodiversity' is not used as a term, hence indicating its lack of traction outside of scientific, policy-making and environmental activism groups. The closest category (which is woefully inadequate) was 'destruction of trees and ecosystems'. This environmental concern declined in each successive survey, from a high of 32.8 per cent in 1992 to 21.1 per cent in 1999 (Lothian, 2002). There is a significant gap between scientific and popular perceptions on biodiversity, thus making it difficult to address a particular aspect of biodiversity conservation, that is, urban biodiversity.

There is another important gap within much of the scientific and popular literature on biodiversity, habitats and cities. This is the perception that cities necessarily reduce all forms of biodiversity, and that 'the environment' is the area of wildlife outside of cities. As Low (2002) has demonstrated, cities support many forms of wildlife, partly because animals adapt to the structures provided by cities. A few examples provided by Low (2002) include peregrine falcons using bridges and high-rise buildings for their nests, swallows using telephone wires rather than trees from which to observe and hunt prey, and the green and golden bellfrog occupying the polluted Brickpit at Homebush in Sydney. While it is clear that cities directly and indirectly contribute to biodiversity loss, it is also the case that they provide habitats and food for particular species. As Low (2002) has correctly identified, cities are not places of no nature, they are places of a new nature.

Finally, the most urgent gap to be filled by scientific research is, arguably, the relationship between biodiversity and climate change (see chapter 9). The existence and likelihood of greater climate change is crucial for biodiversity. Changes such as hotter temperatures, less rainfall, higher evaporation rates, greater intensity of cyclones and larger areas of flood inundation will have (depending on specific locations) significant impacts on vegetation growth, breeding, the carrying capacity of different regions and the likelihood of species being destroyed by sudden events.

AUSTRALIA AND BIODIVERSITY

The idea of biodiversity came to prominence at the United Nations Conference on Environment and Development in Rio de Janeiro in 1992. The Convention on Biological Diversity was one of five major documents signed at the conference. Australia was one of the signatories to the Convention. The Convention has since been ratified by 176 countries, including Australia on 18 June 1993 (Australian and New Zealand Environment and Conservation Council, 1996b; Healey, 2001).

In Australia, the Commonwealth government developed the National Strategy for the Conservation of Australia's Biological Diversity in 1992. Various Australian states have also developed biological conservation strategies. Some of these strategies, for example in Victoria, include a specific section on urban biodiversity, while others such as those in New South Wales do not (see National Parks and Wildlife Service NSW, 1999). The conservation of biodiversity in Australia is particularly important because of the number of endemic species (that is, those species that occur naturally only in Australia). For example, 93 per cent of frogs, 90 per cent of freshwater fish, 89 per cent of reptiles, 85 per cent of flowering plants, 84 per cent of mammals and 45 per cent of Australian birds are endemic. These percentages in themselves are crucial, but when combined with the realisation that Australia is a developed and politically stable country (unlike many of the other biodiverse-rich countries in the world), this makes our position unique.

Discussions about biodiversity in Australia tend to focus on 'the bush'. For example, Hutton and Connors (1999) in a section on biodiversity refer mainly to the campaigns for World Heritage-listing and to arid lands and rangelands. The only urban component of this discussion was the campaign for World Heritage-listing of the Blue Mountains area west of Sydney. This campaign was successful with the announcement in December 2000 at the 24th Session of the World Heritage Committee meeting in Cairns that over one million hectares of land had been inscribed on the World Heritage List. Yencken and Wilkinson (2000) take a broader perspective, referring to land, water and urban biodiversity issues. This broader perspective is important because it is too easy to overlook urban biodiversity issues (see EPA NSW, 2000).

AUSTRALIA'S LARGEST CITIES AND BIODIVERSITY

The locations of Australia's largest cities coincide with areas of biodiversity. It is no accident that these areas were generally higher in the density of Aboriginal settlement. The biodiversity supported gathering and hunting cultures.

Simply put, the contribution of cities to biodiversity loss encompasses three components. These are the stock of biodiversity within the actual city boundaries, the loss of biodiversity in the hinterland of the city, and the ecological footprint of the city that is responsible for biodiversity loss in areas well beyond the city.

The reality is more complex, as it is the 'zone of influence' of urban (and often suburban or exurban development) that changes the biodiversity of an area and the near hinterland (Odell, et al, 2003). This zone of influence is the impact of human activities, including automobile traffic, night lights and the increase in cat and dog population. The outward expansion of Australian cities, both physically and in their activities such as weekend vacations to nearby towns, impacts on biodiversity.

SYDNEY

Taking each of the five major Australian cities in turn, beginning with the largest, it is apparent that Sydney is crucial for biodiversity, but has experienced substantial biodiversity loss over the past 200 or more years. That loss is continuing. The Sydney Region contains over 2000 vascular, or higher-order, endemic plant species, which is more than the entire Great Britain (which contains 1600 species) (cited in Healey, 2001). Bridgman et al (1995) highlight the loss of vegetation and wetlands in the first 200 years of European settlement in the Sydney Region. Blue gum forests had declined from 11 000 hectares in 1788 to less than a hectare in 1988. The decline in turpentine-ironbark was even greater, from 35 000 hectares to less than a hectare over the same period (in Bridgman, et al, 1995). The demise of the Cumberland Plain woodland, from an estimated 107 000 hectares in 1788 to 6 hectares in 1988 (Bridgman, et al, 1995) is significant given the battle to save the ADI site (see box 10.1 below). These figures are disputed by Druce (2001), but the same general trend of decline is noted. For example, Druce (2001, 63) claims that there were originally 122 634 hectares of Cumberland Plain woodland, with 10 832 hectares remaining, of which only 217.8 are in conservation reserves.

Little (2001) noted that the Sydney urban area, as defined by census collection districts, grew from 1524 square kilometres in 1991 to 1615 square kilometres in 1996, which, after adjustments for accuracy, equals about an increase of 1380 hectares per year. This is mostly in the west, south-west and north-west. The expansion of Sydney directly affects agricultural land and biodiversity on remnant bushland in the Sydney Region. Only 5 per cent of native vegetation remains in Western Sydney (a key site of urban growth), and only about 20 per cent of that remaining native vegetation is protected in reserves (Kravchenko, 2001). About 30 per cent of known native species in the Sydney Region are designated as threatened or vulnerable (Kravchenko, 2001), and as previously noted about the inadequacies of our science, we do not even know what we are losing and how important that loss may be.

The loss of biodiversity would be greater if not for the efforts of largely volunteer conservation groups. The Ryde–Hunters Hill Flora and Fauna Preservation Society has been instrumental in the protection and regeneration of the Field of Mars Reserve in Ryde. This area contains, in addition to small mammals, reptiles, frogs and birds, a small remnant of turpentine-ironbark that was once in abundance in the Sydney Region. Another example of the important work done by volunteer conservation groups is the Blue Mountains Wildplant Rescue Service. This group rescues plants before they are destroyed by bulldozers, and cares for them until the plants can be sold and replanted by organisations such as the Roads and Traffic Authority, State Rail and bush regeneration groups (Woodford, 2003). The Blue Mountains is an area of high biodiversity, such that remnant bush in urban areas have been known to support as many as 500 plants of 61 different species on a single home site (Woodford, 2003). The protection of biodiversity cannot be achieved by largely volunteer groups rescuing plants for replanting elsewhere. The World Heritage status for the Blue Mountains will, hopefully, offer a better framework for the protection of biodiversity in this part of the Sydney Region.

Box 10.1 The Australian Defence Industries (ADI) site

The Australian Defence Industries (ADI) site is 1500 hectares of land that was formerly owned by the Commonwealth government. It is located in Western Sydney, in the local government areas of Blacktown and Penrith. The site is significant because of the biodiversity. It is the last remaining significant area of Cumberland Plain woodland in Sydney, and hence the world. Kangaroos and emus inhabit the site. It was listed for preservation by the Australian Heritage Commission in 1999.

The site is a significant battle over preservation versus urban development. The social status of the western suburbs, in contrast with the wealthier eastern and northern suburbs of Sydney, was emphasised by environmentalists campaigning to preserve the ADI site. At the 2001 federal election, the Save the ADI Site Party contested a small number of seats in Western Sydney, and the Prime Minister's seat of Bennelong on the wealthy north shore of Sydney Harbour, to highlight the issue. Under pressure, the Howard government agreed to save more of the site, but over 40 per cent of the site is still proposed for urban development. If this occurs, the fragmentation of the site, plus the impact of introduced animals and plants, will likely impact heavily on the biodiversity and preservation value of the portions of the ADI site that are not intended for urban development. While out of the media spotlight at the moment, the battle to preserve the entire ADI site continues.

MELBOURNE

There have been numerous studies of biodiversity in Melbourne (see McDonnell, Williams and Kahs, 1999, for an overview). In Melbourne the loss of biodiversity includes some 70 plant species already extinct, with many others listed as rare, threatened or endangered (McDonnell, Williams and Kahs, 1999). Despite the loss of plants and wetlands, particularly in inner Melbourne, an incredible amount of biodiversity remains in the Greater Melbourne area. Some of this biodiversity has been enhanced by regeneration projects, such as in Organ Pipes National Park, which was originally declared for protection in 1972 to preserve geological formations but has since become an example of successful bush regeneration (Taylor, 1999).

Another site of immense biodiversity in Melbourne is the Western Treatment Plant, more popularly known as the Werribee Wetlands, which commenced as a sewage farm in 1897 (Low, 2002). It is now a Ramsar-listed wetland, which means that it is a wetland that is listed under the United Nations Convention on Wetlands of International Importance. In 1992 it was found to be first of 659 Victorian wetlands for the numbers and variety of waterfowl present (Low, 2002). The Werribee Wetlands is an example of human-created habitats that may not be appealing on many other environmental and aesthetic grounds, but have become a crucial site for birds.

BRISBANE

Brisbane is situated on the Brisbane River, near where it enters Moreton Bay. This bay is a Ramsar-listed wetland. It is a crucial site because it is 'where the faunas of northern and southern Australia meet' (Davie, et al, 1998, xvi). There are 'about 27 species' of animals and plants that are unique to Moreton Bay (Davie, et al, 1998, xvi). The inshore zone is high in species numbers, particularly around the mouth of the Brisbane River where the muddy sands provide suitable habitat for worms, molluscs and crustaceans that form part of ecosystems and food chains (Davie, et al, 1998).

While very important, Moreton Bay is not the only site of biodiversity richness in or near Brisbane. The Brisbane City Council introduced the 1998 Biodiversity Strategy with the aim of conserving natural areas (both publicly and privately owned) and managing threatening processes in a way that involves the community and improves knowledge (Barton, 2000). The Biodiversity Strategy is associated with the Bushland Preservation Levy, which is included as part of rates charges

(Brisbane City Council, 2004). As of 2000, $48 million raised from this levy had been spent to acquire 1588 hectares of land (Barton, 2000). Acquisitions include sections of the Toohey Forest, Belmont Hills Bushland and Brisbane Koala Bushlands (Brisbane City Council, 2004).

Brisbane is, however, the hub of a rapidly growing region known as South-East Queensland which covers 17 local government areas in addition to the Brisbane City Council. Land clearing and other impacts of urban growth mean that 58 per cent of Queensland's birds, 36 per cent of threatened fauna and 22 per cent of Queensland's plants which are listed as rare and threatened are found in South-East Queensland (Queensland Conservation Council, 2004). One of the most significant issues in South-East Queensland is the relationship between urban and future urban zonings, and the applicability of legislation to prevent the loss of biodiversity through the clearing of land. At present, land required for urban growth is not adequately zoned and planned to protect biodiversity.

PERTH

Perth is one city in which the loss of biodiversity, while significant, has been limited by foresight and planning. Perth was fortunate in that following European settlement at the Swan River colony in 1829, a significant area of bushland on Mount Eliza was retained as Kings Park. Similar to Queens Domain in Hobart, or the slightly more distant Belair National Park in Adelaide, these parks have proven to be excellent refuges for rare plants (Low, 2002). The park system was significantly improved by the Stephenson–Hepburn Report in 1955, which initiated the creation of regional parks, particularly around ocean beaches, rivers and river foreshores and areas of scenic value. Wetlands were largely overlooked in environmental planning, with market gardening and playing fields being the designated uses of a number of wetlands (Singleton, 1992). Subsequent plans have largely, if not accidentally, protected the environmental quality of parts of the Perth Metropolitan Region, thereby enabling the retention of biodiversity that would have otherwise been lost. The 1981 System 6 Study (the work for which was done during 1976–79) was important in providing a major conservation input into the urban planning system in Perth and led to the protection of many key environmental areas within the Perth Metropolitan Region (see Singleton, 1992).

These actions were sometimes followed up by local governments. For example, the City of Stirling Green Plan included recommendations to establish, widen and link bushland reserves to 'improve biological diversity of flora and fauna and to preserve the genetic repository of many species' (City of Stirling, 1992). In many cases, as in other Australian cities, community groups are working to conserve and manage urban remnant bushlands (see Stenhouse, 2001). One project that appears to offer potential for biodiversity conservation across a large part of the Perth Metropolitan Region is the Perth Biodiversity Project, which commenced in 1999 and involves state-level organisations and departments and all Perth metropolitan local governments (Perth Biodiversity Project, 2004). The focus of this project is on the numerous areas of remnant bushland that are outside the state-level protection system. The idea is to protect and manage these areas, and to link them with each other and with state protected areas of biodiversity whenever possible (Perth Biodiversity Project, 2004).

ADELAIDE

The Adelaide area is believed to have been the area of greatest biodiversity in South Australia prior to the arrival of Europeans (Bishop and Oliver, 2000). It is estimated that as a result of habitat variety in the Adelaide area, this 185000 hectares, or 0.15 per cent of South Australia, was home to 30 per cent of the state's terrestrial plants, 58 per cent of birds, 32 per cent of terrestrial mammals, 22 per cent of frogs and 20 per cent of both reptiles and freshwater fish (Bishop and Oliver, 2000). Today the Central Hills Face Zone, between Anstey Hill Conservation Park and Belair National Park, is the area where remnant vegetation is relatively unfragmented. While comprising only 5 per cent of Metropolitan Adelaide, this zone contains 25 per cent of the total remnant vegetation in Adelaide (Bishop and Oliver, 2000).

The focus of biodiversity conservation in Adelaide is the Urban Forest Biodiversity Program. This program involves mapping of vegetation change in the region using geographic information systems (GIS). The mapping of vegetation change, and land tenure, is crucial in order to understand what biodiversity has been lost, what remains and how protected is the remaining vegetation. In the case of Adelaide (similar to other Australian cities), much of the coastal plain biodiversity has been lost, significant biodiversity remains in the hills and some coastal mangroves, and the protection of this biodiversity is insufficient. As of 2000, 26 per cent of native vegetation in the Adelaide Metropolitan Region was formally reserved (a figure that was the second lowest of seven biodiversity planning regions in South Australia), 22 per cent is owned by government departments (mostly SA Water and Forestry SA) and 52 per cent (or 12014 hectares) are in private ownership (Bishop and Oliver, 2000). As with other Australian cities, the likelihood of further biodiversity loss is high. Fortunately, in the case of biodiversity conservation but not necessarily for other sustainability initiatives such as introducing green architecture, Adelaide's population growth and household formation is slower than other major Australian cities. This means relatively less development pressure, and the chance to at least reduce the extent of biodiversity loss in Adelaide.

BIODIVERSITY AND SUSTAINABILITY IN AUSTRALIAN CITIES

The major threats to biodiversity in urban areas include habitat loss through clearing for urban development, the intrusion of weeds, the presence of domestic pets that kill native fauna and the presence of feral animals including cats, dogs and foxes, which are now said to be in all the urban bushland reserves of Sydney (Urban Feral Animal Action Group, undated). Other threats to biodiversity include port activities impacting on Moreton Bay, with over 1000 ships using the Port of Brisbane each year, and a need for dredging to maintain the channel depth, thereby creating turbidity and affecting the water quality (Davie, et al, 1998).

Given the importance of biodiversity for sustainability, as identified earlier in this chapter, there are a number of measures that can be taken to influence biodiversity retention and restoration. Fallding (2001, 54–5) claims that 'ten top biodiversity planning principles apply irrespective of the planning scale'. His list is shown in box 10.2.

Box 10.2 Fallding's ten top biodiversity planning principles

1. Identify regional ecological context.
2. Protect communities, ecosystems and supporting processes.
3. Recognise habitat requirements of individual species.
4. Consider all natural areas not just those of highest value.
5. Minimise landscape fragmentation and site disturbance.
6. Promote native species.
7. Protect rare and ecologically important species.
8. Protect unique or sensitive environments.
9. Resolve compatibility of biodiversity with social and economic objectives.
10. Recognise and design for ongoing land management.

Source: Fallding, 2001, 54–5

Fallding's list is a very good start for protecting the existing biodiversity, and for regenerating biodiversity by the promotion of native species. The work of Tim Low (2002), while controversial for some environmentalists, highlights the possibility of non-native species and highly modified environments (including introduced structures such as buildings and telephone wires) being used by native species. At the same time, it is apparent that certain native species of trees and plants may attract some of the larger and aggressive birds. In planning for biodiversity, it is important to consider which particular species may need most careful management. While this may raise accusations of a 'green secular god', it is also clear that if we do not plan to protect and regenerate threatened or endangered endemic species, then extinction is a real possibility.

Planning for biodiversity conservation and restoration in urban areas is a major challenge. There is, fortunately, excellent work being done at present, and despite continued losses of biodiversity through urban expansion, the need to conserve biodiversity in order to become more sustainable is generally accepted. There is also important work being done in Victoria and other states about how to conserve the environment on private property. This issue of property rights and governance structures is crucial because, as has been noted in this chapter, the remnant biodiversity in many Australian cities is privately owned. While there have been additions to the national park and protected areas estate in New South Wales, it is apparent that creating new protected areas close to cities is going to be contentious and expensive to introduce and maintain in the long term. The conservation and restoration of biodiversity requires a range of strategies, including state protection and the enhancement of private protection where appropriate.

SUMMARY

Biodiversity is increasingly being recognised as a major issue for urban sustainability. Australia has a mixed performance on biodiversity conservation (partly due to land clearing in non-urban areas), but as has been demonstrated in this chapter, there are a number of wonderful examples of biodiversity conservation and regeneration. There are, unfortunately, still many threats to biodiversity. The nature of the biodiversity, its extent and the threats vary between cities in Australia. What is common to all cities is our inadequate knowledge about the impacts of climate change on biodiversity and the danger that we do not have adequate knowledge about what biodiversity exists, nor what it does, to even realise what we are losing or have lost. This situation calls for a sense of urgency, humility and caution in planning for other functions in Australia's largest cities.

SECTION 3

FUTURE
DIRECTIONS

This section of the book focuses on processes that are necessary to move Australian cities towards sustainability. The structure of this section has changed significantly during the writing of this book. Section 3 now comprises a single chapter on process and no chapters on the actions each city must take to achieve sustainability. This is because many actions have been suggested throughout the book, and would simply be repeated in different permutations in a chapter located here. Perhaps more importantly, specific actions will become dated as the temporal context changes and new ideas and technology emerge. Bold ideas are needed, critical analysis is required, and situational thinking is necessary to translate ideas so they are appropriate in specific places. Getting the processes operating effectively can enable ongoing learning and improvement in both process and outcomes. Moving towards sustainability is necessarily, therefore, a heuristic process.

CHAPTER 11

PROCESSES FACILITATING SUSTAINABLE CITIES IN AUSTRALIA

INTRODUCTION

Moving towards sustainability is a journey. Yencken and Wilkinson (2000) captured the concept beautifully in the title of their book, *Resetting the Compass*. As the previous ten chapters of this book have highlighted, in relation to Australian cities the compass has already been reset a number of times, but we need to do it again. Given time, a change of one degree can make an enormous, but perhaps insufficient, difference to where we go. The challenge is to reset the compass sufficiently so that we head in the required direction and are accompanied by many fellow travellers.

Unlike in the past where the modernist blueprint plan was prepared and implemented by professionals, we need to have a clear idea of our target, and then to work creatively in an ongoing process on the detail of how to reach that target. This is a heuristic approach that is based on social learning, incorporating feedback into planning and management, and a form of incrementalism in the lived daily lives of people and how we address the details of sustainability.

The target is to make Australian cities more sustainable. This means moving away from the vortex city to a city that exhibits greater self-reliance on a range of key environmental issues such as water, food, waste and energy. This greater self-reliance must be achieved in conjunction with the protection of biodiversity and the improvement of air and water quality. This is no small ask.

The establishment of specific targets and how these targets are to be met will vary from city to city. These processes will be very challenging, for these reasons: not everybody is interested in becoming more sustainable; there is a lack of education and awareness in some parts; some people are currently benefiting from unsustainable practices and can be expected to resist sustainability initiatives. Linking product and process so that ecologically meaningful outcomes can be achieved is very challenging.

This chapter begins by identifying the key process requirements that have been suggested by other authors. It then looks at the scale and process of change, the importance of leadership and of champions and the potential for community-based actions. The following section explores the conflict between statutory plans and the discourse of certainty versus the need for flexibility in planning sustainable cities. The final section investigates sustainability education and how it relates to values, beliefs and actions. Moving towards sustainability requires the willing cooperation of many people. It cannot be achieved by an elite group of planners, designers and 'ideas people'. Even the best planned city that is appropriate for its context will be unsustainable if people adopt unsustainable lifestyles.

PRINCIPLES, PROCESSES AND STRATEGIES

A number of authors have outlined process suggestions for moving towards sustainability or for making cities throughout the world more sustainable. Some of these suggestions are very context-specific and do not translate easily into the Australian situation, but others are potentially appropriate in contemporary Australia. The following section of this chapter summarises the work of four Australian-authored texts: Newman and Kenworthy (1999), Yencken and Wilkinson (2000), Cocks (2003) and Connor and Dovers (2004). The following sections of the chapter build on this work and focus on specific items that need to be addressed in order to improve sustainability.

Newman and Kenworthy (1999) offer four 'new' (this point is debatable) principles for professional praxis to promote sustainable urban change. These principles are recognising values, maximising diversity, crossing boundaries and facilitating organic processes. Recognising values includes at least six core values that matter to a city, namely, the environment, social justice, heritage, the public realm, the urban economy and community matters. Maximising diversity is basically a goal that, if implemented successfully, improves the resilience of a city. Crossing boundaries includes crossing non-ecologically aligned political boundaries in favour of a bioregional approach (see chapter 3 of this book), and crossing academic disciplinary boundaries. Finally, facilitating organic processes includes valuing and restoring natural processes within cities, and encouraging community-based processes to shape our cities.

Yencken and Wilkinson (2000), in discussing sustainability at the national level in Australia, have provided six reasons why current policies will not achieve ecological sustainability. In summary these reasons are:

- Existing policies do not deal comprehensively with the identified problems.
- Many programs are inadequately resourced and implemented.
- There is no effective legislative or administrative base.
- Existing policies have not seriously begun to tackle the issues of population/consumption/technology, energy and material flows/wastes.
- There is a lack of systematic monitoring, feedback and changing of programs where necessary.
- '[T]here have been very few unambiguous successes in reversing adverse environmental trends' (Yencken and Wilkinson, 2000, 314).

Following from this analysis, Yencken and Wilkinson (2000, 315) advocate 'two ways forward, both of which are important'. These are to improve the existing programs following their evaluation, and to 'recast the whole strategic direction of environmental policy by setting purposeful targets for all key aspects of environmental degradation' (Yencken and Wilkinson, 2000, 315). In short, the approach is to build on successes and to set clear targets whilst leaving the details of their achievement to the creative processes of those people responsible for meeting the targets.

Cocks (2003, 214) has identified four main challenges for humans to move towards what he called a 'deep future'. These four challenges are:

- nursing the world through endless change
- raising the quality of social learning
- confronting near-future threats and opportunities
- anticipating deep-future challenges.

Cocks (2003), drawing on authors such as Anthony Giddens, has also offered useful insights on institutional and social change. These include the potential for institutional change to occur slowly through purposive individual actions, and rapidly at a time of crisis. Institutions often change superficially as an initial response to a major problem, but then are faced with the dilemma of resorting to tradition or following the stated ideals of the institution (Cocks, 2003). For Cocks, the hope for the future appears to come from education that develops a population which wants to learn, has a love of knowledge, is curious, accepts the need for ongoing change, values collective action and has a low dependency on tradition as a source of beliefs. This is the type of society that is more likely to recognise and confront the threats and opportunities posed by new technologies, new scientific discoveries, the accumulative impact of urbanisation processes, and so on.

Connor and Dovers (2004) emphasise that despite the deep and diverse roots of ecological sustainability, the concept was only clearly articulated in 1987 by the World Commission on Environment and Development and was stated as an international and national policy agenda for the first time at the Earth Summit in Rio De Janeiro in 1992. They argue that today there is not a shared vision of a sustainable future, and that such a vision is unlikely to occur. Given this context, Connor and Dovers emphasise the need for institutional change. They provide case studies of a number of examples of institutional change, including the introduction of the *Resource Management Act 1991* in New Zealand. This example is particularly pertinent for the current discussion because it highlights that attempting to address sustainability concerns is far more complex than simply tinkering with traditional forms of environmental management or urban planning. This means that social investment in education, training and human resource management is necessary. The New Zealand example is also relevant because '[although] no perfect set of rules and institutional arrangements can be created for achieving sustainability ... attempts must be made and adaptation anticipated' (Connor and Dovers, 2004, 128). The *Resource Management Act* has been the subject of five amendment acts, which comprise 191 pages addressing 369 sections of the legislation (Connor and Dovers, 2004).

All of these, and no doubt many other, authors have something to offer in thinking about sustainable cities in Australia. This book has highlighted the history of Australian cities and the ideas that may have influenced the development of these cities. It has also identified and explained important issues that must be addressed in Australian cities in order to make these cities more sustainable. Each chapter in section 2 of the book has offered ideas on how to move towards sustainability. This chapter, drawing on the above authors, emphasises that the suggestions made to date should eventually become dated, and hopefully, superceded, if we get the change processes working well. While the development of specific ideas and policies for each of Australia's five major cities is necessary, these policies and their implementation will very much depend on institutional structures, the quality of leadership that is available, and the support and involvement of many people who are educated to recognise, address and respond to sustainability challenges.

THE SCALE AND PROCESS OF CHANGE

How should we be thinking about the process of moving towards sustainability? In the first instance it needs to be recognised as a process. As Yencken and Wilkinson (2000) have noted, having clearly defined targets is useful, although Connor and Dovers (2004) are correct in recognising that developing a shared sustainability vision (and hence targets) is very difficult. What are the implications for who sets the targets and who is impacted in the quest to meet the targets? How ecologically meaningful will the targets be if there needs to be widespread agreement about these targets?

These questions could easily lead to the dilution of targets. This may be politically acceptable, but from an ecological perspective targets must be consistent with the seriousness of the problem, meaning that the establishment of easily achievable targets with insufficient ecological worth should be avoided. The setting of such targets requires the integration of scientific knowledge, an understanding of history, the application of values and ethics, and an understanding of the processes of change.

The dilemma for many environmentalists is that the timing and scale of change necessary for sustainability appear beyond the rate of change, and the amount of change, that many other members of society are willing, and able, to undertake. This requires environmental education (as discussed below) and an awareness of political processes so that environmentalists can act ethically and effectively. Unlike Marxists, for whom history appeared to be on their side and the contradictions in capitalism would inevitably lead to socialism and then communism, many environmentalists perceive that time is not on their side. Among the more radical environmentalists, there is a sense that much has been and continues to be lost. For other environmentalists, population growth is closely linked to environmental decline, and the world's and Australia's population continues to grow. The sense of loss is a strong trope in this part of the environmental movement. The risk is that many non-environmentalists will perceive environmentalists as being the 'prophets of doom' (see McCormick, 1995).

By way of contrast, approaches that emphasise hope, the efficacy of human action, and even the potential to economically profit while assisting environmental conservation or restoration, are likely to be viewed more favourably by non-environmentalists. While there may be a tendency for the more optimistic environmentalists to include so-called environmental sceptics (Lomborg, 2001), self-proclaimed 'free market environmentalists' (Simon, 1994) and major business groups who may want limited changes, these approaches can include the work of people who are advocating significant changes. For example, David Suzuki's recent coauthored book (Suzuki and Dressel, 2003) was titled *Good News for A Change*, while the potential for major reductions in energy and resource use have been advocated by von Weizsacker, Lovins and Lovins (1997) in their book *Factor Four: Doubling Wealth-Halving Resource Use.*

What does this suggest about the processes of change? First, it is necessary to inform people of the importance and the current status of an issue, even though this may not be what many people want to hear. In doing so, it is necessary to be aware of the dangers of debilitation, or the 'party on because we're all going to die' attitude. An example of sustainability discourse that represents this step was the Secretary-General of the United Nations, Kofi Annan's, *Millennium Report*. He wrote:

> [W]e must face up to an inescapable reality: the challenges of sustainability simply overwhelm the adequacy of our responses. With some honorable exceptions our responses are too few, too little and too late. (Annan, 2000, 56)

Second, as a number of authors have observed, the processes and rates of change are largely evolutionary in nature (Newman and Kenworthy, 1999; Yencken and Wilkinson, 2000; Cocks, 2003; Connor and Dovers, 2004). Cocks (2003) identifies periods of political instability where revolutionary change is possible, but this approach does not easily build on social learning, and mistakes are likely to be magnified. While evolutionary rather than revolutionary change is the most likely scenario for moves towards sustainability, an educated society with high levels of ecological literacy is likely to be able to move more rapidly towards sustainability, with fewer mistakes along the way. This move can be facilitated by leaders and champions who themselves possess critical thinking skills, openness to change and a desire to include others in a shared project.

LEADERS AND CHAMPIONS

Leadership is crucial for the move towards sustainability. By leadership I mean people with vision who are able to initiate and manage change processes, and in doing so be recognised as leaders who take other people on the journey towards sustainability.

Leadership, in this sense of the term, is not about having a title (although it may help), nor legal power (again, it is useful), nor about administration (which is very necessary to be done by someone). Leadership is sometimes conflated with 'top-down' approaches, and judged by some environmentalists, community activists, and so on, to be an imposition on grassroots organising and community action. There is no doubt that this can easily occur, especially when people in positions of authority do not respect other individuals and communities. Leadership of government departments, educational institutions, environmental organisations and community groups can, however, make the workings of a group or organisation more effective and empower the members and other people. If this leadership is focused on sustainability issues, and in this case, urban sustainability issues given that this is where most Australians live, then it can make a difference.

Leadership and communities are compatible, even though in this chapter they have been addressed in different sections. What varies between 'top-down' impositions and popular local leadership is the style of leadership, the values of grassroots democracy and the conceptions of power (that is, power held through positions and titles or power derived from performance and in trust from people). Geographically based communities and communities of interest can benefit from leadership in their own organisations, but also from effective leadership at other levels ranging from the global to local government. Local urban sustainability is often facilitated by the global conferences and agreements that are then passed into law at the national and state levels in Australia.

Champions differ from leaders in that while they are high-profile people (unlike some leaders) who may be leaders in other fields of endeavour, champions are people who 'lend' their name and image to promote a cause. In the late 1990s, Australian Rules football coach Mick Malthouse and fashion designer Liz Davenport were both important in the battle to prevent the logging of old-growth forests in south-west Western Australia. The support of champions can help to attract media attention, provide legitimacy and galvanise politicians and other decision-makers to change policies, plans and institutional arrangements. The support of champions is also often important for community and grassroots activists who may be experiencing the slog that is a necessary part of most campaigns.

COMMUNITY AND GRASSROOTS ACTIVISM

The term 'community' often has positive connotations. Williams (1983, 76) has observed that community, 'unlike all other terms of social organization ... never seems to be used unfavourably, and never to be given any positive or opposing term'. Even allowing for the sectarian use of the term 'community' in cities such as Belfast, and the increasing tendency of government and developers to portray communities as embodying nimbyism, it appears that Williams' observation remains substantially accurate 20 years later.

This is important for sustainability because many theories of organising, governance and the implementation of sustainability are based on community and local areas, local governments and grassroots citizenship. As was noted in chapter 3, the implementation of Agenda 21 (which is derived from the global-level policy of the United Nations) required the development of Local Agenda 21 by local governments. From a different perspective, notions of bioregionalism focus on local autonomy and the principle of subsidiary – that is, enabling decisions to be made at the lowest possible level. Other, more design-oriented approaches to sustainable cities have focused on the development of community through the process of design and the creation of landscapes that often reflect the imagined communities of previous eras (for example, the work of some new urbanists).

Individuals and communities are crucial in the move towards sustainability. The actions of millions of local residents in saving water, reducing electricity consumption and walking and cycling rather than driving cars can improve sustainability, while conversely even the best designed and built city will not be sustainable if individuals and communities live unsustainable lifestyles. Communities are crucial because they provide local leadership, local role models and sometimes local 'police' in fostering cultures of sustainability, racism, apathy, greed, and so on.

For these reasons, the social learning that Cocks (2003) emphasises as being important for human survival is particularly important in communities. The problem, however, is not simply that it is lacking in communities, although in some traditional or dysfunctional communities it often is lacking, but that it is sometimes overwhelmed by other voices. In a study examining communities and planning in England between 1979 and 1996, a recurring relationship was found to exist between planners and communities in that planners generated community through adversity. As has been noted, 'the community formed is one based on opposition, rather than one based on creative desires. The focus and attributes emphasized in such a community may not be conducive to long-term progressive social relations' (McManus, 2001, 51).

The generation of communities of adversity may also result in the emergence of 'umbrella groups' that unite or at least help coordinate the work of isolated community groups who may be opposed to partic-ular development proposals. Save Our Suburbs Inc was incorporated on 23 January 1998 in Melbourne (Lewis, 1999). This organisation was formed to protect Melbourne suburbs, and the existing residents of those suburbs, from the increased densities (often achieved through the demolition of existing housing) being introduced across Melbourne. Similar organisations exist in other Australian cities.

In Sydney, the Protectors of Public Lands was formed in September 2001 as a coalition of community action groups, environ-mental organisations and local councils that works on a decision-making process of consensus (Protectors of Public Lands, 2003). This coalition attempts to prevent the sale or long-term lease of significant public lands to private developers, a process which has been occurring at all levels of government so that governments can appear fiscally responsible. The coalition lobbies on behalf of its member community groups, who continue to lead the campaign on their local site that is of public significance.

Technically-oriented readers may suggest that this emphasis on community and the ways in which communities can organise seems vague, but the acceptance of new technology, or so-called hard plan-ning and engineering solutions, is increasingly dependent on supportive communities who are receptive to change. A growing number of communities are demanding change in the form of a greater emphasis in planning and management on sustainability issues. Increasing the social capital of communities to respond to the challenges of sustainability is an important step in accelerating the rate of change so that it is ecologically meaningful but not socially destructive. Part of this challenge involves addressing the tensions between the need for certainty and the need for flexibility in order to move towards sustainability.

CERTAINTY, FLEXIBILITY AND SUSTAINABILITY

Sustainability involves uncertainty, and this is one state of mind that many people find difficult to accept. Politicians who are aware of this limitation may exploit it by promoting policies that are said to provide certainty. Many communities want certainty because they are worn down by the continual fighting and uncertainty about particular development proposals. Business advocates favour certainty because it enables them to make more long-term decisions. 'Certainty' is what the urban planning system provides through its statutory zoning schemes, whereas strategic policies and rolling five-year land release programs are designed to provide flexibility and quick responses to changing political-economic conditions.

Flexibility is what many corporations and government departments (including planning departments) have been aspiring to in recent years. Rapid changes in a city's competitiveness, in demographic shifts and in the external environment require rapid and effective responses. Much of the government restructuring of departments has been justified on the grounds of increasing flexibility and an increased ability to respond to new challenges as they arise.

Before specifically considering moving towards sustainability, it is useful to understand how tension between certainty and flexibility is currently being addressed in the planning of our cities. While there is variation between states, current planning practice often includes the use of statutory instruments and policy instruments, with the former providing certainty and the latter providing flexibility. To cite one example, the statutory plan for Perth is the 1963 Metropolitan Region Scheme (as amended), while state planning policies (which have no legal effect) provide the direction but also maintain a degree of flexibility in that they can be changed or updated as is considered necessary. Flexibility is also achieved by the use of a rolling five-year land release program, which is undertaken in accordance with the policies and with the statutory scheme. As is the situation in other Australian cities, this approach is generally efficient for managing urban growth, protecting those environments deemed most valuable, maintaining a high quality of life and managing short- and medium-term issues.

The tension between certainty and flexibility is crucial when we consider issues of sustainability because of the time frame and the type of knowledge involved. The longer time frames, in a rapidly changing world, means that our confidence in our ability to predict the future should be constrained. Whereas in the past urban planners identified trends, developed predictions with some degree of certainty and were often found to be wrong (see chapters 2 and 3 above), it is more likely that our knowledge about the future is 'possibilistic knowledge' (as Cocks, 2003, 225 refers to it). By this he means that we cannot be certain, or even speak with a sense of probability, about most aspects of the future: 'possibilistic knowledge in the form of scenarios is the only knowledge we can have about the future, especially the deep future' (Cocks, 2003, 225). In relation to sustainable cities in Australia, this implies that we need to be responsive to change, and that education for sustainability is vital in order to prepare future generations to face and respond to the sustainability challenges of their lifetime.

EDUCATION FOR SUSTAINABILITY

One of the frequently cited solutions for social and environmental problems is the need to provide education (see Palmer, 1998). The suggestion is almost trite, if it were not for the recognition that there are many different types of educational approaches and that some very important work has already been done in the fields of environmental and sustainability education. One key step is to move from seeing education as teaching to seeing it as learning. This move, and the progression from environment to sustainability (which integrates ecological, economic, social and cultural considerations), is reflected in the NSW Council on Environmental Education's (2001) *Learning for Sustainability* report.

When discussing education there are numerous questions to consider such as how, for what purpose, for who and by who. There is not the space here to engage in an exploration of all of these issues, but there are some key points to be made about sustainability education in Australia. First, it should be taught as part of formal education in the schools and tertiary education sectors. There are certain university degree programs, such as urban planning, architecture and engineering, where sustainability should be a keystone concept. There is little likelihood of the next generation of urban professionals having a positive influence and contribution on sustainability issues if they receive inadequate education in this area. There are many other degrees where sustainability should at least appear, in order to embed the concept in an educated society that is then prepared to address and respond to sustainability challenges. This approach is consistent with the Talloires Declaration of 1990 on sustainability in higher education (Bekessy, et al, 2003).

Education and learning for sustainability extends beyond formal schooling and tertiary institutions. The existence of field sites, interpretative centres and other forms of education outside of the classroom is crucial for learning in the environment, about the environment. It is part of a lifelong learning approach. It also fits in, but is not synonymous with, the more controversial approach of education for the environment. This latter form of education is acceptable, but it should be rigorous, comprehensive, based on scientific and critical thinking, and open to being challenged.

In the specific area of sustainable cities, Australia is fortunate that it does have educational institutions, professional associations, some museums and many other resources that can be mobilised to research, develop and educate about sustainable cities. These are the type of resources that can improve the sustainability of cities today, and educate the coming generations so that they can improve on our efforts.

SUMMARY

This chapter has addressed many of the 'soft' parts of sustainability, that is, the ongoing processes of education, community development, leadership, and so on. It would not have been too difficult to have devised specific actions that each of Australia's five largest cities must address in order to be considered more sustainable, but that approach is based on modernist thinking. There is no doubt that specific plans and actions are necessary, but importantly, who is to develop and implement them, is there a role for community action towards sustainability outside of government plans, and who is to judge their success or failure and to consider the lessons learned from this process?

In this chapter I have argued that increasing and improving education for sustainability is crucial in order to develop a constituency that is prepared to face hard challenges, can live with possibilistic knowledge and can respond creatively to sustainability issues. Many changes will be required in the coming years because moving towards sustainability is not merely a matter of adding another consideration to an ever lengthening list of boxes to tick. It requires a rethink of what we are doing, why we are doing it and how we are doing it. These are ongoing processes. Without them, as a society we will not move towards sustainability, neither in our cities nor in other parts of Australia.

CONCLUSION

Our urban future must become a more sustainable future, or else we eventually may not have a future at all. As has been highlighted in this book, Australia's largest cities face a number of crucial sustainability challenges. Many of these are with us today, some are just around the corner and others are not even on the radar screen at the moment. The challenges vary significantly between the major cities, but so does the capacity to meet these challenges. In Australia we are lucky compared to many other countries that clearly do not have the history, institutional capacity, resources and an educated populace to face and respond to these challenges.

This book has endeavoured to show how we have reached the current scenario of cities that are unsustainable. Sometimes this has occurred because of previous planning ideas that were implemented to improve our cities. Sustainable cities is, after all, the latest in a long tradition of social justice, aesthetic and technologically-oriented approaches that have aimed to address the perceived problems with cities and offer a better way into the future. It has been argued that we can learn from these previous attempts, develop a sense of humility about our current endeavours and yet respond with the urgency and commitment required to address the ecological sustainability concerns identified in this book.

This book has sought to provide an explanation of the ways in which Australia's five largest cities are unsustainable in relation to a number of important issues, and a compilation of a number of issue-specific suggestions and considerations of process that may be important in the future. It has been argued that the future of Australia, as with much of the world, is about the development of sustainable cities. This is crucial for the majority of Australians who will be living in cities, and particularly the metropolitan areas and 'greater regions' of the five largest cities. The development of sustainable cities is also very important for other parts of Australia, and the world, because Australian cities are ever expanding vortices that are increasingly reliant on the natural services provided within their hinterland and the 'distant elsewhere'. This is unsustainable.

Given the need to move from vortex cities to sustainable cities, it has been argued in this book that Australian cities will be more sustainable if they reduce their inputs from nature (both inside of and particularly from outside of the city) and their exports of waste back to nature, and at the same time protect ecosystems, biodiversity and the life support systems of nature that fall within urban boundaries. A number of suggestions have been included in this book as to how this may be achieved, but throughout the book the heuristic nature of social learning, responding to ecological feedback and incorporating it into decision-making has been emphasised. In other words, moving towards sustainability requires more than a 'product-based approach' to addressing the challenges facing our largest cities.

In the previous chapter it was argued that improving education for sustainability is crucial in order to develop a constituency that will face hard challenges, can live with possibilistic knowledge and respond creatively to sustainability issues. It was noted that sustainability generally, and sustainable cities as the subject of this particular book, requires a rethink of what we are doing, why we are doing it and how we are doing it. Further, it was recognised that these are ongoing processes. This book is a small, but hopefully influential, contribution to this ongoing dialogue.

REFERENCE LIST

Aberley, D, 1999, 'Interpreting bioregionalism: a story from many voices' in McGinnis, M (ed), *Bioregionalism*, Routledge, London, pp 13–42.

Albrecht, G, 2000, 'Rediscovering the Coquun: towards an environmental history of the Hunter River', address given to the River Forum 2000, Wyndham Estate, Hunter Valley.

—— 1998, 'Indicators of sustainability', paper presented to the Newcastle City Council Sustainability Indicators Project, 25 June 1998.

Alexander, I, 1994, 'DURD revisited? Federal policy initiatives for urban and regional planning 1991–94', *Urban Policy and Research*, 12 (1) 6–26.

—— 1986, 'Land use and transport planning in Australian cities: capital takes it all' in McLoughlin, B and Huxley, M (eds), *Urban Planning in Australia – Critical Readings*, Longman Cheshire, Melbourne, pp 113–30.

Alexander, I, and Houghton, S, 1995, 'New investment in Urban Public Transport 2: evaluation of the Northern Suburbs Railway in Perth', *Australian Planner*, 35 (2), 82–7.

Allen, D, 1999, 'Editorial: Industrial Ecology', *Environmental Progress*, 18 (1) 3.

Andrews, C, 1999, 'Putting Industrial Ecology into place: evolving roles for planners', *Journal of the American Planning Association*, 65 (4) 364–75.

Annan, K, 2000, *We the Peoples: The Role of the United Nations in the 21st Century (The Millennium Report)*, United Nations, New York.

Apps, D, 2003, 'Climate change warnings', *PM*, ABC radio transcript, updated 5 June 2003, accessed 8 December 2003, <www.abc.net.au/pm/content/2003/s873238.htm>.

AtKisson, A, 1999, *Believing Cassandra: An Optimist Looks at a Pessimist's World*, Scribe Publications, Melbourne.

Australasian Railway Association Inc, 2003, *Year Book and Industry Directory*, Australasian Railway Association Inc, Melbourne.

—— 2002, *Year Book and Industry Directory*, Australasian Railway Association, Inc, Melbourne.

—— 2001, *Year Book and Industry Directory*, Australasian Railway Association, Inc, Melbourne.

—— 2000, *Year Book and Industry Directory*, Australasian Railway Association, Inc, Melbourne.

—— 1999, *Year Book and Industry Directory*, Australasian Railway Association, Inc, Melbourne.

Australian Academy of Technological Sciences and Engineering, 1997, *Urban Air Pollution in Australia*, Australian Academy of Technological Sciences and Engineering, Parkville, Victoria.

Australian and New Zealand Environment and Conservation Council, 1996, *National Strategy for the Conservation of Australia's Biodiversity*, Department of the Environment, Sport and Territories, Canberra.

Australian Bureau of Statistics, 2004a, *Population up in Capital City Fringes and the Coast*, Publication 3218.0, Australian Bureau of Statistics, Canberra.

—— 2004b, *Year Book Australia: Population – How Many People Live in Australia's Coastal Areas*, Publication 1301.0, Australian Bureau of Statistics, Canberra.

—— 2003a, *Year Book Australia, 2003*, Australian Bureau of Statistics, Canberra.

—— 2003b, *Census of Population and Housing: Selected Social and Housing Characteristics*, Publication 2016.0, Australian Bureau of Statistics, Canberra.

—— 2003c, *Melbourne and Sydney Experience Largest Population Growth, but Brisbane Records the Fastest Growth*, Publication 3218.0, Australian Bureau of Statistics, Canberra.

—— 2003d, 'Transport: Special article – Environmental impacts of Australia's transport system' in *Year Book Australia, 2003*, Australian Bureau of Statistics, Canberra, pp 735–43.

—— 2001, *2001 Census of Population and Housing*, Australian Bureau of Statistics, Sydney.

—— 1999, *Household and Family Projections, Australia*, Publication 3236.0, Australian Bureau of Statistics, Canberra.

—— 1997, *Australian Transport and the Environment*, Publication 4605.0, Australian Bureau of Statistics, Canberra.

—— 1997, *Year Book Australia*, Australian Bureau of Statistics, Canberra.

—— 1996, *1996 Census of Population and Housing*, Australian Bureau of Statistics, Sydney.

Australian Greenhouse Office, 2004, *National Greenhouse Gas Inventory 2002*, Australian Greenhouse Office, Canberra.

—— 2003, *Climate Change: An Australian Guide to the Science and Potential Impacts*, Australian Greenhouse Office, Canberra.

—— 2002, *National Greenhouse Gas Inventory: Analysis of Trends and Greenhouse Indicators 1990 to 2000*, Australian Greenhouse Office, Canberra.

Australian Greenhouse Office and International Council for Local Environmental Initiatives (ICLEI), 2003, *Cities for Climate Protection*[TM] *Australia, 2002 Program Report*, Australian Greenhouse Office, Canberra.

Australian Population Institute, 2003, 'Apop: The Australian Population Institute Inc', last updated 15 September 2003, accessed 26 February 2004, <www.apop com.au>.

Australian State of the Environment Committee, 2001, *Australia State of the Environment 2001*, report to the Minister for the Environment and Heritage, CSIRO Publishing on behalf of the Department of Environment and Heritage, Canberra.

Australian Urban and Regional Development Review, 1995, *Timetabling for Tomorrow: An Agenda for Public Transport in Australia: Strategy Paper No 2*, Australian Urban and Regional Development Review, Canberra.

AVJennings Limited, 2003, Submission to the Productivity Commission, letter from Tim Redway to Gary Banks, 25 September 2003, <www.pc.gov.au/inquiry/housing/subs/sub035.pdf>.

Bachels, M, and Newman, P, 2001, 'Cities back on track: using a systems approach for sustainable city policy' in Laird, P, Newman, P, Bachels, M and Kenworthy, J, *Back on Track: Rethinking Transport Policy in Australia and New Zealand*, UNSW Press, Sydney, pp 133–55.

Badcock, B, 2002, *Making Sense of Cities: A Geographical Survey*, Arnold, London.

Badcock, B and Browett, M, 1992, 'Adelaide's heart transplant, 1970–88: the redeployment of capital in the renovation and redevelopment submarkets', *Environment and Planning A*, 24 (8) 1167–90.

Barton, A, 2000, 'Brisbane City Council Biodiversity Strategy', paper presented to Biodiversity in Urban Environments Conference, Adelaide, June 2000, last updated 2000, accessed 26 February 2004, <www.urbanforest.on.net/pdf/conference–Abarton.pdf>.

Beatley, T, 2000, *Green Urbanism: Learning from European Cities*, Island Press, Washington DC.

Beaverstock, J, Taylor, P and Smith, R, 1999, 'A roster of world cities', *Cities*, 16 (6) 445–58.

Bekessy, S, Burgman, M, Wright, T, Leal Filho, W and Smith, M, 2003, 'Universities and Sustainability', *Tela: Environment, Economy and Society*, Issue 11, Australian Conservation Foundation, Melbourne.

Bell, S and Morse, S, 2001, 'Breaking through the glass ceiling: who really cares about sustainability indicators?', *Local Environment*, 6 (3) 291–310.

—— 1999, *Sustainability Indicators: Measuring the Immeasurable*, Earthscan, London.

Berke, P, et al, 2003, 'Greening development to protect watersheds: does New Urbanism make a difference?', *Journal of the American Planning Association*, 69 (4) 397–413.

Birch, E, 2002, 'Five generations of the Garden City' in Parsons, K and Schuyler, D, (eds), *From Garden City to Green City: The Legacy of Ebenezer Howard*, John Hopkins University Press, Baltimore, pp 171–200.

Blowers, A, (ed), 1993, *Planning for a Sustainable Environment: A Report by the Town and Country Planning Association*, Earthscan, London.

Bold, WE, 1914, *Report of Tour Round the World*, Perth City Council, Perth.

Boyden, S, Millar, S, Newcombe, K and O'Neill, B, 1981, *The Ecology of the City and its People: The Case of Hong Kong*, ANU Press, Canberra.

Bradstock, R, Gill, A, Kenny, B and Scott, J, 1998, 'Bushfire risk at the urban interface estimated from historical weather records: consequences for the use of prescribed fire in the Sydney region of south-eastern Australia', *Journal of Environmental Management*, 52, 259–71.

Brennan, A, 1998, 'Bioregionalism – a misplaced project?', *Worldviews: Environment, Culture, Religion*, 2, 215–37.

Bridgman, H, Warner, R and Dodson, J, 1995, *Urban Biophysical Environments*, Oxford University Press, Melbourne.

Brindle, R, 1992, 'Toronto – paradigm lost?', *Australian Planner*, 29, 123–30.

Brisbane City Council, 2004, 'Brisbane City Council – Bushland Preservation Levy', accessed 23 March 2004, <http://www.brisbane.qld.gov.au>.

Brown, L, Gardner, G and Halweil, B, 2000, *Beyond Malthus: Nineteen Dimensions of the Population Challenge*, Earthscan, London.

Bulkeley, H, 2000, 'The formation of Australian climate change policy' in Gillespie, A and Burns, W (eds), *Climate Change in the South Pacific: Impacts and Responses in Australia, New Zealand and Small Island States*, Kluwer Academic Publishers, Dordrecht, pp 33–50.

Bunker, R, 2002, 'In the shadow of the city: the fringe around the Australian metropolis in the 1950s', *Planning Perspectives*, 17, 61–82.

—— 1990, 'Urban design in a metropolitan setting: a case study of Adelaide' in *Town Planning Review*, 61 (1) 21–40.

Burgess, J, Clark, J and Harrison, C, 1998, '"Respondents'" evaluations of a contingent valuation survey: a case study of an economic evaluation of the wildlife enhancement scheme, Pevensey Levels in East Sussex', *Area*, 30, 19–27.

Burgess, R, Carmona, M and Kolstee, T, (eds) 1997, *The Challenge of Sustainable Cities: Neoliberalism and Urban Strategies in Developing Countries*, Zed Books, London.

Burnley, I, 1980, *The Australian Urban System: Growth, Change and Differentiation*, Longman Cheshire, Melbourne.

Burnley, I and Murphy, P, 2004, *Sea Change: Movement from Metropolitan to Arcadian Australia*, UNSW Press, Sydney.

Busby, R, 1976, *The Book of Welwyn: The Story of the Five Villages and the Garden City*, Barracuda Books, Chesham.

Button, K, 2002, 'City management and urban environmental indicators', *Ecological Economics*, 40 (2) 217–33.

Callenbach, E, 1975, *Ecotopia: The Notebooks and Reports of William Weston*, Banyan Tree, Oakland, California.

Callon, M, 1986, 'Some elements of a sociology of translation: domestication of the scallops and fishermen of St Brieux Bay' in Law, J (ed), *Power, Action and Belief: A New Sociology of Knowledge*, Methuen, London, pp 196–233.

Capello, R, Nijkamp, P and Pepping, G, 1999, *Sustainable Cities and Energy Policies*, Springer-Verlag, Berlin.

Carmichael, G and McDonald, P, 2003, 'Fertility trends and differentials' in Khoo, S-E and McDonald, P (eds), *The Transformation of Australia's Population 1970–2030*, UNSW Press, Sydney, pp 40–76.

Cervero, R, 2003, 'Growing smart by linking transportation and land use: perspectives from California', *Built Environment*, 29 (1) 66–78.

Christoff, P, 2000, 'Ecological modernisation, ecological modernities' in Young, S (ed), *The Emergence of Ecological Modernisation: Integrating the Environment and the Economy?*, Routledge, London, 209–231.

City of Melbourne, 2004, *City Plan 2010*, accessed 1 March 2004, <http://www.melbourne.vic.gov.au/cityplan/infopage.cfm>.

City of Stirling, 1992, *Green Plan – Urban Bushland Conservation Strategy*, accessed 14 October 2003, <http://www.stirling.wa.gov.au/planning/greenPlan/GREEN%20PLAN2a.htm>.

Cleland, K, 2000, *Commission of Inquiry, Environment and Planning: Woodlawn Waste Management Facility, Mulwaree Shire, Collex Waste Management Pty Limited*, Office of the Commissioners of Inquiry for Environment and Planning, Sydney.

Cocks, D, 2003, *Deep Futures: Our Prospects for Survival*, UNSW Press, Sydney.

Coleman, A, 1985, *Utopia on Trial: Vision and Reality in Planned Housing*, Hilary Shipman, London.

Commoner, B, 1971, *The Closing Circle*, Bantam Books, New York.

Connor, R and Dovers, S, 2004, *Institutional Change for Sustainable Development*, Edward Elgar Publishing, Cheltenham.

Cooper, M, 1999, 'Spatial discourses and social boundaries: re-imagining the Toronto Waterfront' in Low, S (ed), *Theorizing the City: The New Urban Anthropology Reader*, Rutgers University Press, New Jersey, pp 403–38.

Corbett, J and Corbett, M, 2000, *Designing Sustainable Communities: Learning from Village Homes*, Island Press, Washington DC.

Cossins, G, 1990, 'Surface hydrology: water supply and flooding' in Davie, P, Stock, E and Low Choy, D (eds), *The Brisbane River: A Source-Book for the Future*, Australian Littoral Society Inc in association with the Queensland Museum, Brisbane, pp 55–62.

Crane, R and Schweitzer, L, 2003, 'Transport and sustainability: the role of the built environment', *Built Environment*, 29 (3) 238–52.

Crombie, D, 1992, *Regeneration – Toronto's Waterfront and the Sustainable City: Final Report*, Ministry of Supply and Services, Ottawa.

Cronon, W, 1991, *Nature's Metropolis: Chicago and the Great West*, Norton, New York.

CSIRO (Commonwealth Scientific and Industrial Research Organisation), 2001, *Climate Change: Projections for Australia*, CSIRO, Melbourne.

Cutter, S and Renwick, W, 2004, *Exploitation, Conservation, Preservation: A Geographic Perspective on Natural Resource Use*, 4th ed, John Wiley & Sons, Hoboken, New Jersey.

Daly, H and Cobb, J Jr, 1994, *For the Common Good: Redirecting the Economy Toward Community, the Environment, and a Sustainable Future*, 2nd ed, Beacon Press, Boston.

Davie, P, et al, 1998, *Wild Guide to Moreton Bay: Wildlife and Habitats of a Beautiful Australian Coast – Noosa to the Tweed*, Queensland Museum, Brisbane.

Davies, A, 2003, 'Smartening up the sprawl', *Sydney Morning Herald*, 3–4 May 2003, p 39.

Davison, G, 1970, 'Public utilities and the expansion of Melbourne in the 1880s', *Australian Economic History Review*, 10 (2) 169–89.

Deakin, D, (ed), 1989, *Wythenshawe: The Story of a Garden City*, Phillimore, Chichester.

Department of Environment and Conservation NSW, 2003, *New South Wales State of the Environment 2003*, Department of Environment and Conservation NSW, Sydney.

Department of Infrastructure, Planning and Natural Resources, 2003, *Metropolitan Development Program: Managing Sydney's Urban Growth*, DIPNR, Sydney.

De Villiers, P, 1997, 'New Urbanism: a critical review', *Australian Planner*, 34 (1) 30–4.

Dickens, C, 1856, Gibson, J (ed), 1983, *Hard Times*, MacMillan Education, London.

Diesendorf, M, 2003, *Australia's Polluting Power: Coal-Fired Electricity and its Impact on Global Warming*, World Wildlife Fund, Sydney.

—— 2000, 'Sustainability and Sustainable Development' in Dunphy, D, et al (eds), *Sustainability: The Corporate Challenge for the 21st Century*, Allen & Unwin, Sydney, pp 19–37.

Dollery, B and Marshall, C, 2003, 'Future directions for Australian local government' in Dollery, B, Marshall, N and Worthington, A (eds), *Reshaping Australian Local Government: Finance, Governance and Reform*, UNSW Press, Sydney, pp 231–50.

Downton, PF and Ede, S, 1995, 'Reshaping the great Australian Dream', *Streetwise*, 23, pp 3–8.

Druce, M, 2001, 'Recovery planning – can it bring the bush back to Western Sydney?' in Newton, S (ed), *Bushland or Buildings? The Dilemma of Biodiversity Conservation in Urban Areas*, Nature Conservation Council of NSW Inc, Sydney, pp 63–6.

Duany, A and Talen, E, 2002, 'Transect planning', *Journal of the American Planning Association*, 68, 245–66.

Dunn, K, McGuirk, P and Winchester, H, 1995, 'Place making: the social construction of Newcastle', *Australian Geographical Studies*, 33 (2) 149–66.

Ecologically Sustainable Development Steering Committee, 1992, *National Strategy for Ecologically Sustainable Development*, Australian Government Publishing Service, Canberra.

Ecumenical Housing, 2001, *Creating Better Futures for Residents of High-Rise Public Housing in Melbourne*, Ecumenical Housing, Melbourne.

Engels, F, 1892 (originally 1845), *The Condition of the Working Class in England in 1844*, George Allen & Unwin, London.

Environment Australia, 2003, 'The WasteWise construction program' in Trewin D (ed), *Environment by Numbers: Selected Articles on Australia's Environment*, Australian Bureau of Statistics, Canberra, pp 143–4.

—— 2002, *Environmental Impact of End-of-Life Vehicles: An Information Paper*, Environment Australia, Canberra.

Environment Protection Authority, New South Wales, 2000, *Industry Sector: Solid Waste Landfills Compliance Performance Report*, EPA NSW, Sydney.
—— 2000, *New South Wales State of the Environment 2000 Report*, EPA NSW, Sydney.
EPA NSW – see Environment Protection Authority, New South Wales
Erkman, S, 1997, 'Industrial ecology: an historical view', *Journal of Cleaner Production*, 5 (1/2) 1–10.
Fallding, M, 2001, 'Planning around biodiversity' in Newton, S (ed), *Bushland or Buildings? The Dilemma of Biodiversity Conservation in Urban Areas*, Nature Conservation Council of NSW Inc, Sydney, pp 53–7.
Filion, P, 2003, 'Towards Smart Growth: the difficult implementation of alternatives to urban dispersal', *Canadian Journal of Urban Research*, 12 (1), Supplement, pp 48–70.
Flint, K, 1999, 'Institutional Ecological Footprint Analysis: a case study of the University of Newcastle', Honours thesis, University of Newcastle, Newcastle.
Foran, B and Poldy, F, 2002, *Future Dilemmas: Options to 2050 for Australia's Population, Technology, Resources and Environment*, Working Paper Series 02/01, CSIRO Sustainable Ecosystems, Canberra.
Forster, C, 1999, *Australian Cities: Continuity and Change*, 2nd ed, Oxford University Press, Melbourne.
Foster, I, 2002, *Farmnote : Climate Change Projections and Impacts for WA*, Western Australia Department of Agriculture, Perth, No 5 of 2002.
Frawley, K, 1999, 'A green vision: the evolution of Australian environmentalism' in Anderson, K and Gale, F (eds), *Cultural Geographies*, 2nd ed, Addison Wesley, Melbourne, pp 265–93.
Freestone, R, 2002, 'Greenbelts in city and regional planning' in Parsons, K and Schuyler, D, (eds), *From Garden City to Green City: The Legacy of Ebenezer Howard*, John Hopkins University Press, Baltimore, pp 67–98.
—— 2000, 'From city improvement to the city beautiful' in Hamnett, S and Freestone, R (eds), *The Australian Metropolis: A Planning History*, Allen & Unwin, Sydney, pp 27–45.
—— 1998, 'The City Beautiful: towards an understanding of the Australian experience', *Journal of Architectural and Planning Research*, 15 (2) 91–108.
—— 1997, 'Melbourne and the City Beautiful Movement 1900–1930' in Dingle, T (ed), *The Australian City – Future/Past: The Third Australian Planning History/Urban History Conference Proceedings*, 11–14 December 1996, Monash University, Melbourne, pp 223–32.
—— 1996, 'Sulman of Sydney: modern planning in theory and practice 1980–1930', *Town Planning Review*, 67 (1) 45–63.
—— 1981, 'Planning for profit in urban Australia 1900–1930: a descriptive prologomenon', *Antipode*, 13 (1) 15–26.
Friends of the Earth, Hong Kong, 2002, '"Agenda 2047" – a community dialogue', *One Earth*, 49, 17–25.
Frost, L, 1991, *The New Urban Frontier: Urbanisation and City Building in Australasia and the American West*, UNSW Press, Sydney.
Fulton, W, 2002, 'The garden suburb and the new urbanism' in Parsons, K and Schuyler, D, (eds), *From Garden City to Green City: The Legacy of Ebenezer Howard*, John Hopkins University Press, Baltimore, pp 159–170.
Gargett, K and Marsden, S, 1996, *Adelaide: A Brief History*, State History Centre, Adelaide.
Garnaut, C, 2000, in Hamnett, S and Freestone, R (eds), *The Australian Metropolis: A Planning History*, Allen & Unwin, Sydney, pp 46–64.

Gibbs, D, Deutz, P and Proctor, A, 2002, 'Sustainability and the local economy: the role of eco-industrial parks,' paper presented to Ecosites and Eco-centres in Europe, Brussels, 19 June 2002, <http://www.hull.ac.uk/geog/PDF/ECOIND1.pdf>

Gillespie, P and Mason, D, 2003, *NSW Agriculture Environmental Planning and Management Sub-Program: The Value of Agriculture in the Sydney Region*, NSW Agriculture, Sydney.

Giradet, H, 1999, 'Big foot, small world', *The New Internationalist*, 313, 16–17.

Gleeson, B, 2001, *Towards a National Planning Framework for Australia*, Issues Paper 8, Urban Frontiers Program, University of Western Sydney, Sydney.

Gleeson, B and Low, N, 2000, *Australian Urban Planning: New Challenges, New Agendas*, Allen & Unwin, Sydney.

—— 2000, 'Is planning history?' in Freestone, R (ed), *Urban Planning in a Changing World*, E & FN Spon, London, pp 269–84.

Godschalk, D, 2004, 'Land use planning challenges', *Journal of the American Planning Association*, 70 (1) 5–13.

Golledge, R, 1960, 'Sydney's metropolitan fringe: a study in urban-rural relations', *Australian Geographer*, 7, 243–55.

Government Statistician's Office, 1957, *Official Year Book of Western Australia, 1957*, Government Statistician's Office, Perth.

Graedel, T and Allenby, BR, 1995, *Industrial Ecology*, Prentice Hall, New Jersey.

Graham–Taylor, S, 2002, 'Myth and reality: the quality of Perth's air' in Gaynor, A, Trinca, M and Haebich, A (eds), *Country: Visions of Land and People in Western Australia*, Western Australian Museum, Perth, pp 213–25.

Grant, J, 2000, 'Industrial Ecology: planning a new type of industrial park', *Journal of Architectural and Planning Research*, 17 (1) 64–81.

Griffiths, T, 2001, *Forests of Ash: An Environmental History*, Cambridge University Press, Cambridge.

Gunton, R, 2000, 'The role and function of State Rail in Sydney's transport system' in Warren Centre for Advanced Engineering, *Sustainable Transport in Sustainable Cities: The Way We Live, The State of Play*, Warren Centre for Advanced Engineering, Sydney, pp 57–67.

Hajer, M, 1995, *The Politics of Environmental Discourse: Ecological Modernization and the Policy Process*, Oxford University Press, Oxford.

Hamilton, C, 2001, *Running from the Storm: The Development of Climate Change Policy in Australia*, UNSW Press, Sydney.

—— 2000, 'Climate change policies in Australia' in Gillespie, A and Burns, W (eds), *Climate Change in the South Pacific: Impacts and Responses in Australia, New Zealand and Small Island States*, Kluwer Academic Publishers, Dordrecht, pp 51–78.

Hamnett, S, 2000, 'The late 1990s: competitive versus sustainable cities' in Hamnet, S and Freestone, R, (eds), *The Australian Metropolis: A Planning History*, Allen & Unwin, Sydney, pp 168–88.

Hardy, D, 2000, 'Quasi utopias: perfect cities in an imperfect world' in Freestone, R (ed), *Urban Planning in a Changing World*, E & FN Spon, London, pp 61–77.

Harrison, C and Wood, P, (eds) 1992, *Art in Theory 1900–1990: An Anthology of Changing Ideas*, Blackwell, Oxford.

Harvey, D, 1996, *Justice, Nature and the Geography of Difference*, Blackwell, Oxford.

—— 1989, *The Condition of Postmodernity*, Basil Blackwell, Oxford.

Haughton, G, 1994, 'Birth pangs in Utopia: the plans for an international, high-tech sustainable city in Australia', *Geography*, 79 (1) 42–52.

Haughton, G and Hunter, C, 1994, *Sustainable Cities*, Jessica Kingsley Publishers, London.

Haveri, A and Siirila, S, 1999, 'Two growing urban regions: a comparison of growth patterns and growth management strategies in the Helsinki region and the Brisbane region', *Fennia*, 177 (2) 107–22.

Healey, J (ed), 2001, *Issues in Society: Biodiversity*, Spinney Press, Sydney.

Hebbert, M, 2003, 'New Urbanism – the movement in context', *Built Environment*, 29 (3) 193–209.

Hicks, P, 2001, 'History of the zone rebate', *Department of the Parliamentary Library, Research Note*, 26, 2000–01.

Hill, D, 2001, *Urban Rail in Adelaide*, presentation by David Hill, Australasian Railway Association Inc Manager – Research, to the ARA/LLDCN South Australian Infrastructure Conference in Adelaide, 31 May 2001.

Hine, M, 2003, 'The South Australian Partnership for Local Agenda 21– collaboration for change', paper presented to the Sustaining our Communities – International Local Agenda 21 Conference, Adelaide, 2003.

Hodge, A, 2003, 'Russian "roulette" on Kyoto', *Australian*, 4 December 2003, p 8.

Hoffman, A, 2003, 'Linking social systems analysis to the industrial framework', *Organization and Environment*, 16 (1) 66–86.

Honadle, G, 1999, *How Context Matters: Linking Environmental Policy to People and Place*, Kumarian Press, Hartford.

Hough, M, 1995, *Cities and Natural Processes*, Routledge, London.

House of Representatives Standing Committee for Long Term Strategies, 1994, *Australia's Population 'Carrying Capacity': One Nation – Two Ecologies*, Australian Government Publishing Service, Canberra.

Howard, E, 1898 (1945 ed, Osborne, F, ed), *Garden Cities of Tomorrow*, Faber and Faber, London.

Hugo, G, 2003, 'Changing patterns of population distribution' in Khoo, S-E and McDonald, P (eds), *The Transformation of Australia's Population 1970–2030*, UNSW Press, Sydney, pp 185–218.

Houghton, J, Jenkins, G and Ephraums, J, (eds), 1990, *Climate Change: The IPCC Scientific Assessment*, Cambridge University Press, Cambridge.

Hutchings, A, 2000, 'From theory to practice: the inter-war years' in Hamnett, S and Freestone, R (eds), *The Australian Metropolis: A Planning History*, Allen & Unwin, Sydney, pp 65–79.

Hutton, D and Connors, L, 1999, *A History of the Australian Environmental Movement*, Cambridge University Press, Melbourne.

Huxley, M, 2000, 'Planning practice and social theory: a guide to further reading' in McLoughlin, JB and Huxley, M (eds), *Urban Planning in Australia: Critical Readings*, Longman Chshire, Melbourne, pp 333–44.

—— 1994, 'Panoptica: utilitarianism and land-use control' in Gibson, K and Watson, S (eds), *Metropolis Now: Planning and the Urban in Contemporary Australia*, Pluto Press, Sydney, pp 148–60.

—— 1986, 'Planning practice and social theory: a guide to further reading' in McLoughlin, JB and Huxley, M (eds), *Urban Planning in Australia: Critical readings*, Longman Cheshire, Melbourne, pp 333–44.

Inoguchi, T, Newman, E and Paoletto, G (eds), 1999, *Cities and the Environment: New Approaches for Eco-Societies*, United Nations University Press, Tokyo.

Intergovernmental Panel on Climate Change (IPCC), 2001, *Climate Change 2001*, Cambridge University Press, Cambridge.

—— 1996, *Climate Change 1995*, Cambridge University Press, Cambridge.

International Press Service Association, 1929, *Who's Who in Australia, 1929: Biographical Sketches and Photos of Representative Commercial, Professional, Financial, Pastoral and Businessmen of Australia*, International Press Service Association, Sydney.

Jay, M, 1999, 'Does practice make perfect? Debate about principles versus practice in New Zealand local government planning', *Planning Practice and Research*, 14 (4) 467–79.

Jefferson, M, 1917, 'The distribution of British cities and the Empire', *Geographical Review*, 4, 387–94.

Joint Venture for More Affordable Housing, 1989, *New Choices in Housing: Guidelines for Cost-Effective Residential Land Development*, Commonwealth of Australia, Canberra.

Jones, R, Pittock A and Whetton, P, 2000, 'The potential impacts of climate change' in Gillespie, A and Burns, W (eds), *Climate Change in the South Pacific: Impacts and Responses in Australia, New Zealand and Small Island States*, Kluwer Academic Publishers, Dordrecht, pp 7–32.

Johnson, C, 2003, *Greening Sydney: Landscaping the Urban Fabric*, Government Architect Publications, Sydney.

Kenworthy, J, 1991, 'The land use and transit connection in Toronto: some lessons for Australian cities', *Australian Planner*, 28, 149–54.

Kenworthy, J and Newman, P, 1994, 'Toronto – paradigm regained', *Australian Planner*, 31, 137–47.

Kerr, J, 2003, 'Motorway takes toll on road trips, *Sydney Morning Herald*, 2 April 2003, p 8.

Kleiner, F, Mamiya, C and Tansey, R, 2001, *Gardner's Art Through the Ages*, 11th ed, Harcourt College Publishers, Fort Worth.

Kogarah Council, 2004, 'Kogarah Town Square Re-development', accessed 8 March 2004, <http://www.kogarah.nsw.gov.au/www/...h-town-square-redevelopment.html>.

Korhonen, J, 2002, 'Two paths to Industrial Ecology: applying the product-based and geographical-based approaches', *Journal of Environmental Planning and Management*, 45, (1) 39–57.

Kravchenko, P, 2001, 'Failing to act – the missing framework for urban bushland conservation and management' in Newton, S (ed), *Bushland or Buildings? The Dilemma of Biodiversity Conservation in Urban Areas*, Nature Conservation Council of NSW Inc, Sydney, pp 106–15.

Krockenberger, M, 2003, speech presented by Michael Krockenberger to the National Population Summit, Adelaide, 21 November 2003.

Kronsell, A, 2000, 'A sustainable impact on the EU? An analysis of the making of the Fifth Environmental Action Program' in Young, S (ed), *The Emergence of Ecological Modernisation: Integrating the Environment and the Economy?*, Routledge, London, 87–105.

Laird, P, 2001, 'Australian Transport and Energy Data (Appendix A)' in Laird, P, Newman, P, Bachels, M and Kenworthy, J, *Back on Track: Rethinking Transport Policy in Australia and New Zealand*, UNSW Press, Sydney, pp 177–84.

Lambert, A and Boons, F, 2002, 'Eco-industrial parks: stimulating sustainable development in mixed industrial parks', *Technovation*, 22 (8) 471–84.

Lay, M, 1992, *Ways of the World: A History of the World's Roads and the Vehicles that Used Them*, Primavera Press, Sydney.

LeGates, R, and Stout, F (eds), *The City Reader*, Routledge, London.

Lennon, M, 2000, 'The revival of metropolitan planning' in Hamnett, S and Freestone, R, (eds), 2000, *The Australian Metropolis: A Planning History*, Allen & Unwin, Sydney, pp 149–67.

Lenzen, M, 1999, 'Total requirements of energy and greenhouse gases for Australian transport', *Transportation Research Part D*, 4, 265–90.

Ley, D and Murphy, P, 2001, 'Immigration in gateway cities: Sydney and Vancouver in comparative perspective', *Progress in Planning*, 55 (3) 119–94.

Ley, D and Tutchener, 2001, 'Immigration, globalisation and house prices in Canada's gateway cities', *Housing Studies*, 16 (2) 199–224.

Ley, D, Tutchener, J and Cunningham, G, 2002, 'Immigration, polarization, or gentrification? Accounting for changing house prices and dwelling values in gateway cities', *Urban Geography*, 23 (8) 703–27.

Little, S, 2001, 'Urban development: planning for biodiversity conservation' in Newton, S (ed), *Bushland or Buildings? The Dilemma of Biodiversity Conservation in Urban Areas*, Nature Conservation Council of NSW Inc, Sydney, pp 123–37.

Logan, M, 1986, 'Urban Planning, policy and management' in McLoughlin, JB and Huxley, M, *Urban Planning in Australia: Critical Readings*, Longman Cheshire, Melbourne, pp 131–56.

Lomborg, B, 2001, *The Skeptical Environmentalist: Measuring the Real State of the World*, Cambridge University Press, Cambridge.

Lothian, A, 2002, 'Australian attitudes towards the environment: 1991 to 2001', *Australian Journal of Environmental Management*, 9, 45–61.

Low, T, 2002, *The New Nature: Winners and Losers in Wild Australia*, Viking, Melbourne.

Lloyd, C, 1995, 'Water, sewerage and drainage' in Troy, P (ed), *Technological Change and the City*, Federation Press, Sydney, pp 54–77.

Luketina, D and Bender, M, 2002, 'Incorporating long-term trends in water availability in water supply planning', *Water Science and Technology*, 46 (6–7) 113–20.

Lund, H, 2003, 'Testing the claims of New Urbanism: local access, pedestrian travel, and neighboring behaviors', *Journal of the American Planning Association*, 69 (4) 414–29.

Maher, C, 1982, *Australian Cities in Transition*, Shillington House, Melbourne.

Maitland, B, 1997, 'Lost cities of the borehole seam' in Moore, RJ and Ostwald, M, (eds) and Chawner, A (photography), *Hidden Newcastle: Urban Memories and Architectural Imaginaries*, Gadfly Media, Sydney, pp 73–87.

Maitland, B and Stafford, D, 1997, 'Newcastle–Coalfield Coalition' in Dingle, T (ed), *The Australian City – Future/Past: The Third Australian Planning History/Urban History Conference Proceedings*, 11–14 December 1996, Monash University, Melbourne, pp 365–71.

Marshall, A, 2003, 'A tale of two towns tells a lot about this thing called New Urbanism', *Built Environment*, 29 (3) 227–37.

May, P, 2003, 'Amalgamation and virtual local government' in Dollery, B, Marshall, N and Worthington, A (eds), *Reshaping Australian Local Government: Finance, Governance and Reform*, UNSW Press, Sydney, pp 79–97.

McCarty, J, 1970, 'Australian capital cities in the nineteenth century', *Australian Economic History Review*, 10 (2) 107–37.

McDonald, P, 2003, 'Australia's future population: population policy in a low-fertility society' in Khoo, S-E and McDonald, P (eds), *The Transformation of Australia's Population 1970–2030*, UNSW Press, Sydney, pp 266–79.

McDonnell, M, Williams, N and Kahs, A, 1999, *A Reference Guide to the Ecology and Natural Resources of the Melbourne Region: A Bibliography of the Biodiversity Literature for Scientists, Teachers, Policy Makers, Planners and Natural Resource Managers*, Australian Research Centre for Urban Ecology, Melbourne.

McInerney, J, 1993, *The Future of Australia Lies in its Cities*, New College Institute for Values Research, University of NSW, Working Paper No 2, Sydney.

McKormick, J, 1995, *The Global Environmental Movement*, 2nd ed, John Wiley and Sons, Chichester.

McLoughlin, JB, 1992, *Shaping Melbourne's Future? Town Planning, the State and Civil Society*, Cambridge University Press, Melbourne.

McManus, P, in press, 'In whose interest? Consent, dissent and the Sydney 2000 Olympic Games' in Cryle, D and Hillier, J (eds), *Consensus and Consent*, Queensland University Press, Brisbane.

—— 2002a, 'Out of place: agriculture in Australian cities', paper presented to the Institute of Australian Geographers Annual Conference, Canberra, 2002.

—— 2002b, 'Your car is as welcome as you are: a history of transportation and planning in the Perth Metropolitan Region' in Gaynor, A, Trinca, M and Haebich, A (eds), *Country: Visions of Land and People in Western Australia*, Western Australian Museum, Perth, pp 187–211.

—— 2001, 'One step forward and two steps back: urban policy and community planning in England since 1979' in Yiftachel, O, Little, J, Hedgcock, D and Alexander, I (eds), *The Power of Planning: Spaces of Control and Transformation*, Kluwer Academic Publishers Dordrecht, pp 45–55.

—— 2000 'Beyond Kyoto: media representation of an environmental issue', *Australian Geographical Studies*, 38 (3) 306–19.

—— 1998, 'Sustainability, planning and urban form: the approaches of Troy, Newman and Kenworthy, Trainer and Rees', *Australian Planner*, 35 (3) 162–8.

—— 1996, 'Contested terrains: politics, stories and discourses of sustainability', *Environmental Politics*, 5 (1) 48–73.

—— 1992, 'Toronto – a model city?', *Australian Urban Studies*, 20 (3) 9–11.

McManus, P and Pritchard, B, 2001, 'Regional policy: towards the Triple Bottom Line', *Australasian Journal of Regional Studies*, 7 (3) 249–60.

McShane, C, 1994, *Down the Asphalt Path: The Automobile and the American City*, Columbia University Press, New York.

Mees, P, 2003, 'The attempt to revive metropolitan planning in Melbourne', paper presented to the Planning with Diversity Conference, Adelaide, 2003.

—— 1994, 'Toronto – paradigm re-examined', *Urban Policy and Research*, 12 (3) 146–63.

Mercer, D and Jotkowitz, B, 2000, 'Local Agenda 21 and barriers to sustainability at the local government level in Victoria, Australia', *Australian Geographer*, 31 (2) 163–81.

Meyer, B, 2000, 'The shape of Sydney, 1801–2001' in Warren Centre for Advanced Engineering, *Sustainable Transport in Sustainable Cities: The Way We Live, The State of Play*, Warren Centre for Advanced Engineering, Sydney, pp 33–43.

Miller, C, 2003, 'Measuring quality: the New Zealand experience', *Built Environment*, 29 (4) 336–42.

Miller, GT Jr, 2002, *Sustaining the Earth*, 5th ed, Wadsworth, Belmont, California.

Miller, M, 2002, 'The origins of the Garden City neighbourhood' in Parsons, K and Schuyler, D, (eds), *From Garden City to Green City: The Legacy of Ebenezer Howard*, John Hopkins University Press, Baltimore, pp 99–130.

—— 1989, *Letchworth – The First Garden City*, Phillimore, Chichester.

Millett, M, 2002, 'Carr resists tide of migrants as Sydney heads for 5 million', *Sydney Morning Herald*, 3 July 2002, p 7.

Minnery, J, 2001, 'Inter-organisational approaches to regional growth management: a case study of South East Queensland', *Town Planning Review*, 21 (1) 25–44.

Miranda, M and Aldy J, 1998, 'Unit pricing of residential municipal solid waste: lessons from nine case study communities', *Journal of Environmental Management*, 52, 79–93.

Moffatt, I, 1999, 'Edinburgh: a sustainable city?', *The International Journal of Sustainable Development and World Ecology*, 6, 135–48.

Morison, I, 2000, 'The corridor city: planning for growth in the 1960s' in Hamnett, S and Freestone, R (eds), *The Australian Metropolis: A Planning History*, Allen & Unwin, Sydney, pp 113–30.

Mouritz, M, 2000, 'Water sensitive urban design – Where to now?', keynote address presented at the Water Sensitive Urban Design Workshop, Melbourne, 30–31 August 2000.

Mulligan, M and Hill, S, 2001, *Ecological Pioneers: A Social History of Australian Ecological Thought and Action*, Cambridge University Press, New York.

Nankervis, M, 2003, 'Measuring Australian planning: constraints and caveats', *Built Environment*, 29 (4) 315–26.

National Bureau of Statistics of the People's Republic of China, 2000, *China – Census 2000*, Zhongguo tong ji chu ban she, Beijing.

National Land and Water Resources Audit, 2002, *Australia's Natural Resources 1997–2002 and Beyond*, National Land and Water Resources Audit, Canberra.

National Parks and Wildlife Service NSW, 2001, *Biodiversity Planning Guide for NSW Local Government: Edition One*, National Parks and Wildlife Service NSW, Sydney.

—— 1999, *NSW Biodiversity Strategy*, National Parks and Wildlife Service NSW, Sydney.

Newcastle City Council, 1997, *State of the Environment Report*, Newcastle City Council, Newcastle

Newman, P, 1992, 'The rebirth of Perth's suburban railways' in Hedgcock, D and Yiftachel, O (eds), *Urban and Regional Planning in Western Australia*, Paradigm Press, Perth, pp 174–87.

Newman, P and Kenworthy, J, 1999, *Sustainability and Cities: Overcoming Automobile Dependence*, Island Press, Washington DC.

Newman, P, Kenworthy, J and Bachels, M, 2001, 'How we compare: patterns and trends in Australian and New Zealand cities' in Laird, P, Newman, P, Bachels, M and Kenworthy, J, *Back on Track: Rethinking Transport Policy in Australia and New Zealand*, UNSW Press, Sydney, pp 133–55.

Newman, P, Kenworthy, J and Vintilla, P, 1992, *Housing, Transport and Urban Form, Background Paper 2 for National Housing Strategy*, Institute for Science and Technology Policy, Murdoch University, Perth.

Newman, P, et al, 1996, 'Human settlements' in *Australia State of the Environment Report*, Department of Environment, Sport and Territories, Australian Government Publishing Service, Canberra.

Newton, PW, et al, 2001, *Human Settlements: Australia State of the Environment 2001 (Theme Report)*, CSIRO Publishing on behalf of the Department of Environment and Heritage, Canberra.

NSW Council on Environmental Education, 2001, *Learning for Sustainability: NSW Government Environmental Education Plan 2002–05*, NSW Government, Sydney.

NSW Parliament, Legislative Council, 2000, Albury–Wodonga Development Repeal Bill, Second Reading, *Parliamentary Debates (Hansard)*, No 71, 23 May 2000, pp 5486–9.

Odell, E, Theobald, D and Knight, R, 2003, 'Incorporating ecology into land use planning: the songbirds' case for clustered development', *Journal of the American Planning Association*, 69 (1) 72–81.

O'Neill, B, Mackellar FL and Lutz, W, 2001, *Population and Climate Change*, Cambridge University Press, Cambridge.

O'Rourke, C, 2003, 'New lungs for city – a breath of fresh air for us', *Sydney Morning Herald*, 11 March 2003, p 7.

O'Rourke, D, Connelly, L and Koshland, C, 1996, 'Industrial ecology: a critical review', *International Journal of Environment and Pollution*, 6 (2/3) 89–112.

Owen, K, 2002 'The Sydney 2000 Olympics and urban entrepreneurialism: local variations in urban governance', *Australian Geographical Studies*, 40, 323–36.

Palmer, J, 1998, *Environmental Education in the 21st Century: Theory, Practice, Progress and Promise*, Routledge, London.

Palmer, J, Cooper, I, van der Vorst, R, 1997, 'Mapping out fuzzy buzzwords – who sits where on sustainability and sustainable development', *Sustainable Development*, 5 (2) 87–93.

Park, R, 1949, *Poor Man's Orange*, Penguin, Ringwood, Victoria.

—— 1948, *The Harp in the South*, Penguin, Ringwood, Victoria.

Parker, P, 1995, 'From sustainable development objectives to indicators of progress: options for New Zealand communities', *New Zealand Geographer*, 51 (2) 50–7.

Parsons, K and Schuyler, D, 2002, (eds), *From Garden City to Green City: The Legacy of Ebenezer Howard*, John Hopkins University Press, Baltimore.

Pearce, D and Barbier, E, 2000, *Blueprint for a Sustainable Economy*, Earthscan, London.

Peiser, R, 2001, 'Decomposing urban sprawl', *Town Planning Review*, 72 (3) 275–97.

Perth Biodiversity Project, *Perth Biodiversity Project: Councils Caring for Their Natural Communities*, Western Australian Local Government Association, accessed 21 March 2004, <http://www.walga.asn. au/projServices/pbp>.

Pinchot, G, 1901, 'Conservation' in Wall, D (ed), 1994, *Green History: A Reader in Environmental Literature, Philosophy and Politics*, Routledge, London, p 36.

Portney, K, 2002, 'Taking sustainable cities seriously: a comparative analysis of twenty-four US cities', *Local Environment*, 7 (4) 363–80.

Price, S, 2003, 'Improving Western Australian local government implementation of the environmental aims of Agenda 21', paper presented to Sustaining our Communities – International Local Agenda 21 Conference, Adelaide, 2003.

Priemus, H, 1999, 'Sustainable cities: how to realize an ecological breakthrough – a Dutch approach', *International Planning Studies*, 4 (2) 213–36.

Protectors of Public Lands, 2003, 'Protectors of Public Lands', last updated June 2003, accessed 3 March 2004, <http:www.nsw.nationaltrust.org.au/ppl/html>.

Pugh, C, (ed), 2000, *Sustainable Cities in Developing Countries: Theory and Practice at the Millennium*, Earthscan, London.

Pund, G, 2003, 'Suburban planning and the provision of effective bus services', PhD thesis, Macquarie University.

Queensland Conservation Council, 2004, 'Save our bush', accessed 22 March 2004, <http://www.qccqld.org.au/saveourbush/theissue.htm>.

Razzell, W, 1990, 'Water supply' in Davie, P, Stock, E and Low Choy, D (eds), *The Brisbane River: A Source-Book for the Future*, Australian Littoral Society Inc in association with the Queensland Museum, Brisbane, pp 213–16.

Rees, W, 1997, 'Is 'sustainable city' an oxymoron?', *Local Environment*, 2 (3) 303–10.

Reisner, M, 1993, *Cadillac Desert: The American West and its Disappearing Water*, Penguin, New York.

Rich, D, Cardew, R and Langdale, J, 1987, 'Urban development and economic change: the example of Sydney' in Hamnett, S and Bunker, R (eds), *Urban Australia: Planning Issues and Policies*, Alexandrine Press, Oxford, pp 26–41.

Riedy, C, and Diesendorf, M, 2003, 'Financial subsidies to the Australian fossil fuel industry', *Energy Policy*, 31, 125–37.

Robins, N, 1995, *Citizen Action to Lighten Britain's Ecological Footprints*, International Institute for Environment and Development, London.

Rowland, D, 2003, 'An ageing population: emergence of a new stage of life?' in Khoo, S-E and McDonald, P (eds), *The Transformation of Australia's Population 1970–2030*, UNSW Press, Sydney, pp 238–65.

Rudlin, D and Falk, N, 1999, *Building the 21st Century Home: The Sustainable Urban Neighbourhood*, Architectural Press, Oxford.

Rutherford, J, Logan, M and Missen, G, 1966, *New Viewpoints in Economic Geography*, Martindale Press, Sydney.

Saddler, H, Diesendorf, M, and Dennis, R, 2004, *A Clean Energy Future for Australia, A Study by Energy Strategies for the Clean Energy Future Group*, <http://www.wwf.org.au>.

Sale, K, 1985, *Dwellers in the Land: The Bioregional Vision*, Planet Drum, San Francisco.

Salt, B, 2001, *The Big Shift: Welcome to the Third Australian Culture*, Hardie Grant Books, Melbourne.

Sandercock, L, 1975, *Cities for Sale: Property, Politics and Urban Planning in Australia*, Melbourne University Press, Melbourne.

Satterthwaite, D, 1997, 'Sustainable cities or cities that contribute to sustainable development?', *Urban Studies*, 34 (10) 1667–91.

Saunders, P, 2003, 'Canada and Kyoto', *CBC News Online*, updated 12 August 2003, accessed 8 December 2003, <http://www.cbc.ca/news/background/kyoto/canada.html>.

Schubert, D, 2000, 'The neighbourhood paradigm: from garden cities to gated communities' in Freestone, R (ed), *Urban Planning in a Changing World*, E & FN Spon, London, pp 118–38.

Self, P, 1988, 'The resurgence of metropolitan planning in Australia', *The Planner*, 74 (12) 16–19.

Senate Committee, 2002 – see Senate Environment, Communications, Information Technology and the Arts References Committee, 2002

Senate Environment, Communications, Information Technology and the Arts References Committee, 2003, *Plastic Bag Levy (Assessment and Collection) Bill 2002 (No 2) and Plastic Bag (Minimisation of Usage) Education Fund Bill 2002 (No 2)*, ECITARC, Canberra.

—— 2002, *The Value of Water: Inquiry into Australia's Urban Water Management, Report*, ECITARC, Canberra.

—— National Plastic Bags Working Group, 2002, *Plastic Shopping Bags in Australia*, report to the National Packaging Covenant Council, ECITARC, Canberra.

Shane, E M and Graedel, T, 2000, 'Urban environmental sustainability metrics: a provisional set', *Journal of International Planning and Management*, 43 (5) 643–63.

Simmie, J, 1993, *Planning at the Crossroads*, UCL Press, London.

Simon, J, 1981, *The Ultimate Resource*, Princeton University Press, Princeton, New Jersey.

Sinclair, I, 1996, 'A view from the edge: issues in rural and metropolitan fringe planning – Sydney's agricultural land', *New Planner*, 27, 24–25.

Singleton, J, 1992, 'Environmental planning for the Swan Coastal Plain' in Hedgcock, D and Yiftachel, O (eds), *Urban and Regional Planning in Western Australia*, Paradigm Press, Perth, pp 235–51.

60L Green Building, 2004, '60L Green Building', accessed 14 March 2004, <http://www.60lgreenbuilding.com>.

Southworth, M, 2003, 'New Urbanism and the American metropolis', *Built Environment*, 29 (3) 210–26.

Spearritt, P, 2000, *Sydney's Century: A History*, UNSW Press, Sydney.

—— 1978, *Sydney Since the Twenties*, Hale and Iremonger, Sydney.

State of the Environment Advisory Council, 1996, *Australia State of the Environment Report 1996*, CSIRO Publishing, Melbourne.

Stelter, G, 2000, 'Rethinking the significance of the City Beautiful idea' in Freestone, R (ed), *Urban Planning in a Changing World*, E & FN Spon, London, pp 98–117.

Stenhouse, R, 2001, 'Management of urban remnant bushlands by the community and local government', *Australian Journal of Environmental Management*, 8, 37–47.

Stimson, R and Taylor, S, 1999, 'City profile: Brisbane', *Cities*, 16 (4) 285–98.

Stokes, R and Hill, R, 1992, 'The evolution of metropolitan planning in Western Australia' in Hedgcock, D and Yiftachel, O (eds), *Urban and Regional Planning in Western Australia*, Paradigm Press, Perth, pp 111–30.

Sustainable Population Australia, 2003, website last updated 29 March 2004, accessed 29 March 2004, <www.population.org.au>.

Takeda Foundation, 2002, 'The Takeda Award 2001', last updated 4 May 2002, accessed 22 March 2004, <http:www.takeda–foundation.jp/en/award/takeda/2001/fact/03_l.html>.

Talen, E, 1999, 'Sense of community and neighbourhood form: an assessment of the social doctrine of New Urbanism', *Urban Studies*, 36 (8) 1361–79.

Tammemagi, H, 1999, *The Waste Crisis: Landfills, Incinerators and the Search for a Sustainable Future*, Oxford University Press, New York.

Taplin, R, 1999, 'Sydney: sustainable city?' in Walker, K and Crowley, K (eds), *Australian Environmental Policy 2: Studies in Decline + Devolution*, UNSW Press, Sydney, pp 166–85.

Taplin, R and Yu, X, 2000, 'Climate change policy formation in Australia: 1995–1998' in Gillespie, A and Burns, W (eds), *Climate Change in the South Pacific: Impacts and Responses in Australia, New Zealand and Small Island States*, Kluwer Academic Publishers, Dordrecht, pp 95–112.

Taylor, R, 1999, *Wild Places of Greater Melbourne*, CSIRO Publishing and Museum Victoria, Collingwood.

Thompson-Fawcett, M, 2003, 'A New Urbanist diffusion network: the Americo–European connection', *Built Environment*, 29 (3) 253–70.

Tibbits, G (1988) '"The enemy within our gates": slum clearance and high-rise flats' in Howe, R (ed), *New Houses for Old: Fifty Years of Public Housing in Victoria 1938–1988*, Ministry of Housing and Construction, Melbourne, pp 123–62.

Till, K, 2001, 'New Urbanism and nature: green marketing and the neotraditional community', *Urban Geography*, 22 (3) 220–48.

Todd, J, 2002, *Review of Literature on Residential Firewood Use, Wood-Smoke and Air Toxics, Technical Report No 4*, Environment Australia, Canberra.

Town of Seaside, 2003, Town of Seaside website, accessed 25 March 2003, <http://www.stamit.com.au/news/v6n1/sis1.html>.

Tregoning, H, Agyeman, J and Shenot, C, 2002, 'Sprawl, Smart Growth and Sustainability', *Local Environment*, 7 (4) 341–7.

Troy, P, 2001, 'Rethinking our cities', *Financial Review*, 23 March 2001, pp 1–2, 8–9.

Tubby, F, 1998, *Select Committee on Perth's Air Quality*, State Law Publisher, Perth.

Turton, H and Hamilton, C, 2002, *Updating Per Capita Emissions for Industrialised Countries*, Australia Institute, Canberra.

United Nations Population Fund, 2001, *The State of the World Population 2001, Footprints and Milestones: Population and Environmental Change*, United Nations Population Fund, New York.

Urban Feral Animal Action Group, undated, *The Urban Fox: Predator of our Wildlife*, Urban Feral Animal Action Group, Sydney.

Urbinato, D, 1994, 'London's historic "pea-soupers"' in *EPA Journal* (US Environmental Protection Agency), 20 (1–2) 44.

Van Berkel, 2003, 'The Kwinana Industrial Area: an evolving example of an eco-industrial park', presentation to the International Society for Industrial Ecology, Ann Arbor, Michigan, June–July 2003.

Von Weizsaker, E, Lovins, A and Lovins, LH, 1997, *Factor Four: Doubling Wealth – Halving Resource Use: A New Report to the Club of Rome*, Allen & Unwin, Sydney.

Wackernagel, M and Rees, W, 1996, *Our Ecological Footprint: Reducing Human Impact on the Earth*, New Society Publishers, Gabriola Island, Canada.

Ward, S, 2002, 'Ebenezer Howard: his life and times' in Parsons, K and Schuyler, D, *From Garden City to Green City*, John Hopkins University Press, Baltimore, pp 14–37.

Warner, R, 2000, 'Stormwater management in Sydney's urban rivers' in Brizga, S and Finlayson, B (eds), *River Management: The Australian Experience*, John Wiley & Sons, Chichester, pp 173–96.

Watson, R, 1997, *Australasian Impacts of Climate Change: An Assessment of Vulnerability, A Special Report of the IPCC Working Group II*, Australian Greenhouse Office, Canberra.

Wayne, C, 1966, *Overall Review of Transport in Western Australia*, Western Australian Government, Perth.

Weale, A, 1992, *The New Politics of Pollution*, Manchester University Press, Manchester.

Webster, C, 2001, 'Gated cities of tomorrow', *Town Planning Review*, 72 (2) 149–69.

Western Australia Department of Environment, 2004, *Perth Metropolitan Domestic Waste*, information flyer for Sustainable Living Home/Sustainable Living website, Department of Premier and Cabinet.

——2003a, *Strategic Direction for Waste Management in Western Australia*, Western Australia Department of Environment, Perth.

——2003b, *Western Australia's Waste Management and Recycling Fund: Recommendations for the Statutory Review of the Fund*, Western Australia Department of Environment, Perth.

——1998, *Environment Western Australia 1998: State of the Environment Report*, Western Australia Department of Environment, Perth.

Wheeler, S, 2003, 'The evolution of urban form in Portland and Toronto: implications for sustainability planning', *Local Environment*, 8 (3) 317–36.

White, S and Fane, S, 2000, 'Designing cost effective water demand management programs in Australia', *Water Science and Technology*, 46 (6–7) 225–32.

Whittaker, S, 1997, 'Are Australian councils "willing and able" to implement Local Agenda 21?', *Local Environment*, 2 (3) 319–28.

Wilbanks, T, et al, 2003, 'The research strategy: linking the local to the global' in Association of American Geographers Global Change and Local Places Research Team (eds), *Global Change and Local Places: Estimating, Understanding and Reducing Greenhouse Gases*, Cambridge University Press, New York, pp 27–54.

Wills, N, 1945, 'The rural urban fringe: some agricultural characteristics', *Australian Geographer*, 5, 29–35.

Wilmoth, D, 1987, 'Metropolitan planning for Sydney' in Hamnett, S and Bunker, R (eds), *Urban Australia: Planning Issues and Policies*, Alexandrine Press, Oxford, pp 158–84.

Wilson, W, 1989, *The City Beautiful Movement*, John Hopkins University Press, Baltimore.

Wood, R, 2003, 'The structural determinants for change in Australia's greenhouse gas emissions, Honours thesis, University of Sydney, Sydney.

Woodford, J, 2003, 'Beating the bulldozers to protect the diversity of life', *Sydney Morning Herald*, Weekend Edition, 1–2 February 2003, p 13.

World Commission on Environment and Development, 1987, *Our Common Future*, Oxford University Press, Oxford.

World Economic Forum, 2002, *2002 Environmental Sustainability Index*, accessed 20 March 2004, <http://www.ciesin.columbia.edu/indicators/ESI/downloads.html>.

Wright, AG, 2002, *Shaping the Vision and Strategy for Sustainable Waste Management in New South Wales*, Wright Corporate Strategy Pty Ltd, Sydney.

——2000, *Independent Public Assessment – Landfill Capacity and Demand*, Wright Corporate Strategy Pty Ltd, Sydney.

Wright, B, 2001, *Expectations of a Better World: Planning Australian Communities*, Royal Australian Planning Institute, Canberra.

Yencken, D and Wilkinson, D, 2000, *Resetting the Compass: Australia's Journey Towards Sustainability*, CSIRO Publishing, Collingwood.

Yiftachel, O, 2001, 'Introduction: outlining the power of planning' in Yiftachel, O, Little, J, Hedgcock, D and Alexander, I (eds), *The Power of Planning: Spaces of Control and Transformation*, Kluwer Academic Publishers, Dortrecht, pp 1–20.

——1991, *Theory and Practice in Metropolitan Planning: The Case of Perth*, School of Architecture and Planning, Curtin University of Technology, Perth.

Yiftachel, O and Kenworthy, J, 1992, 'The planning of metropolitan Perth: some critical observations' in Hedgcock, D and Yiftachel, O (eds), *Urban and Regional Planning in Western Australia*, Paradigm Press, Perth, pp 131–48.

Yiftachel, O, Little, J, Hedgcock, D and Alexander, I (eds), 2001, *The Power of Planning: Spaces of Control and Transformation*, Kluwer Academic Publishers, Dortrecht.

Young, S, 2000, 'Introduction: The origins and evolving nature of ecological modernisation' in Young, S (ed), *The Emergence of Ecological Modernisation: Integrating the Environment and the Economy?*, Routledge, London, 1–39

Zimmerman, J, 2001, 'The "nature" of urbanism on the New Urbanist frontier: sustainable development or defense of the suburban dream', *Urban Geography*, 22 (3) 249–67.

INDEX

Also published by UNSW Press

FUTURE MAKERS, FUTURE TAKERS
Life in Australia 2050

Doug Cocks

This book tackles the big issues confronting Australians over the coming turbulent times. It identifies, describes and compares the broad socio-political philosophies that make up the country's economic, environmental and social choices. *Future Makers, Future Takers* is a cautiously optimistic book, which will be welcomed by all Australians wanting a considered, non-partisan view of our options for the future and a balanced judgment about where these might lead in terms of quality of life for ordinary Australians by the year 2050 – and beyond.

ISBN 0 86840 473 X